FOUNDATIONS OF

CHINESE

CIVILIZATION

FOUNDATIONS OF CHINESE CIVILIZATION

The Yellow Emperor to the Han Dynasty
(2697 BCE - 220 CE)

Jing Liu

UNDERSTANDING CHINA THROUGH COMICS
VOLUME 1

A GRAPHIC NOVEL HISTORY FROM STONE BRIDGE PRESS
Berkeley CA

Published by
Stone Bridge Press
P.O. Box 8208 • Berkeley, California 94707
TEL 510-524-8732 • sbp@stonebridge.com • www.stonebridge.com

First edition, 2016.

Book design and layout by Linda Ronan.

Printed in the United States of America.

LIBRARY OF CONGRESS CATALOGING-IN-PUBLICATION DATA
Names: Liu, Jing (Author of graphic novels), author, illustrator.
Title: Foundations of Chinese civilization / Jing Liu.
Description: First edition. | Berkeley : Stone Bridge Press, 2016. | Series: Understanding China through comics | Includes bibliographical references and index.
Identifiers: LCCN 2016009755 (print) | LCCN 2016012382 (ebook) | ISBN 9781611720273 (alk. paper) | ISBN 9781611729184 (ebook)
Subjects: LCSH: China—History—Comic books, strips, etc. | Graphic novels.
Classification: LCC DS735 .L576 2016 (print) | LCC DS735 (ebook) | DDC 931—dc23
LC record available at http://lccn.loc.gov/2016009755

CONTENTS

INTRODUCTION

Discussion about China tends to center on its economic growth and for good reason. In just three decades China has gone from third world country to the world's second largest economy and in doing it so has lifted over 600 million people from poverty.

But while this astronomical growth has attracted widespread attention, it is only one story of many and for the curious reader may raise even more questions about China than it answers. Most importantly. . . .

Who exactly are the Chinese?

While there's no easy answer to that question, I would suggest that looking toward China's history, its collective past, is an excellent place to start.

The Understanding China Through Comics series is a work of history that paints a rich and thorough portrait of the Chinese people. Figures both legendary and real, famous battles, and political machinations all feature in its pages, as do nomad invasions, the plight of peasant farmers, and the occasional love story.

One issue with recounting so much history is how to convey it meaningfully. Books in this series draw on disciplines like geography, economics, and philosophy to help contextualize individuals and their actions, as well as identify themes seen again and again throughout Chinese history.

This is especially true for *Foundations of Chinese Civilization*, the first book in this series and the one you hold in your hands now. While thousands of years have seen China change in many ways, much has remained constant. *Foundations of Chinese Civilization* helps establish and explain certain features of China in its earliest years that are still essential to an understanding of the Chinese people today.

So. Who are the Chinese? While a single answer to that question will never suffice, I hope that by exploring China's history readers will begin to understand the complex accumulation of ideas that make the Chinese people who they are today. Use this book to open up further avenues of exploration and inquiry. After all, the power to pursue knowledge rests with you the reader.

J.L.

TIMELINE

2697 BCE	Reign of Yellow Emperor begins*
2070 BCE	Emperor Yu establishes Xia dynasty*
1600 BCE	Shang dynasty overthrows Xia dynasty *
c. 1200 BCE	Oracle bone script first appears
1046 BCE	King Wu defeats Shang dynasty and establishes Zhou dynasty
	Western Zhou dynasty period begins
841 BCE	Leading nobles exile King Li and begin Gong He Regency
827 BCE	King Xuan restores Zhou dynasty
770 BCE	Zhou capital moves east to Luoyang
	Spring and Autumn period of Eastern Zhou dynasty begins
551 BCE	Confucius is born
403 BCE	Warring States period of Eastern Zhou dynasty begins
256 BCE	Qin state captures Zhou capital, ending Zhou dynasty
221 BCE	First emperor unifies China and founds Qin dynasty
210 BCE	First emperor of the Qin dies
207 BCE	Xiang Yu defeats Qin army and Liu Bang attacks Qin capital
206 BCE	Qin dynasty falls
202 BCE	Liu Bang defeats Xiang Yu and founds Han dynasty
	Western Han dynasty period begins
195 BCE	Liu Bang dies after sustaining wounds while fighting rebels
133 BCE	Emperor Wu begins war against Xiongnu nomads
86 BCE	Sima Qian, author of *Records of the Grand Historian*, dies
9 CE	Wang Mang formally establishes Xin dynasty
23 CE	Liu Xiu defeats Xin army
25 CE	Liu Xiu reestablishes Han dynasty
	Eastern Han dynasty period begins
63 CE	Cai Lun, inventor of paper, dies amid palace intrigue
220 CE	Han dynasty falls

*veracity debated by scholars

FOUNDATIONS OF CHINESE CIVILIZATION

5,000 YEARS AT A GLANCE

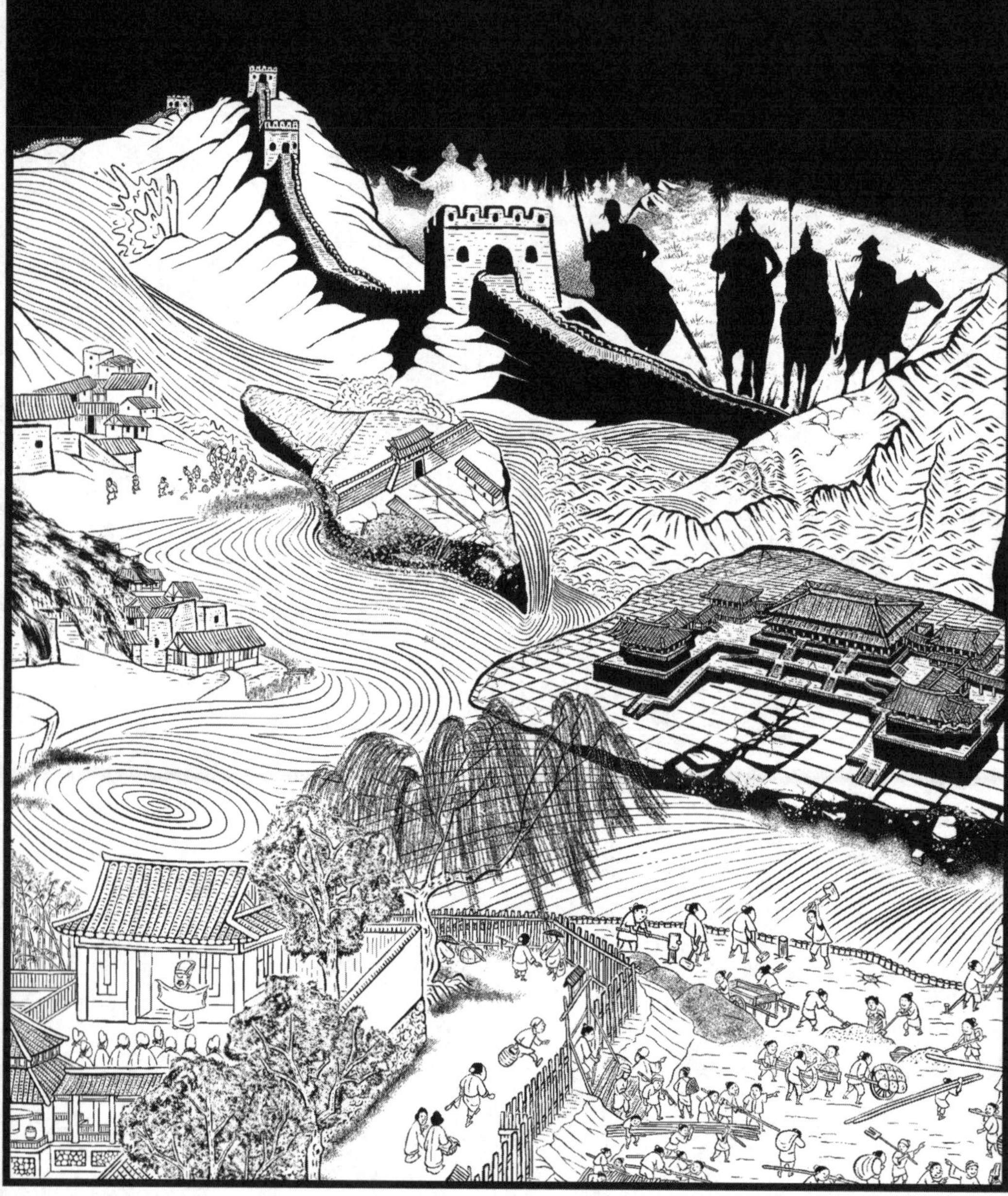

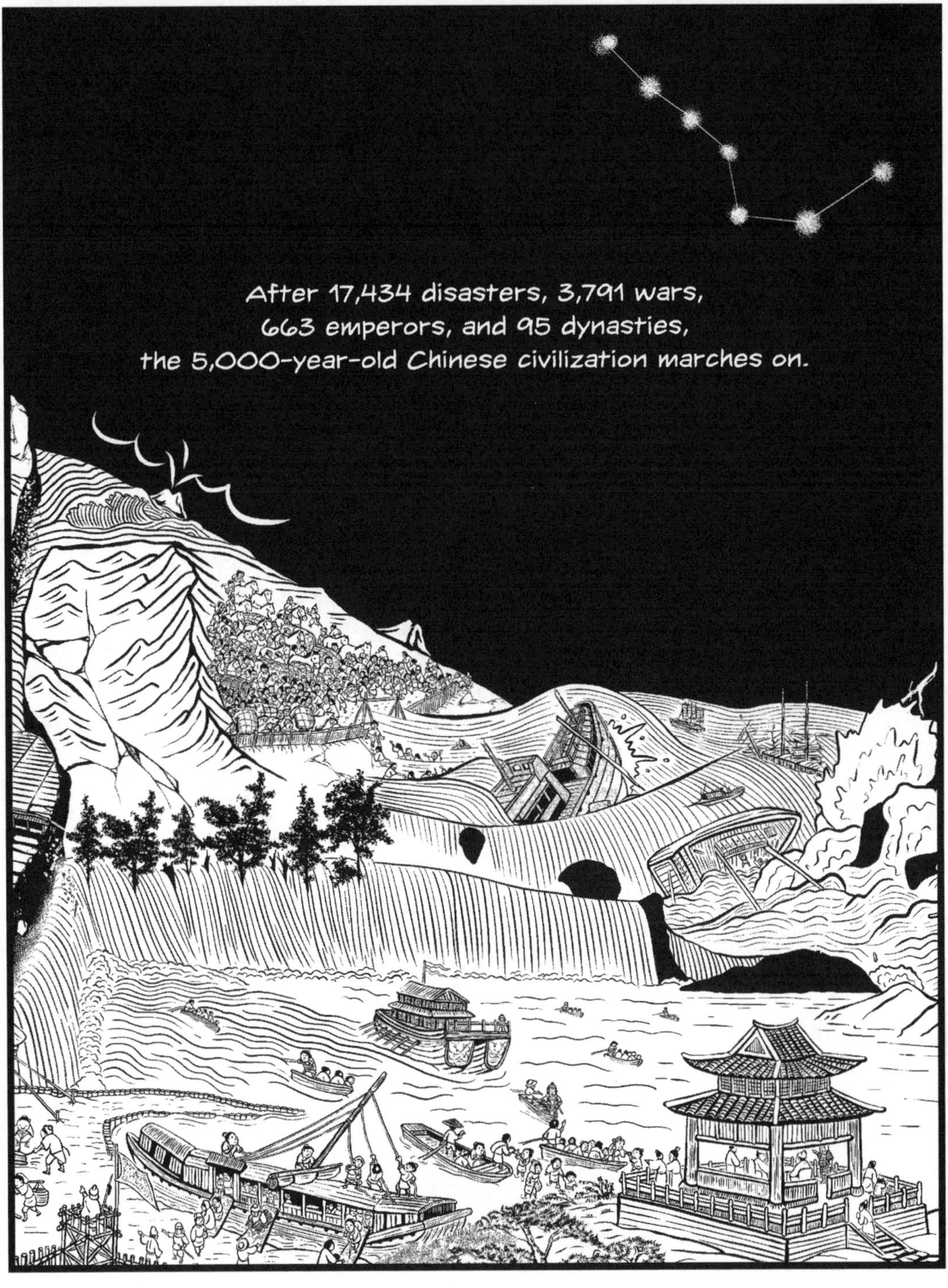
After 17,434 disasters, 3,791 wars,
663 emperors, and 95 dynasties,
the 5,000-year-old Chinese civilization marches on.

Although dynasties decline and collapse, new dynasties are founded and China prospers despite this extraordinary upheaval.

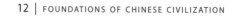

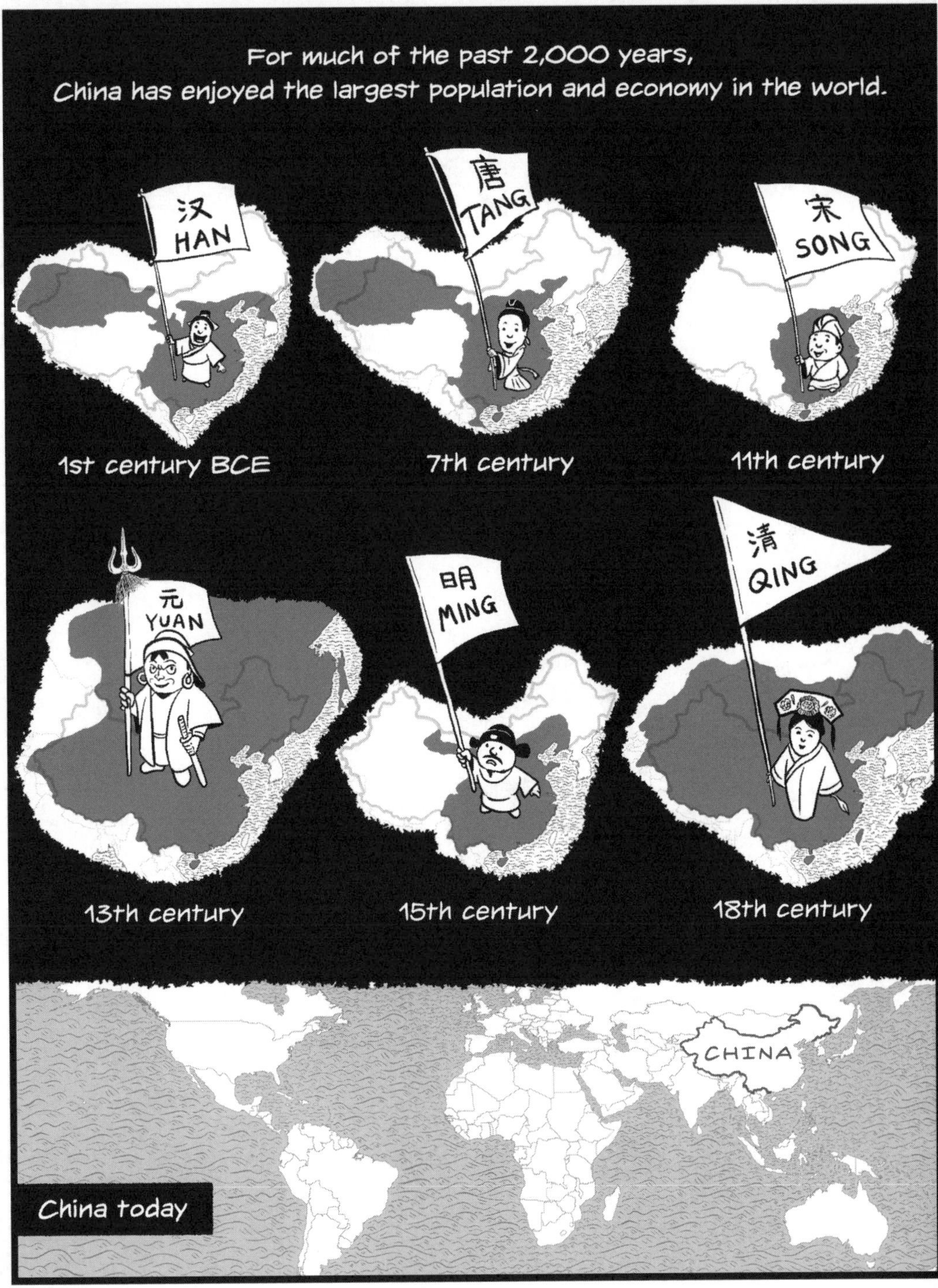
For much of the past 2,000 years,
China has enjoyed the largest population and economy in the world.
汉
HAN
1st century BCE
唐
TANG
7th century
宋
SONG
11th century
元
YUAN
13th century
明
MING
15th century
清
QING
18th century
CHINA
China today

Of the 95 dynasties in China's history, nine were major ones.

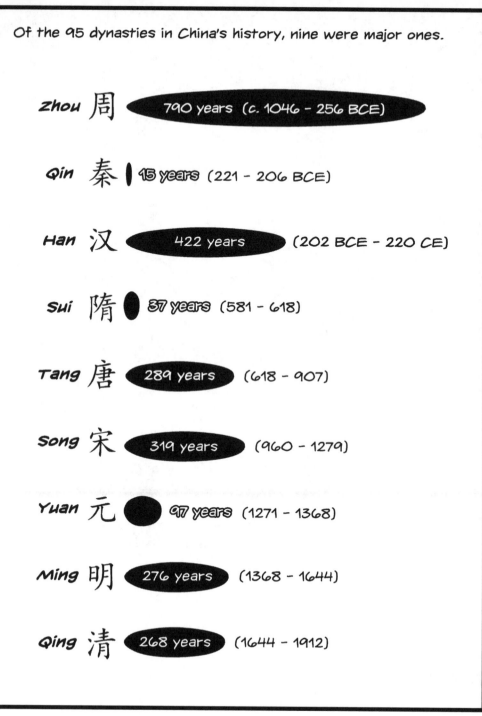

Zhou 周 790 years (c. 1046 – 256 BCE)

Qin 秦 15 years (221 – 206 BCE)

Han 汉 422 years (202 BCE – 220 CE)

Sui 隋 37 years (581 – 618)

Tang 唐 289 years (618 – 907)

Song 宋 319 years (960 – 1279)

Yuan 元 97 years (1271 – 1368)

Ming 明 276 years (1368 – 1644)

Qing 清 268 years (1644 – 1912)

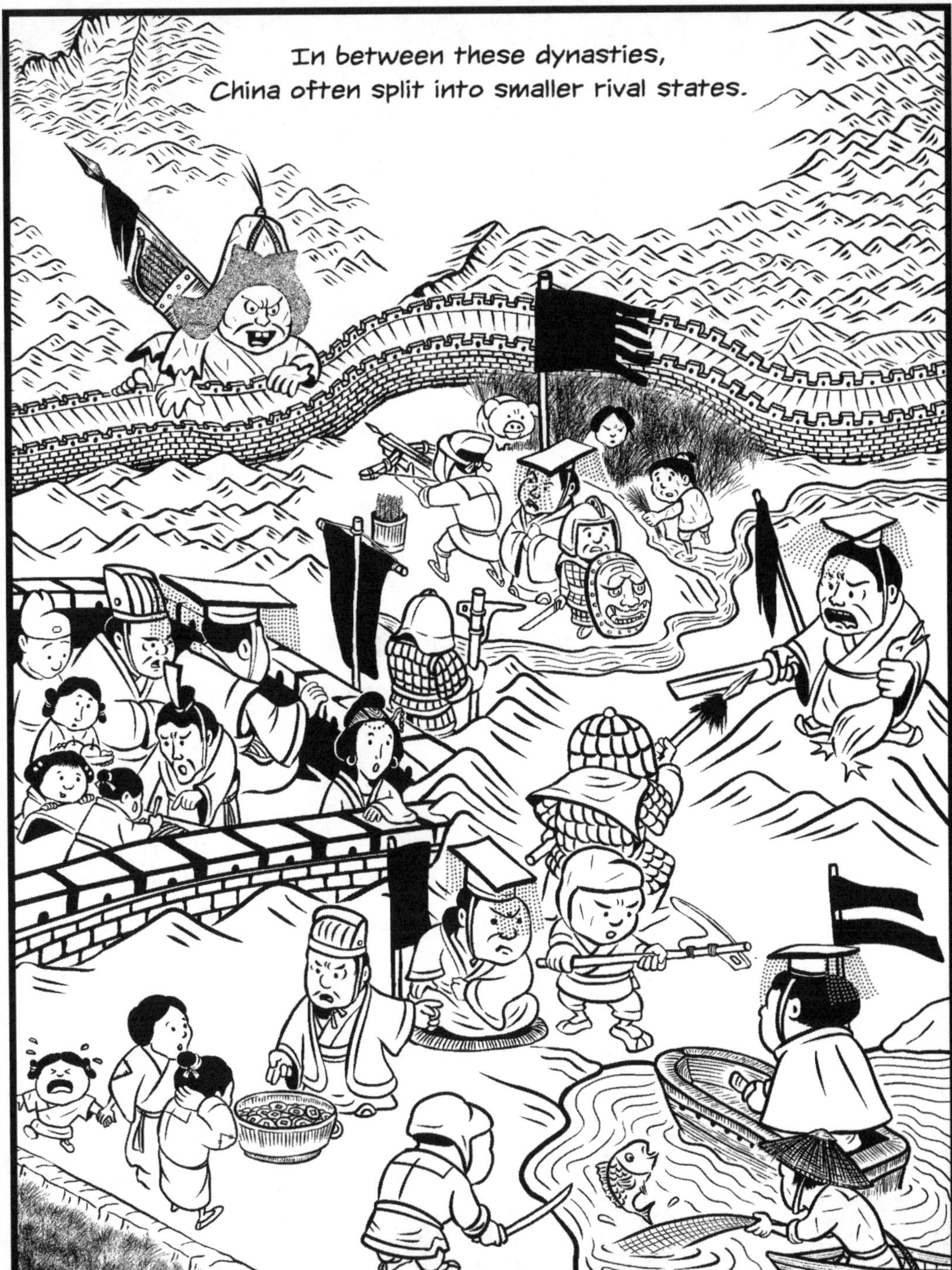
In between these dynasties,
China often split into smaller rival states.

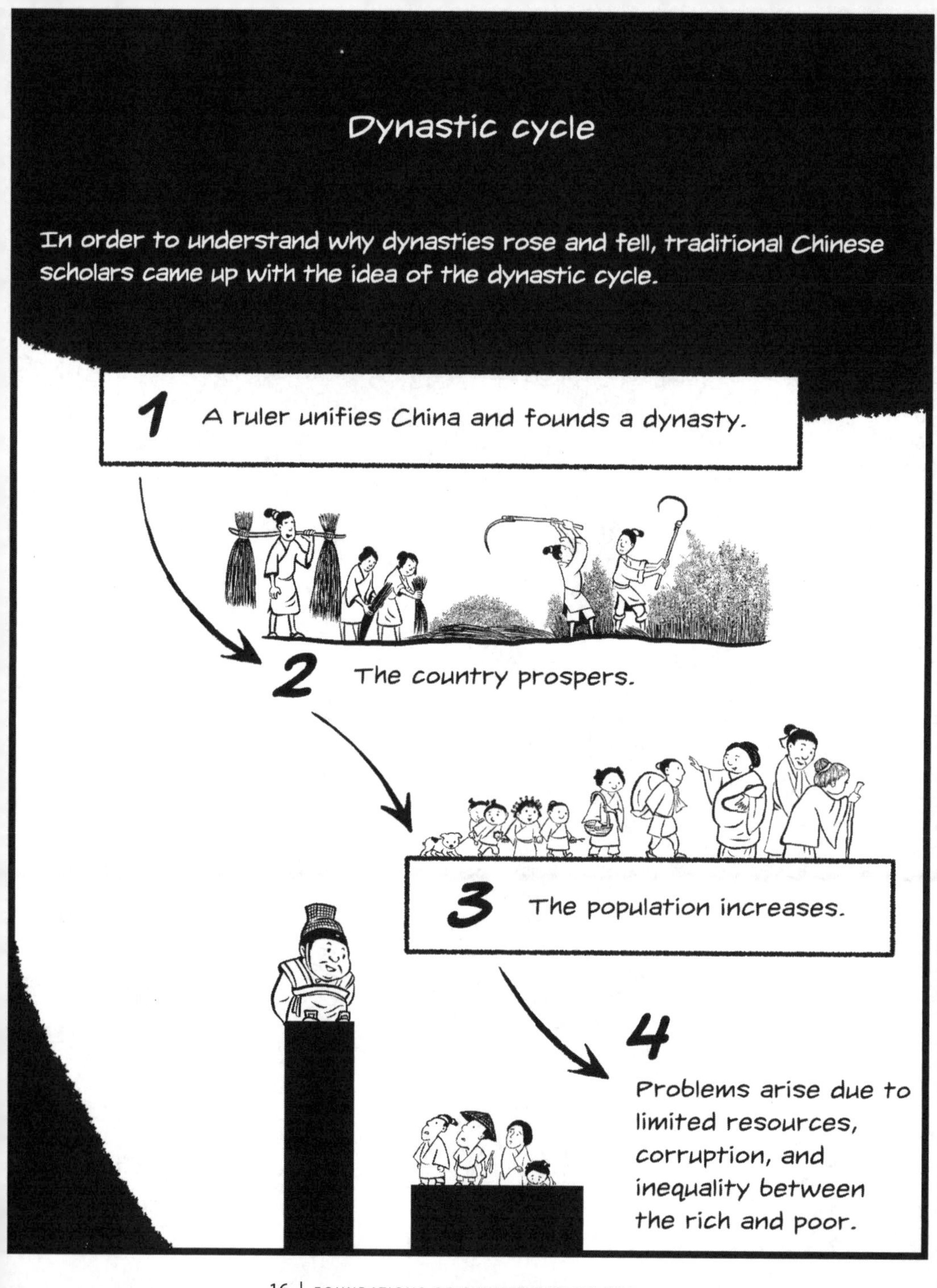
Dynastic cycle
In order to understand why dynasties rose and fell, traditional Chinese scholars came up with the idea of the dynastic cycle.
1 A ruler unifies China and founds a dynasty.
2 The country prospers.
3 The population increases.
4 Problems arise due to limited resources, corruption, and inequality between the rich and poor.

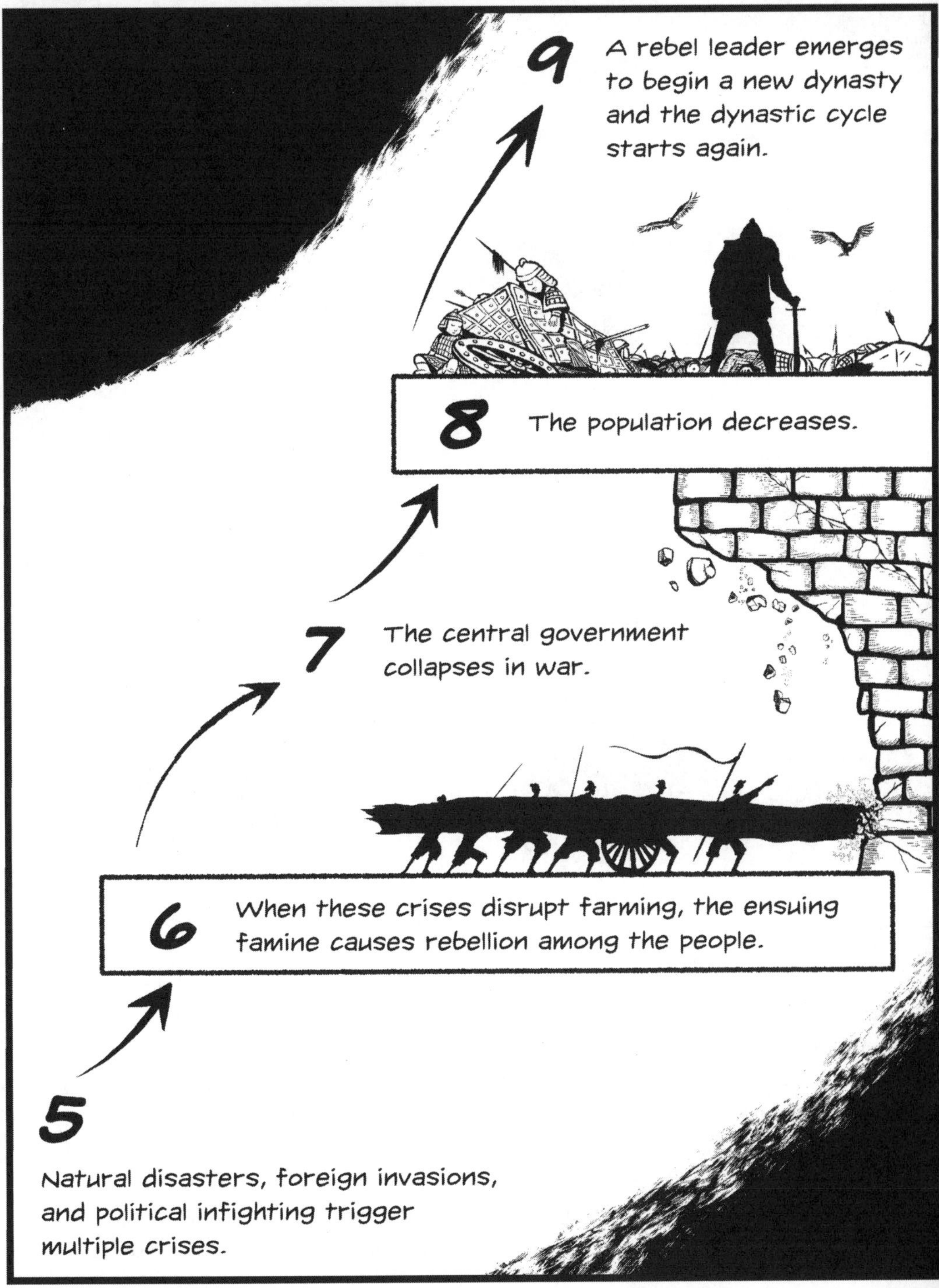
9
A rebel leader emerges to begin a new dynasty and the dynastic cycle starts again.
8
The population decreases.
7
The central government collapses in war.
6
When these crises disrupt farming, the ensuing famine causes rebellion among the people.
5
Natural disasters, foreign invasions, and political infighting trigger multiple crises.

Geography of China

Natural disasters played a vital role in the dynastic cycle.
China's geography makes it extremely vulnerable to such disasters.

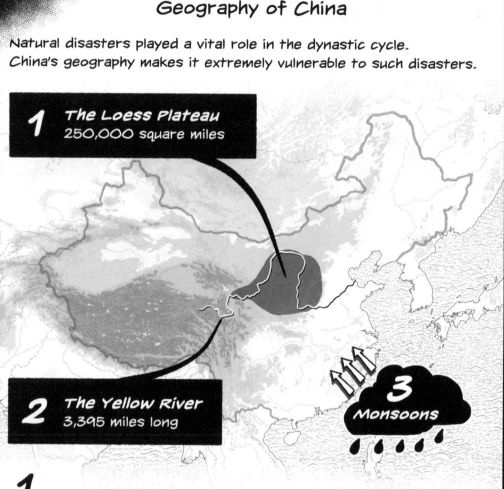

1 **The Loess Plateau**
250,000 square miles

2 **The Yellow River**
3,395 miles long

3 Monsoons

1

The Loess Plateau features the largest accumulation of dust
on earth. It is roughly the size of Texas, or of Germany and
the U.K. combined. The loess is made up of wind-blown desert dust,
as well as deposits from the last Ice Age, which ended around
11,000 years ago.

Loose soil and a lack of vegetation have made the Loess Plateau
more vulnerable to soil erosion than any other region in the world.

2

The Yellow River cuts through the Loess Plateau. The soil gives the river its yellow hue. In its lower reaches, the Yellow River becomes the planet's muddiest river.

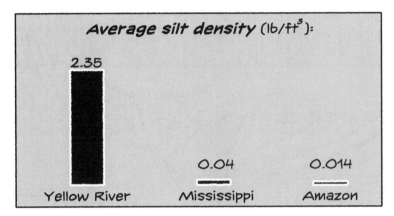

Average silt density (lb/ft³):

- 2.35 — Yellow River
- 0.04 — Mississippi
- 0.014 — Amazon

Silt from the Loess Plateau fills the riverbed and water has to find new ways to reach the sea, causing floods.

3

Seasonal winds, also known as monsoons, compound the problem. During monsoon season, annual rainfall is concentrated in a span of three months during the summer. This intense precipitation often leads to floods followed by droughts.

Because of erosion from the Loess Plateau, silt in the Yellow River, and rain from monsoons, China has suffered 1,621 floods and 1,392 droughts over 2,000 years according to official Chinese histories meticulously compiled by each dynasty.

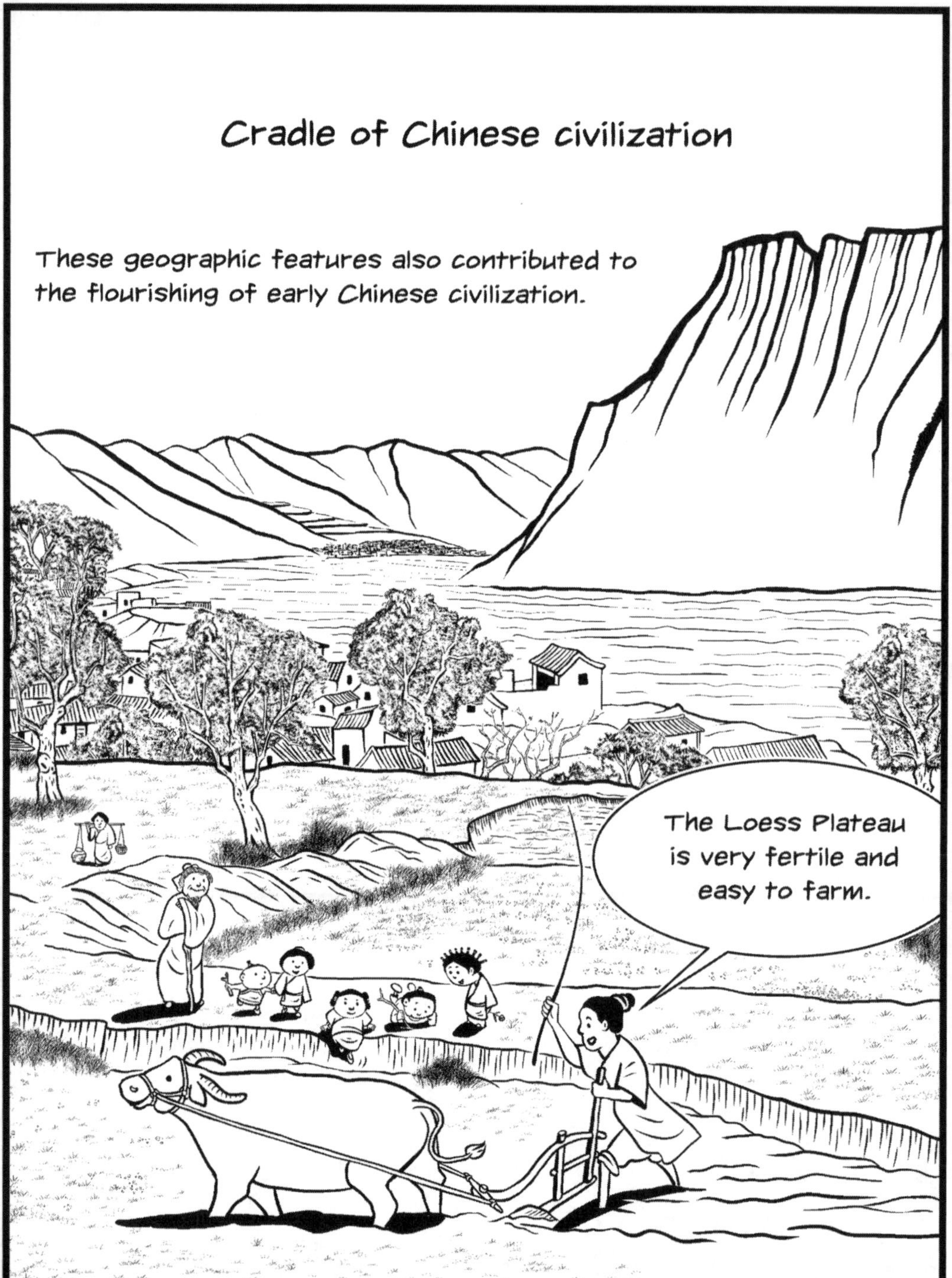
Cradle of Chinese civilization
These geographic features also contributed to the flourishing of early Chinese civilization.
The Loess Plateau is very fertile and easy to farm.

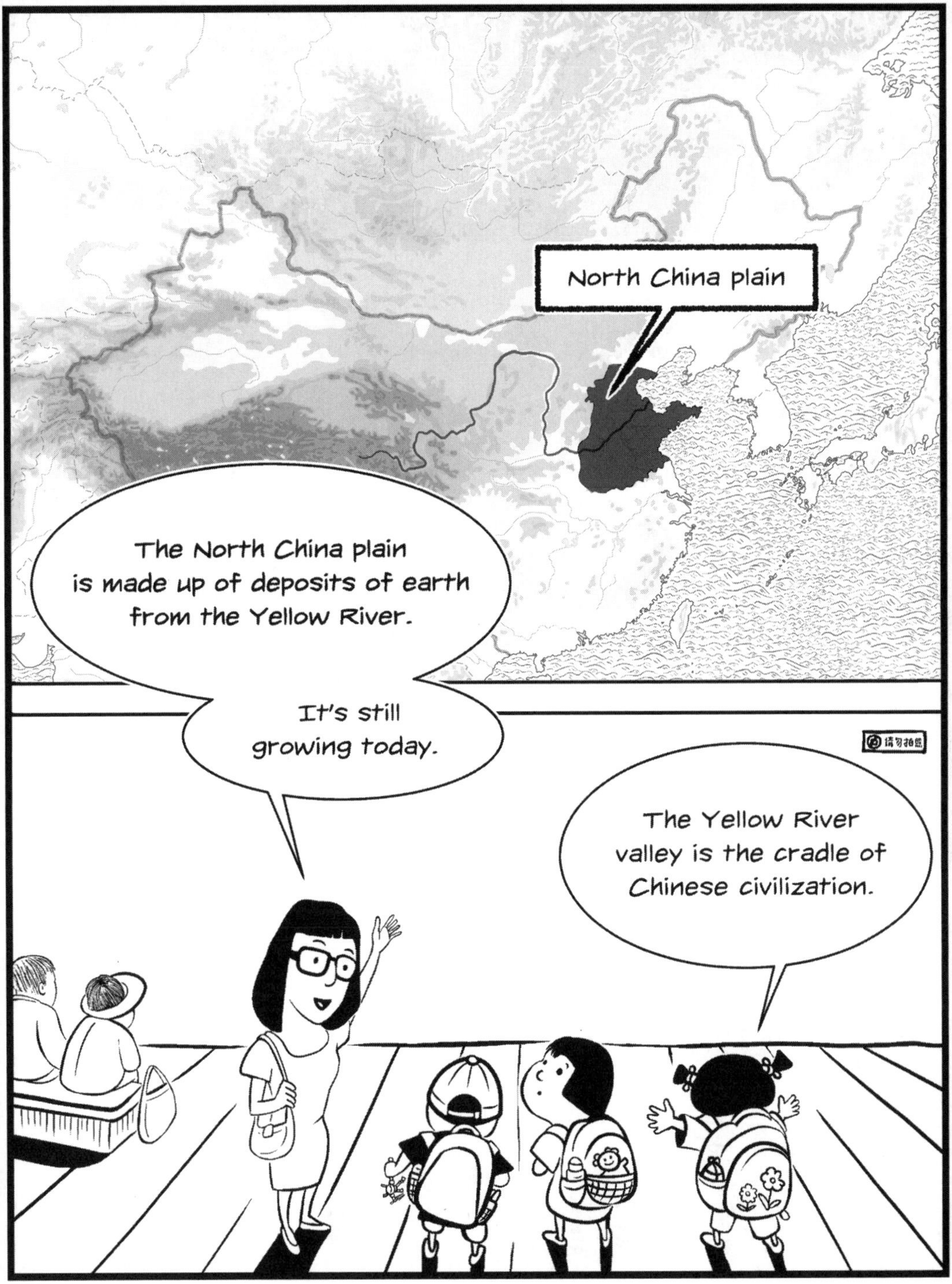
North China plain
The North China plain is made up of deposits of earth from the Yellow River.
It's still growing today.
The Yellow River valley is the cradle of Chinese civilization.

Beyond the 16-inch rain belt

Looking from the North China plain, China's terrain ascends in three sections from east to west.

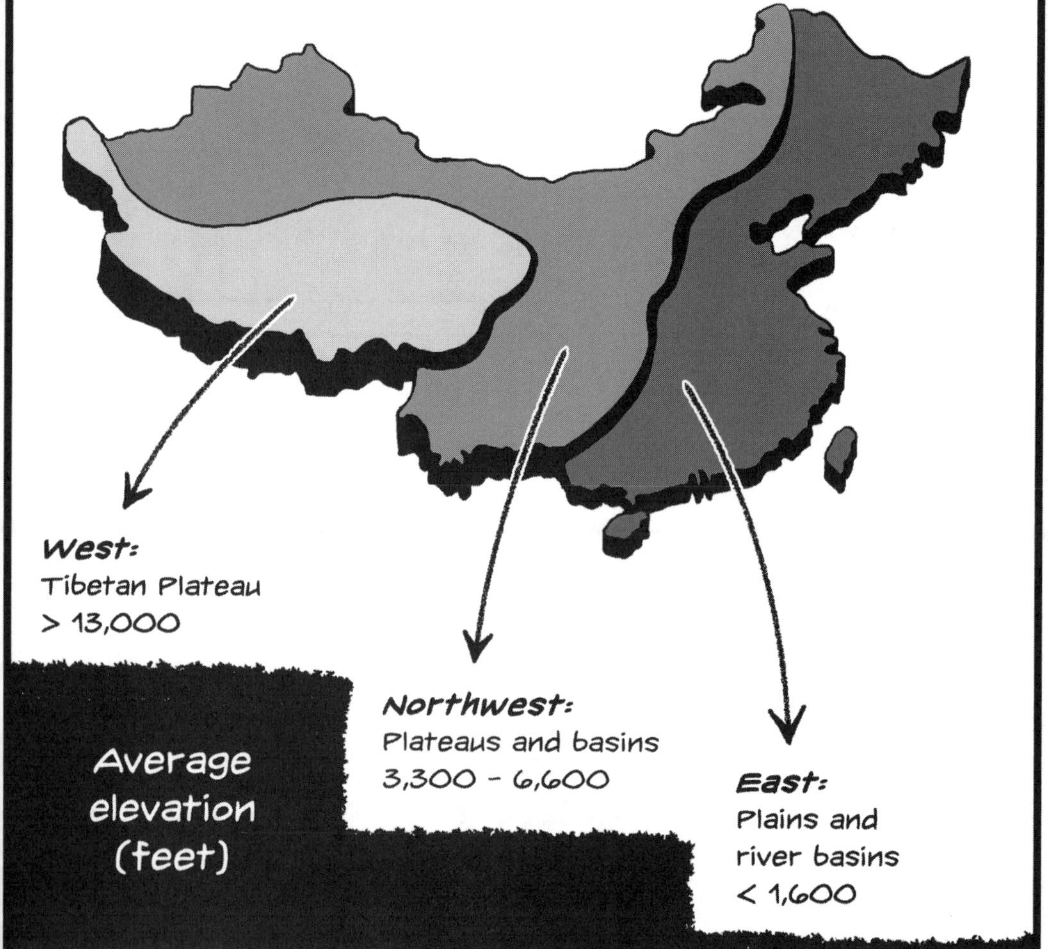
West:
Tibetan Plateau
> 13,000
Northwest:
Plateaus and basins
3,300 - 6,600
East:
Plains and
river basins
< 1,600
Average
elevation
(feet)

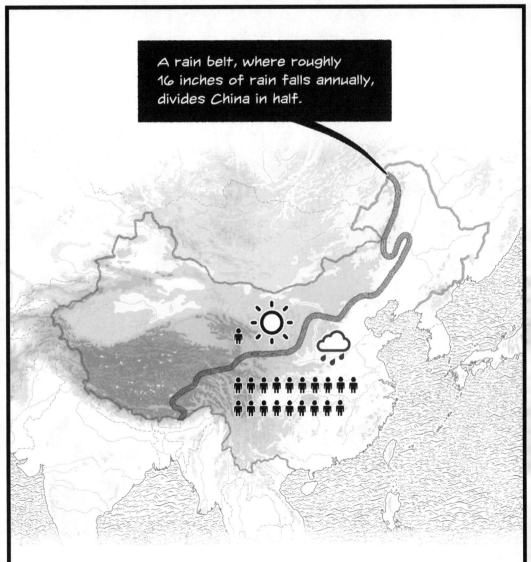

A rain belt, where roughly 16 inches of rain falls annually, divides China in half.

Agricultural production is concentrated to the east of the rain belt line, where more than 16 inches of rain falls each year. The western half of China, where less rain falls because high terrain blocks the summer monsoons, is dry and barren.

Today, due to water shortages, only 5% of Chinese live west of the rain belt.

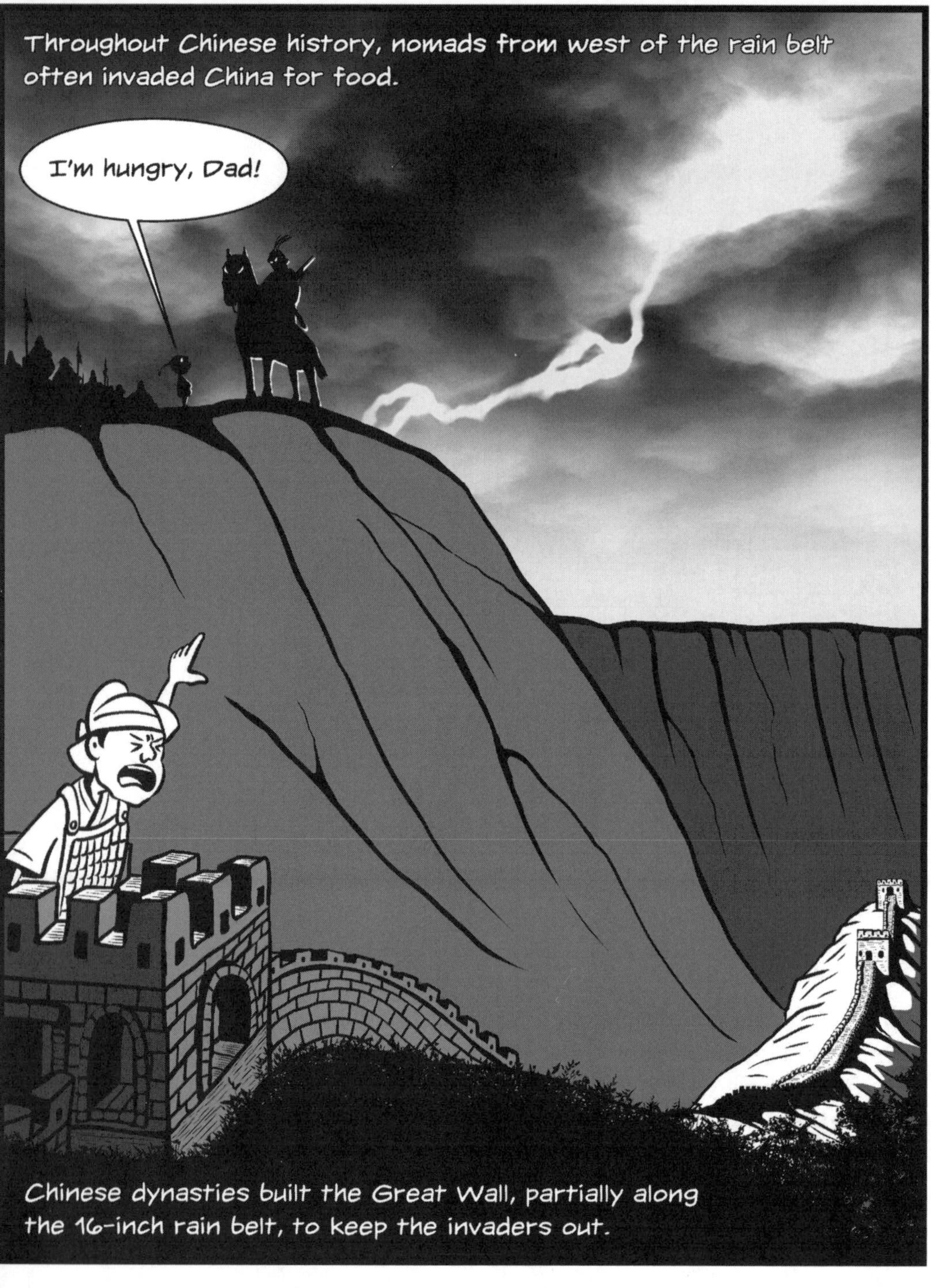
Throughout Chinese history, nomads from west of the rain belt often invaded China for food.
I'm hungry, Dad!
Chinese dynasties built the Great Wall, partially along the 16-inch rain belt, to keep the invaders out.

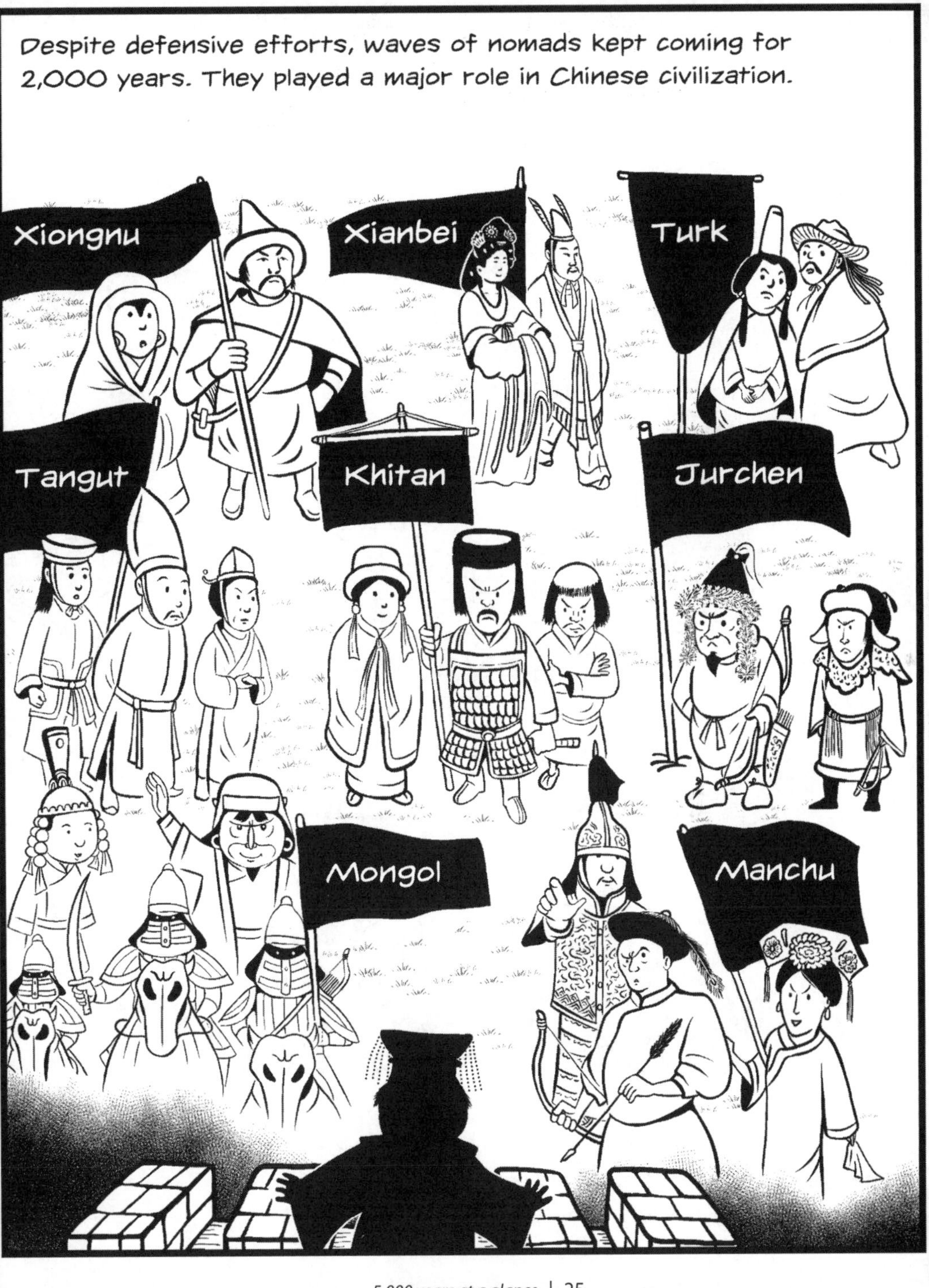
Despite defensive efforts, waves of nomads kept coming for 2,000 years. They played a major role in Chinese civilization.
Xiongnu
Xianbei
Turk
Tangut
Khitan
Jurchen
Mongol
Manchu

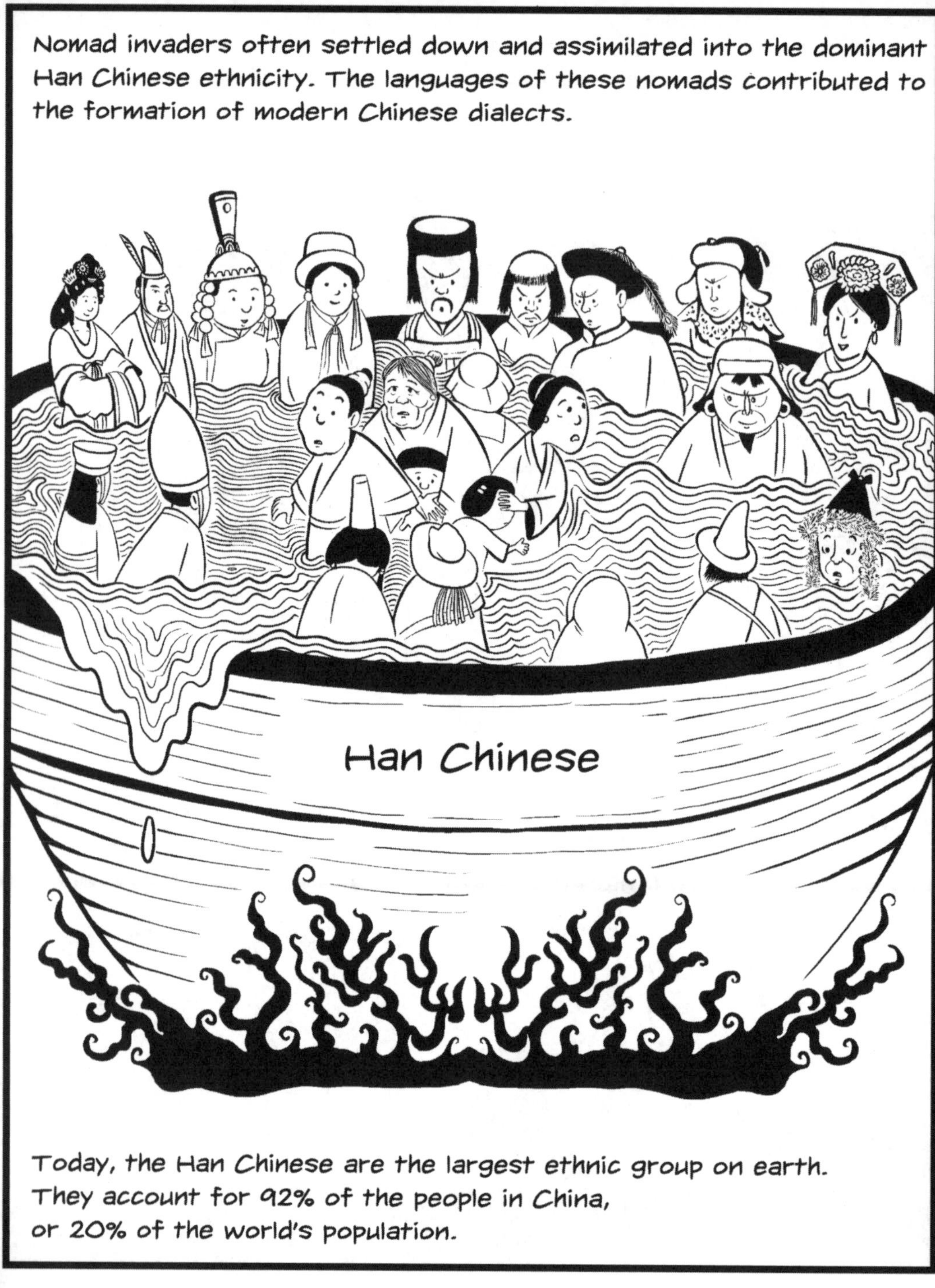
Nomad invaders often settled down and assimilated into the dominant Han Chinese ethnicity. The languages of these nomads contributed to the formation of modern Chinese dialects.
Han Chinese
Today, the Han Chinese are the largest ethnic group on earth. They account for 92% of the people in China, or 20% of the world's population.

Centralization

Having a centralized government for half its history has allowed China to survive as an agriculture-based economy, despite being prone to floods, droughts, and nomad invasions.

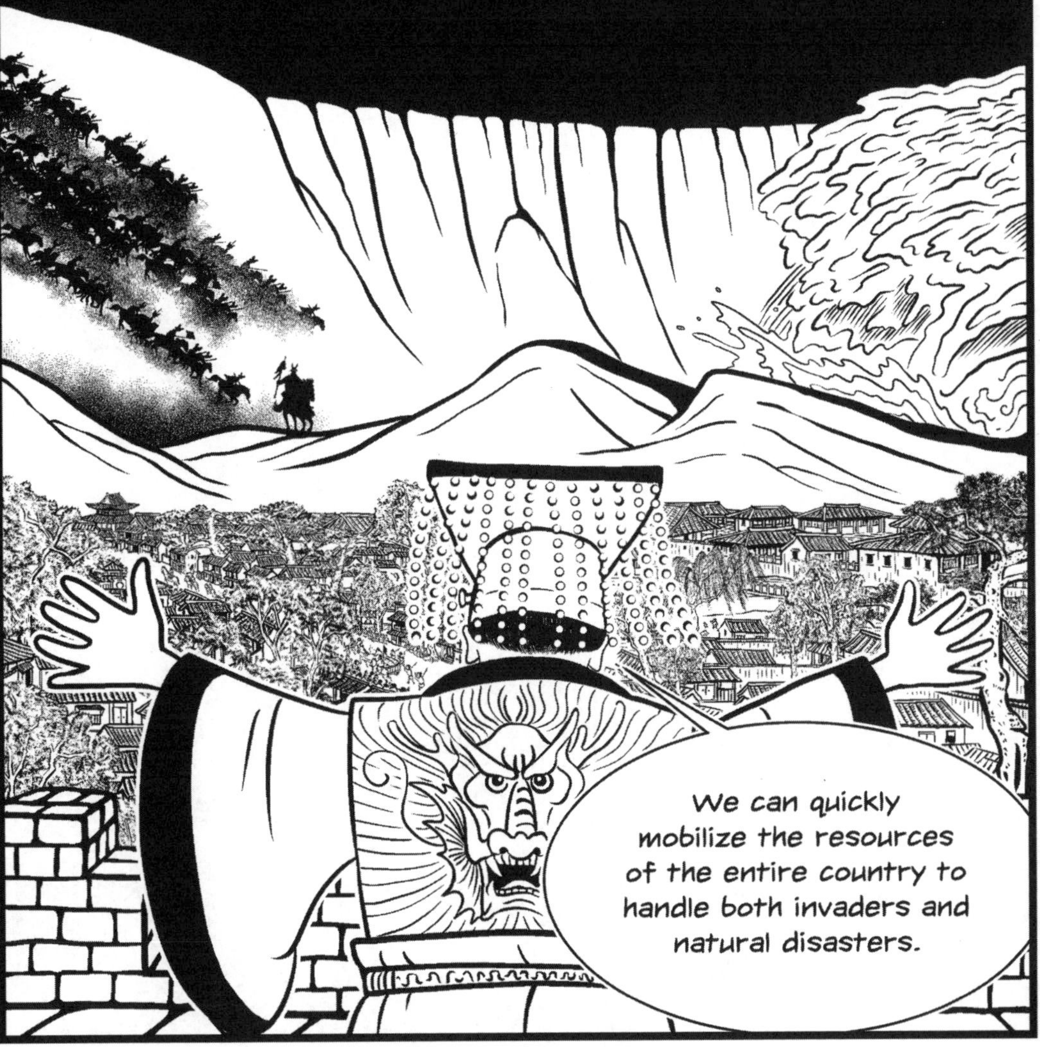
We can quickly mobilize the resources of the entire country to handle both invaders and natural disasters.

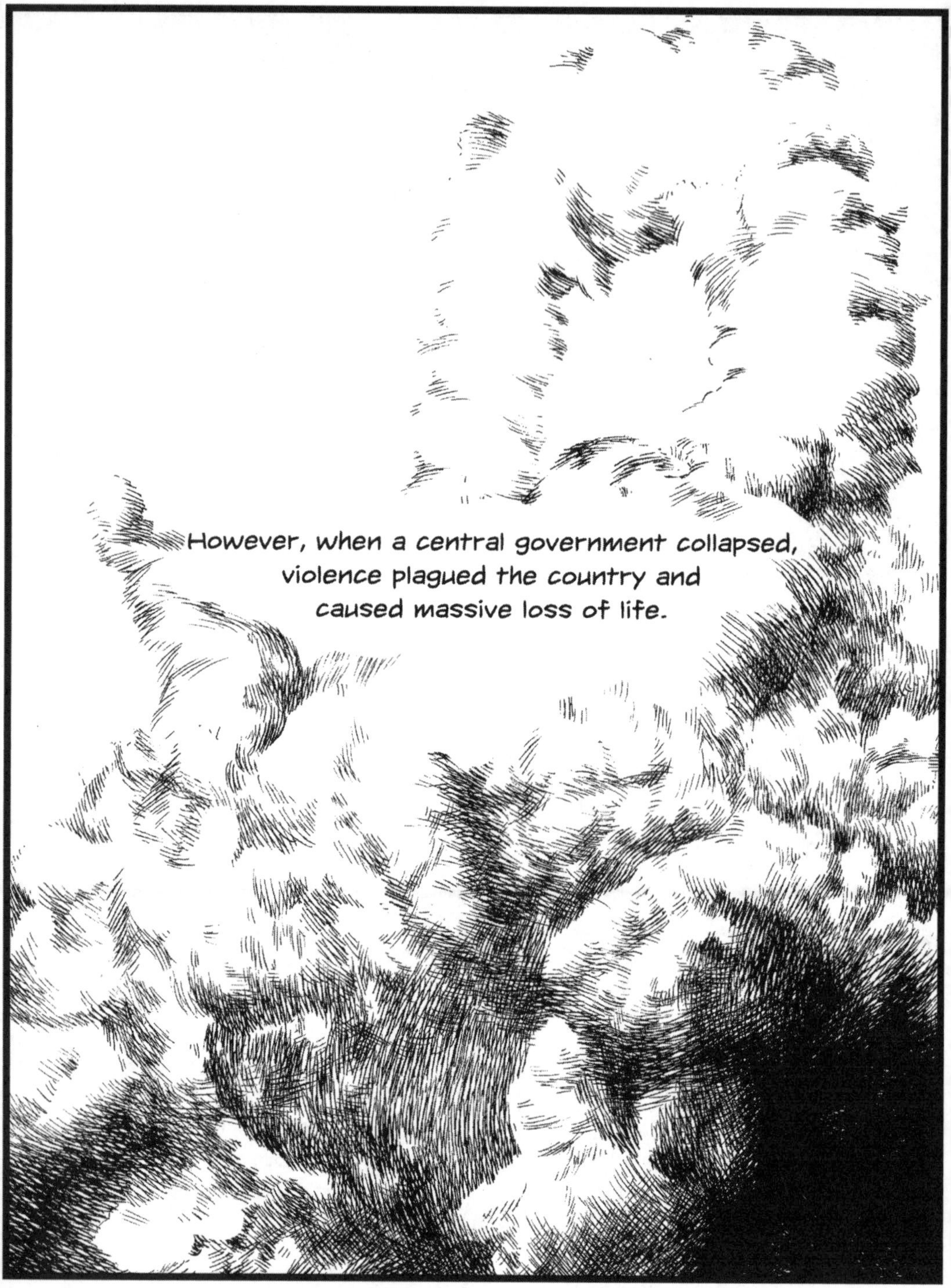
However, when a central government collapsed, violence plagued the country and caused massive loss of life.

As many as 2/3 of the population might perish during a dynastic change.

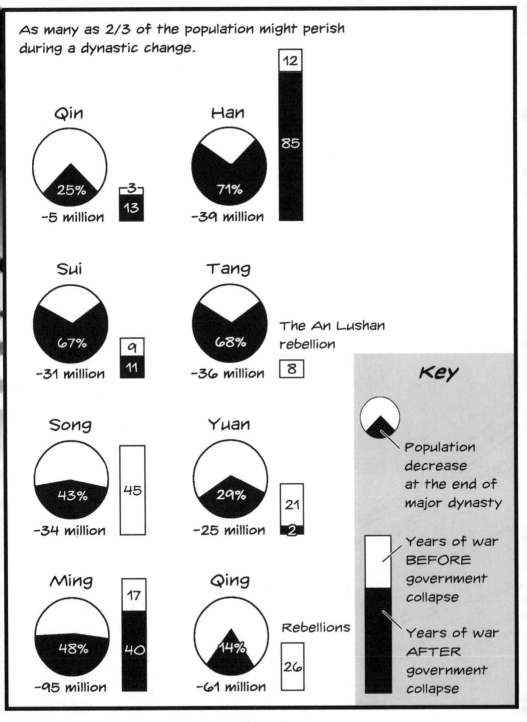

Qin
25%
-5 million
3
13

Han
12
85
71%
-39 million

Sui
67%
-31 million
9
11

Tang
68%
-36 million
The An Lushan rebellion
8

Song
43%
-34 million
45

Yuan
29%
-25 million
21
2

Ming
48%
-95 million
17
40

Qing
14%
-61 million
Rebellions
26

Key

Population decrease at the end of major dynasty

Years of war BEFORE government collapse

Years of war AFTER government collapse

WHO ARE THE CHINESE PEOPLE?

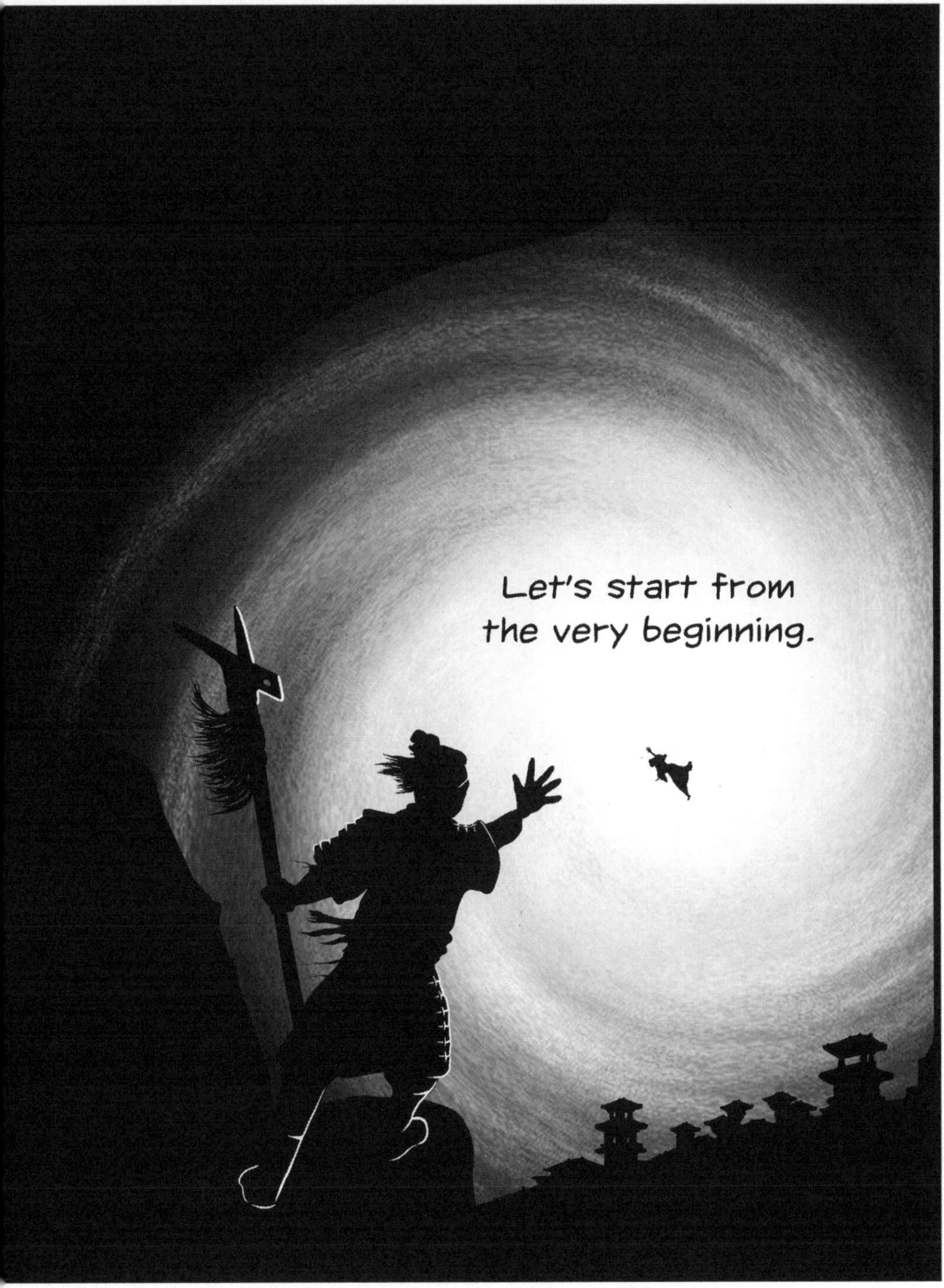
Let's start from
the very beginning.

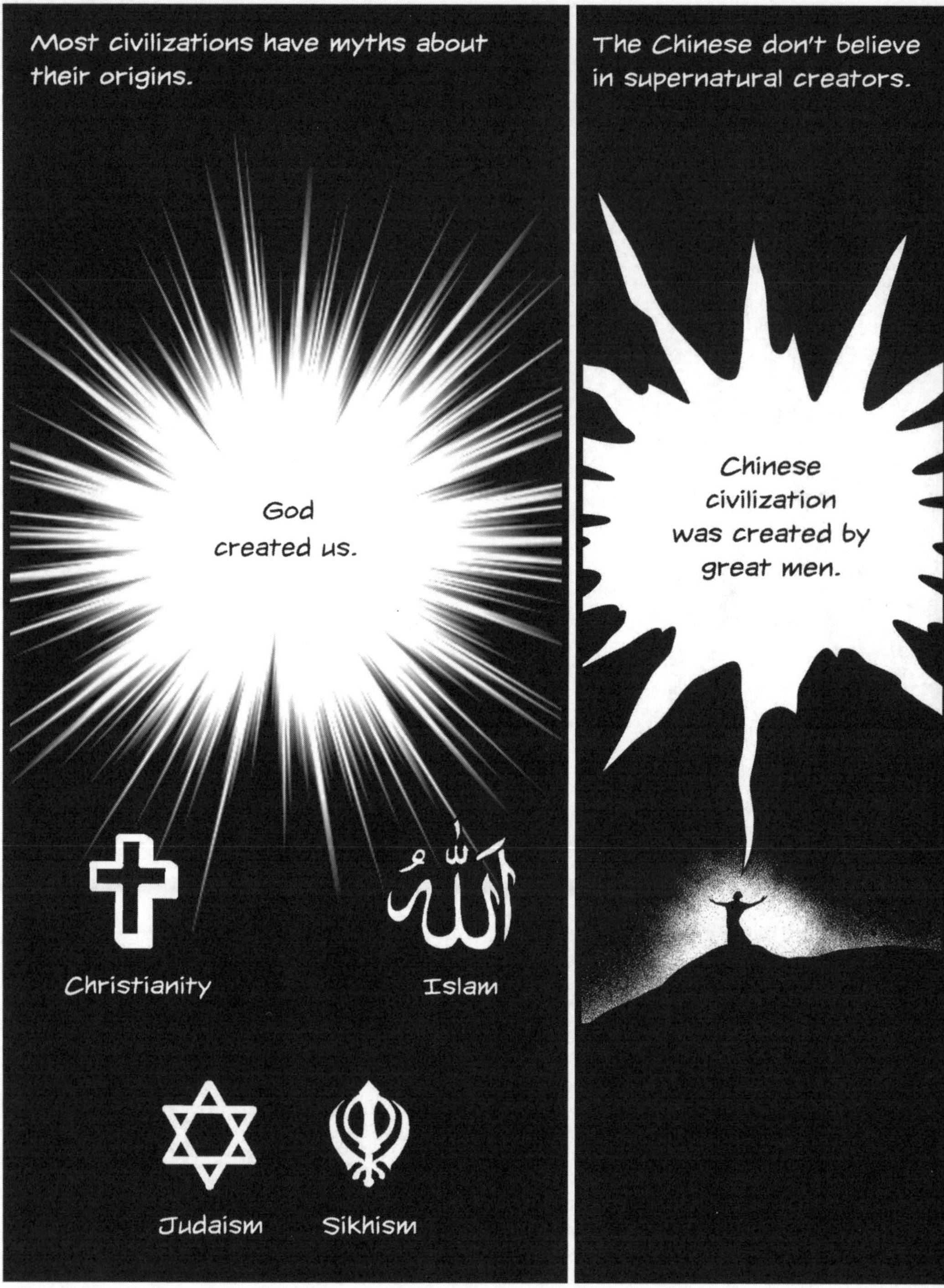
Most civilizations have myths about their origins.
God created us.
Christianity
Islam
Judaism
Sikhism
The Chinese don't believe in supernatural creators.
Chinese civilization was created by great men.

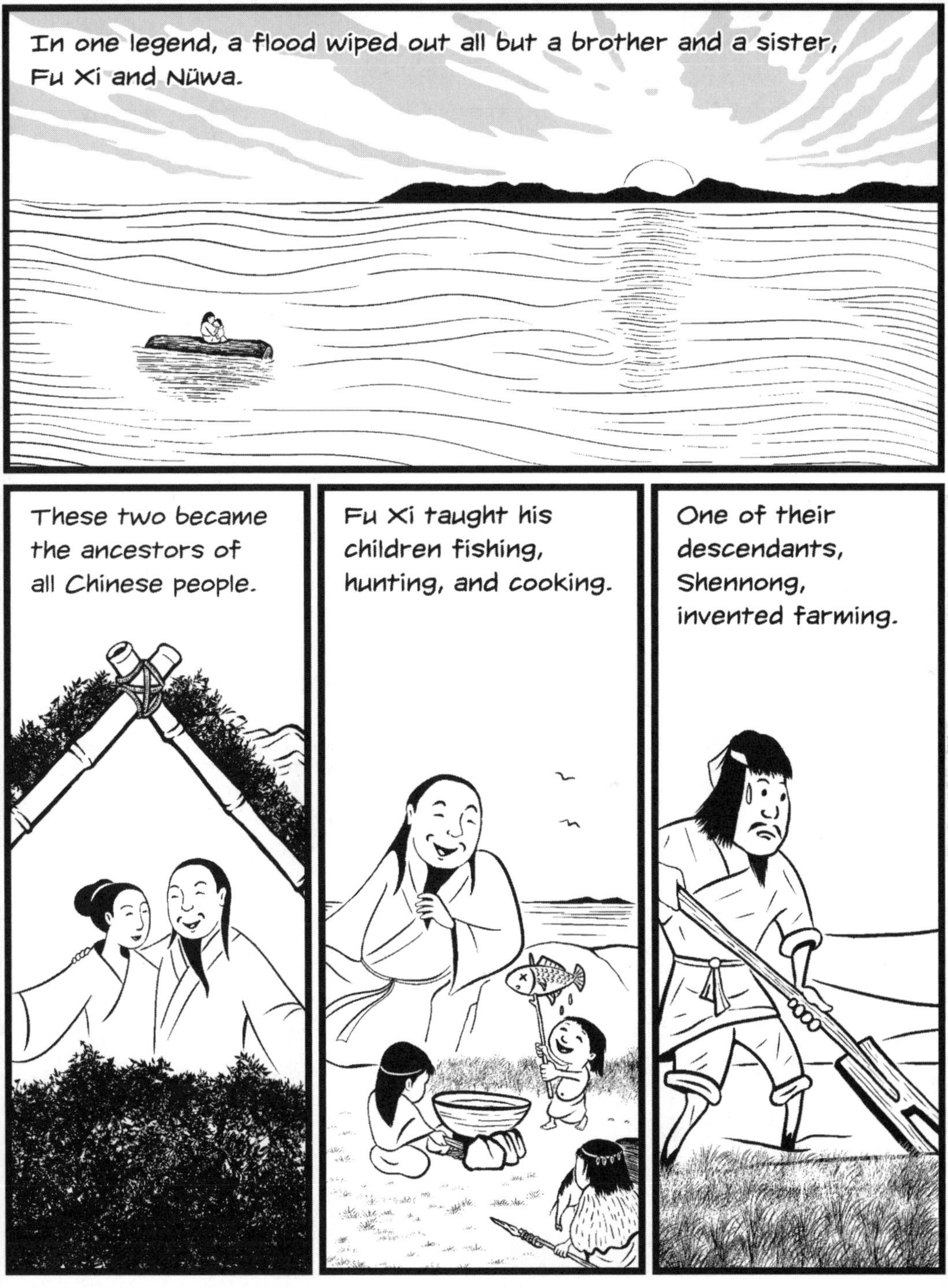
In one legend, a flood wiped out all but a brother and a sister, Fu Xi and Nüwa.
These two became the ancestors of all Chinese people.
Fu Xi taught his children fishing, hunting, and cooking.
One of their descendants, Shennong, invented farming.

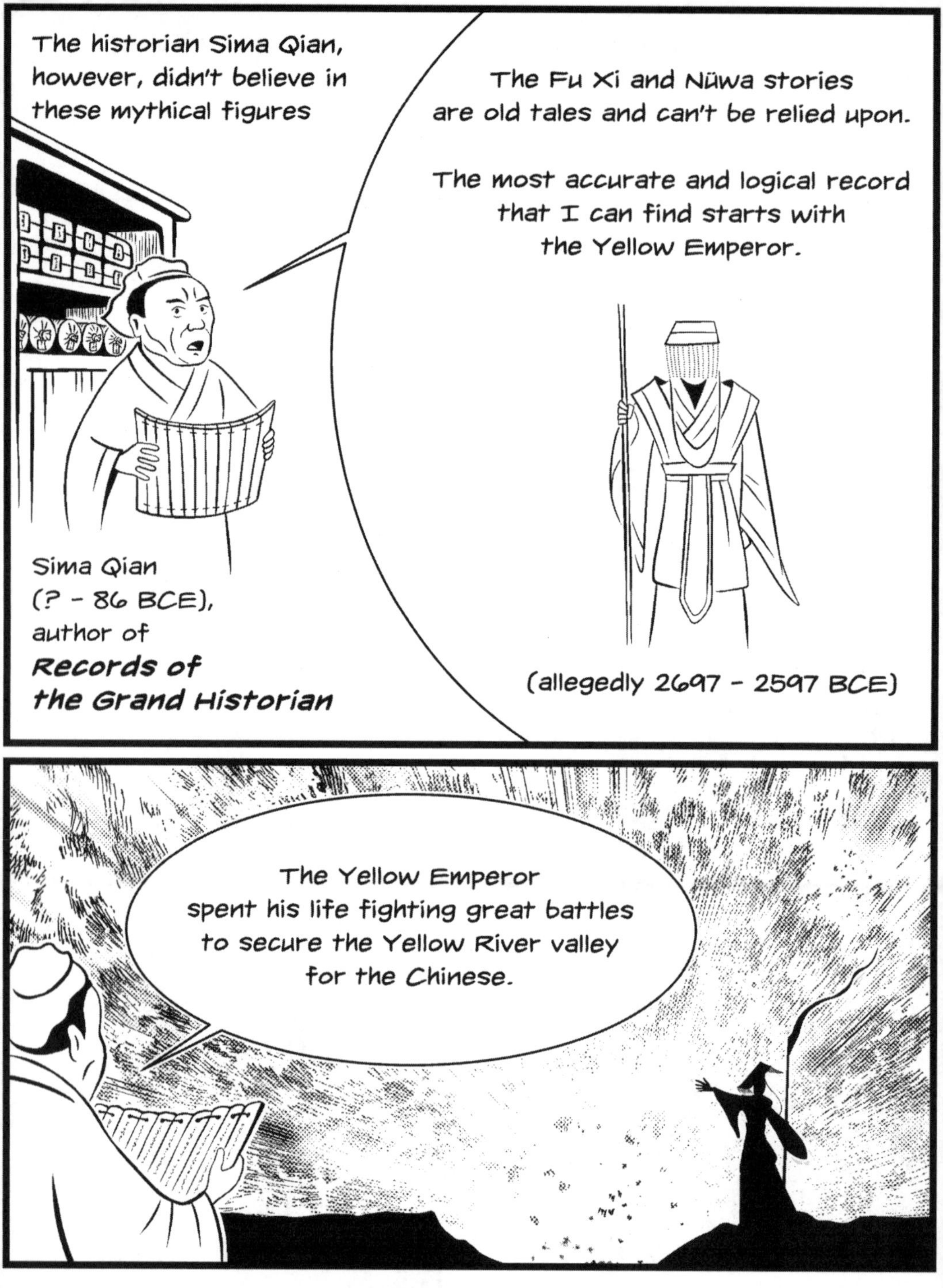

The historian Sima Qian, however, didn't believe in these mythical figures
The Fu Xi and Nüwa stories are old tales and can't be relied upon.
The most accurate and logical record that I can find starts with the Yellow Emperor.
Sima Qian (? - 86 BCE), author of *Records of the Grand Historian*
(allegedly 2697 - 2597 BCE)
The Yellow Emperor spent his life fighting great battles to secure the Yellow River valley for the Chinese.

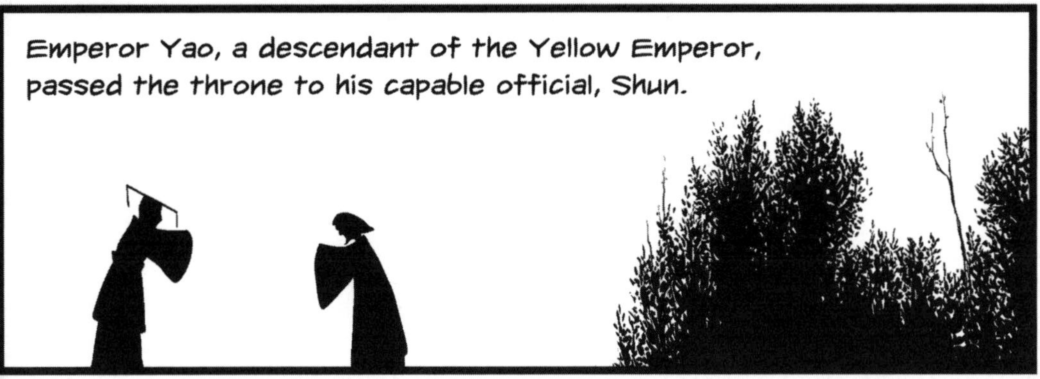
Emperor Yao, a descendant of the Yellow Emperor, passed the throne to his capable official, Shun.

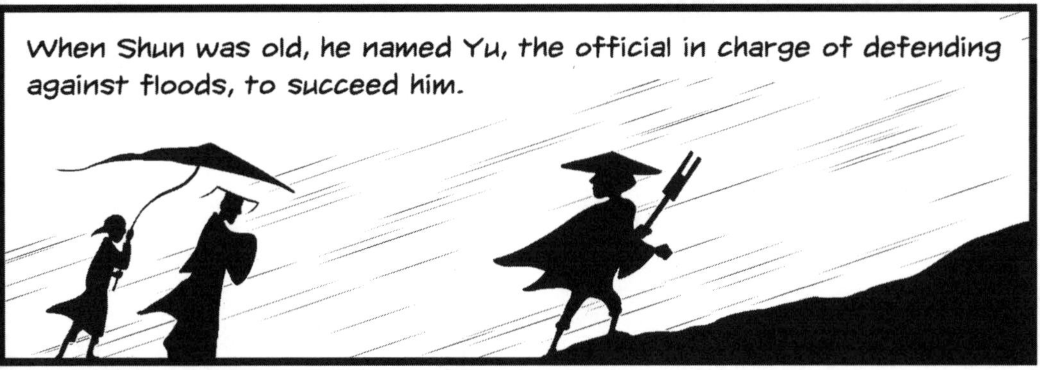
When Shun was old, he named Yu, the official in charge of defending against floods, to succeed him.

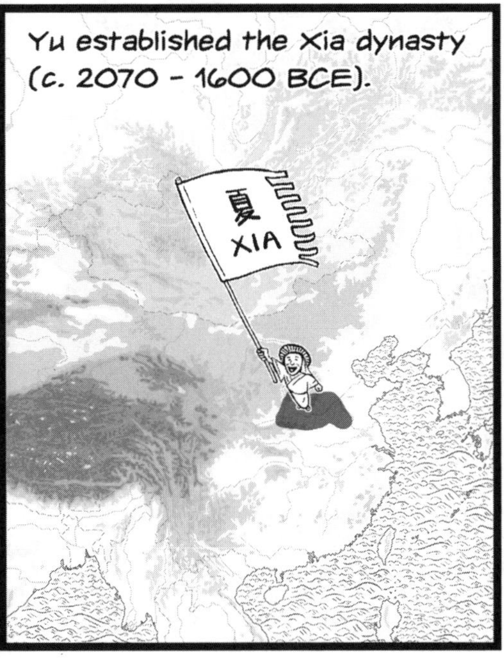
Yu established the Xia dynasty (c. 2070 - 1600 BCE).
夏
XIA

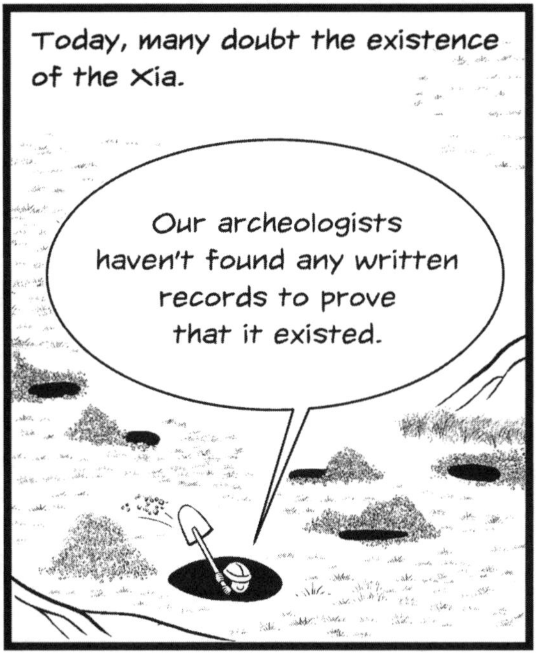
Today, many doubt the existence of the Xia.
Our archeologists haven't found any written records to prove that it existed.

THE SHANG DYNASTY

c. 1600 – 1046 BCE

As history would have it, the Shang followed
the quasi-legendary Xia dynasty.

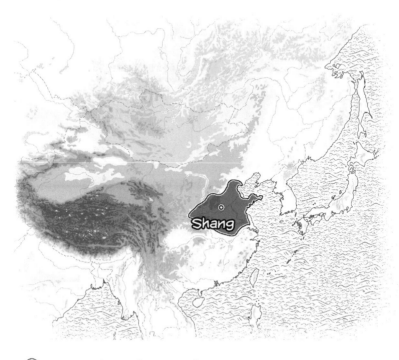

◎ Capital Yin (Anyang)

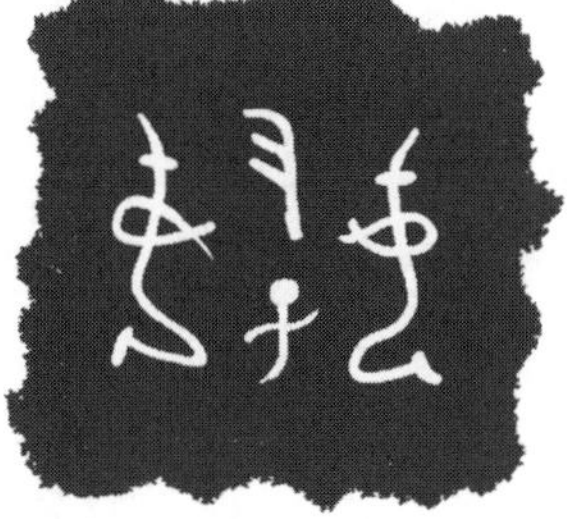

Writing appeared and Chinese civilization made the leap from myth to history.

Ancient Chinese written characters, known as oracle bone script, were carved on animal bones or turtle shells.

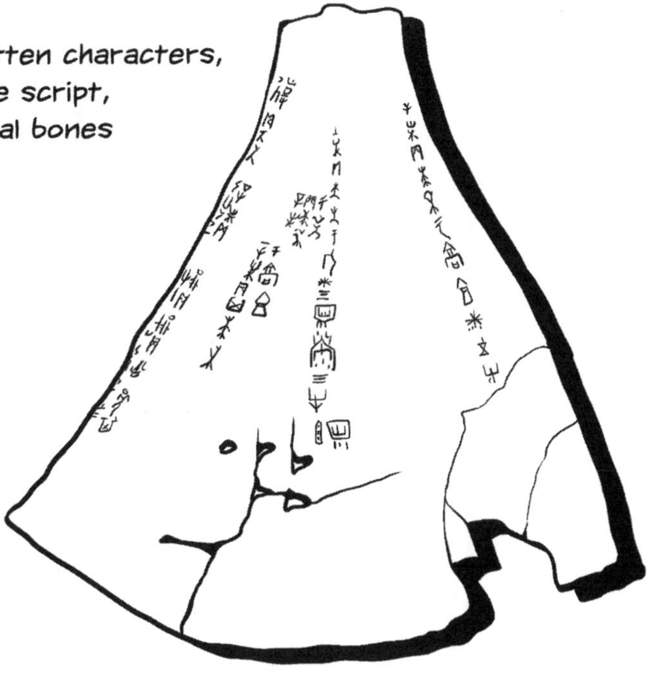

Oracle bone script
(c. 1200 – 1050 BCE)

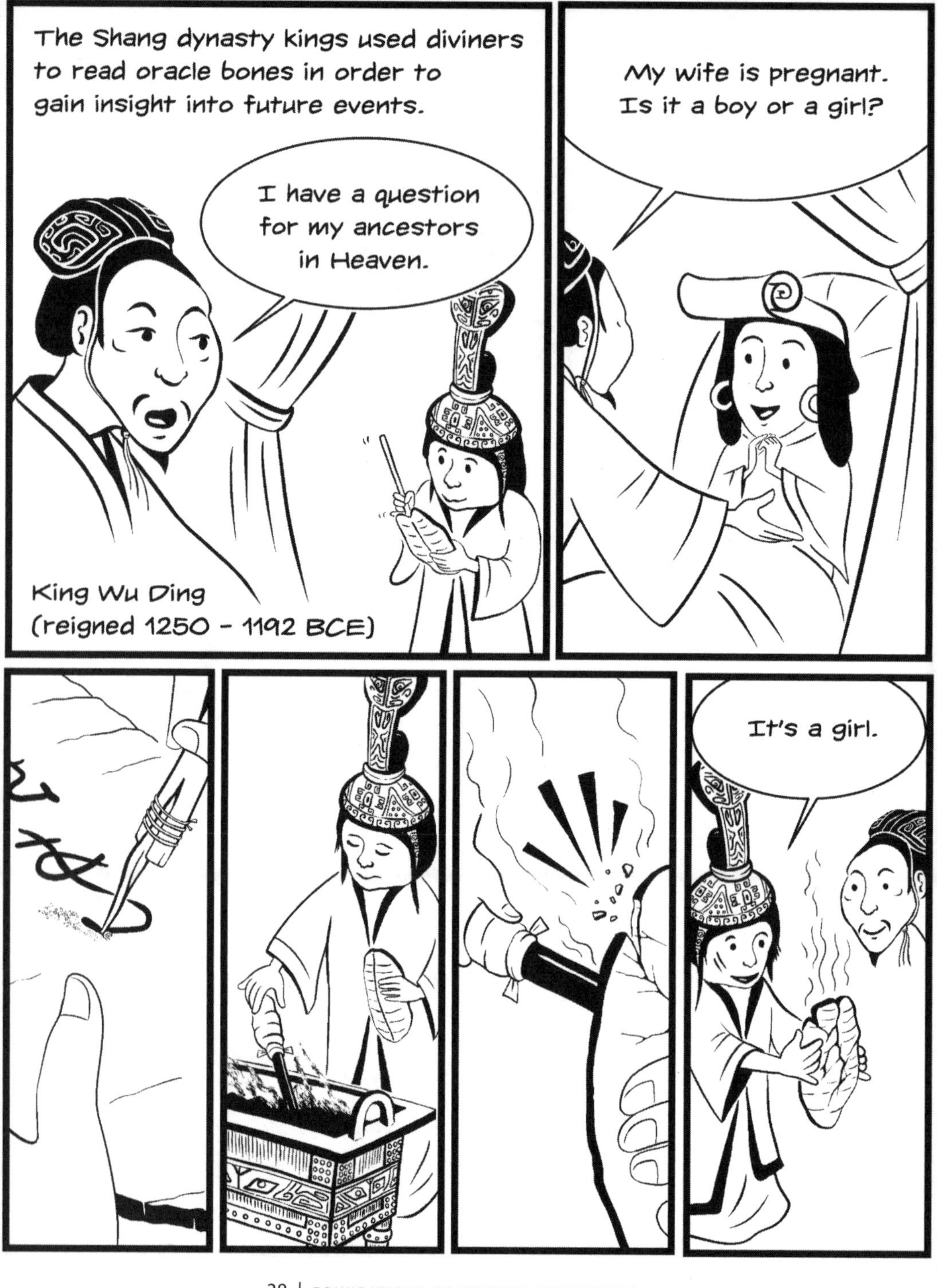
The Shang dynasty kings used diviners to read oracle bones in order to gain insight into future events.
I have a question for my ancestors in Heaven.
King Wu Ding (reigned 1250 - 1192 BCE)
My wife is pregnant. Is it a boy or a girl?
It's a girl.

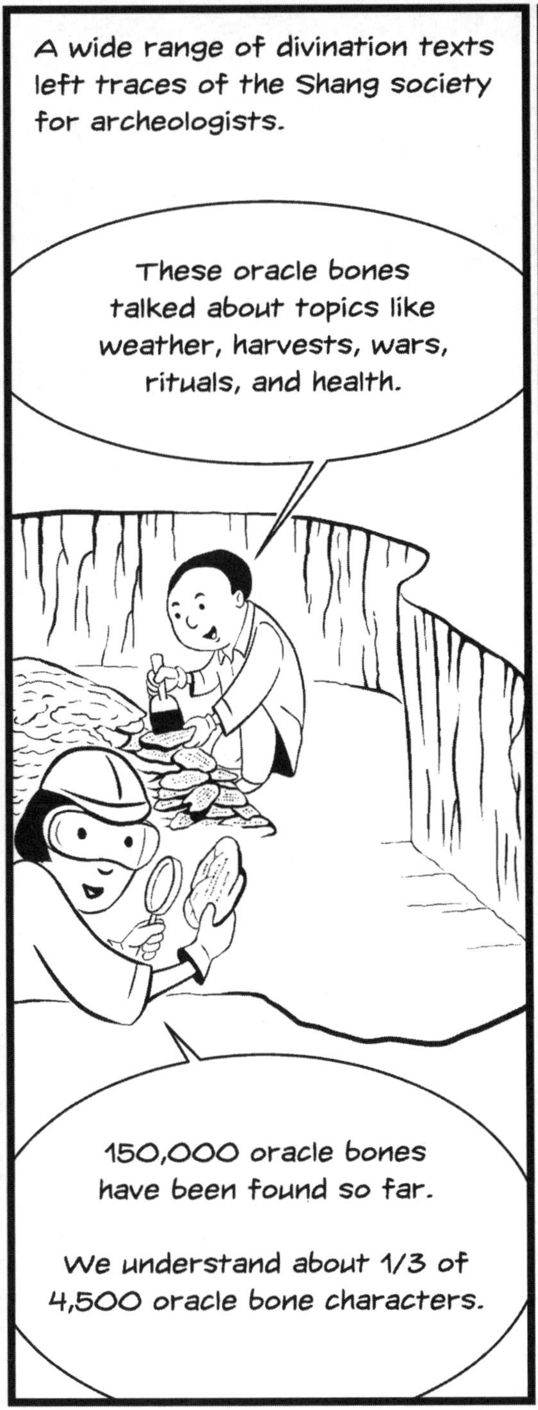
A wide range of divination texts left traces of the Shang society for archeologists.
These oracle bones talked about topics like weather, harvests, wars, rituals, and health.
150,000 oracle bones have been found so far.
We understand about 1/3 of 4,500 oracle bone characters.

Some modern Chinese characters can be traced back to the Shang.

Oracle bone script	Modern Chinese	Core meaning
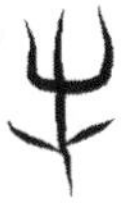	牛	ox
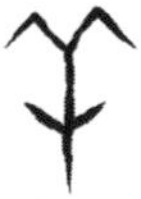	羊	goat
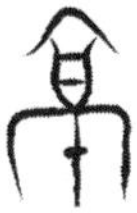	京	capital
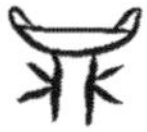	鼎	vessel
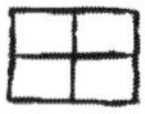	田	field
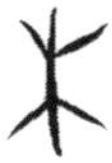	木	tree
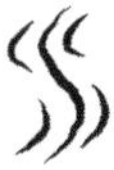	水	water

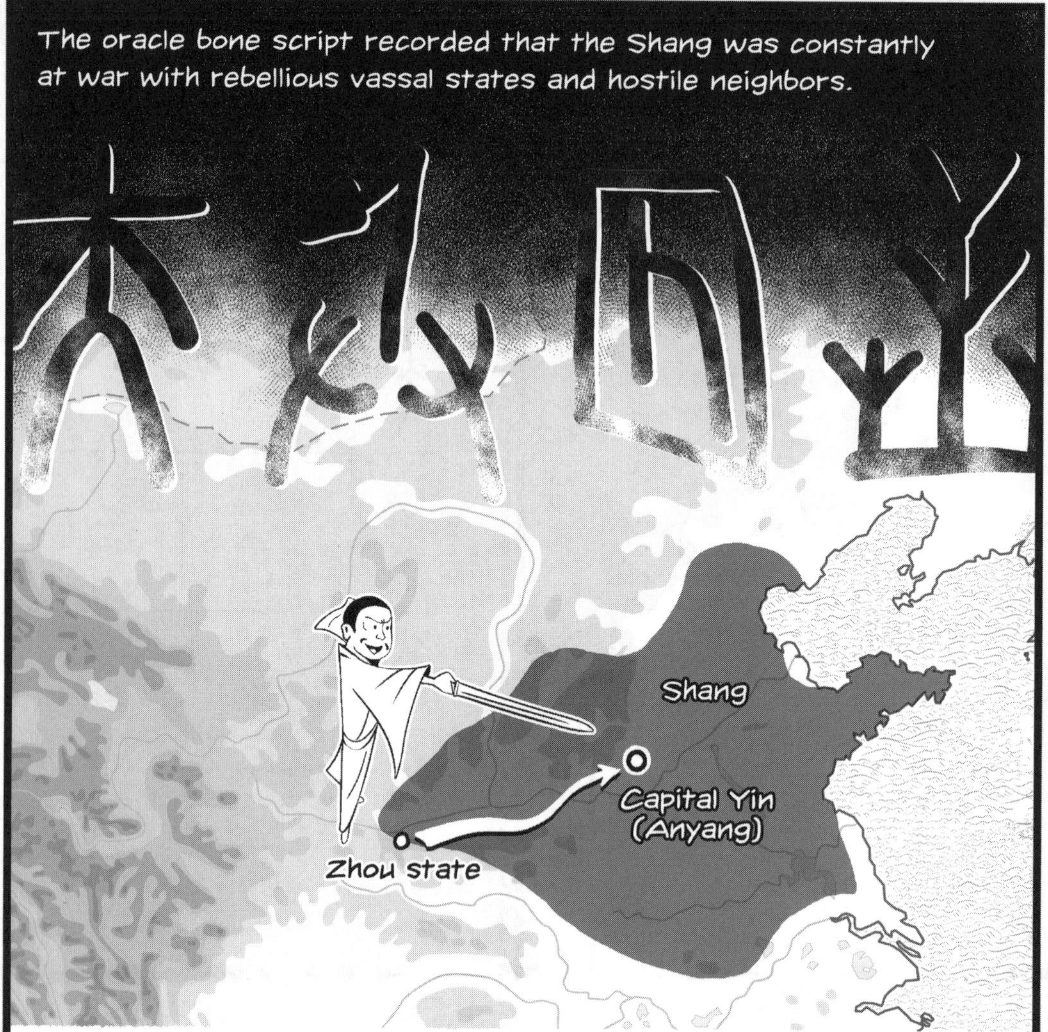
The oracle bone script recorded that the Shang was constantly at war with rebellious vassal states and hostile neighbors.
Shang
Capital Yin (Anyang)
Zhou state

In 1046 BCE, around 800 Shang vassals led by the Zhou state rose up and toppled their Shang overlords.

King Wu of Zhou (reigned 1046 - 1043 BCE) proclaimed the establishment of the Zhou dynasty.

THE ZHOU DYNASTY*

1046 – 256 BCE

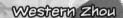

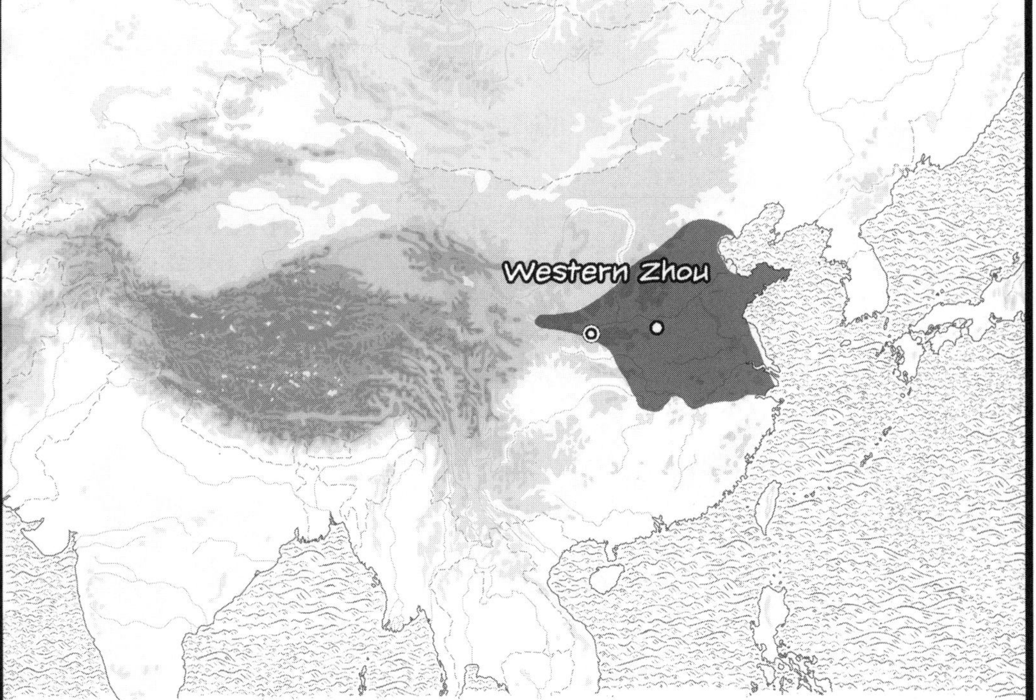

Western Zhou

◎   Capital Haojing (Xi'an)

O   Eastern capital Luoyi (Luoyang)

* The first part of the Zhou dynasty is referred to as
the Western Zhou dynasty and lasted from 1046 to 771 BCE.

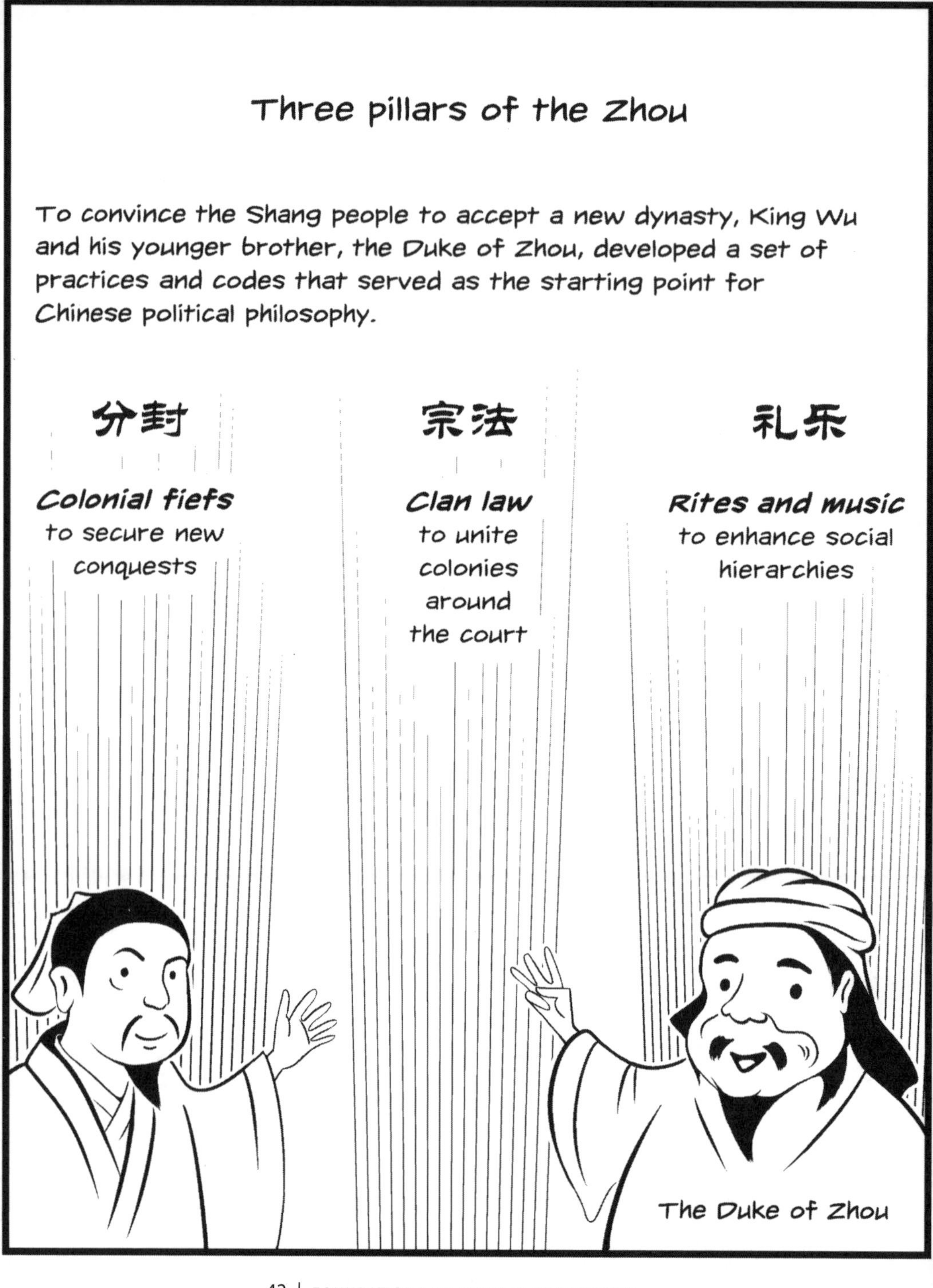
Three pillars of the Zhou
To convince the Shang people to accept a new dynasty, King Wu and his younger brother, the Duke of Zhou, developed a set of practices and codes that served as the starting point for Chinese political philosophy.
分封
Colonial fiefs to secure new conquests
宗法
Clan law to unite colonies around the court
礼乐
Rites and music to enhance social hierarchies
The Duke of Zhou

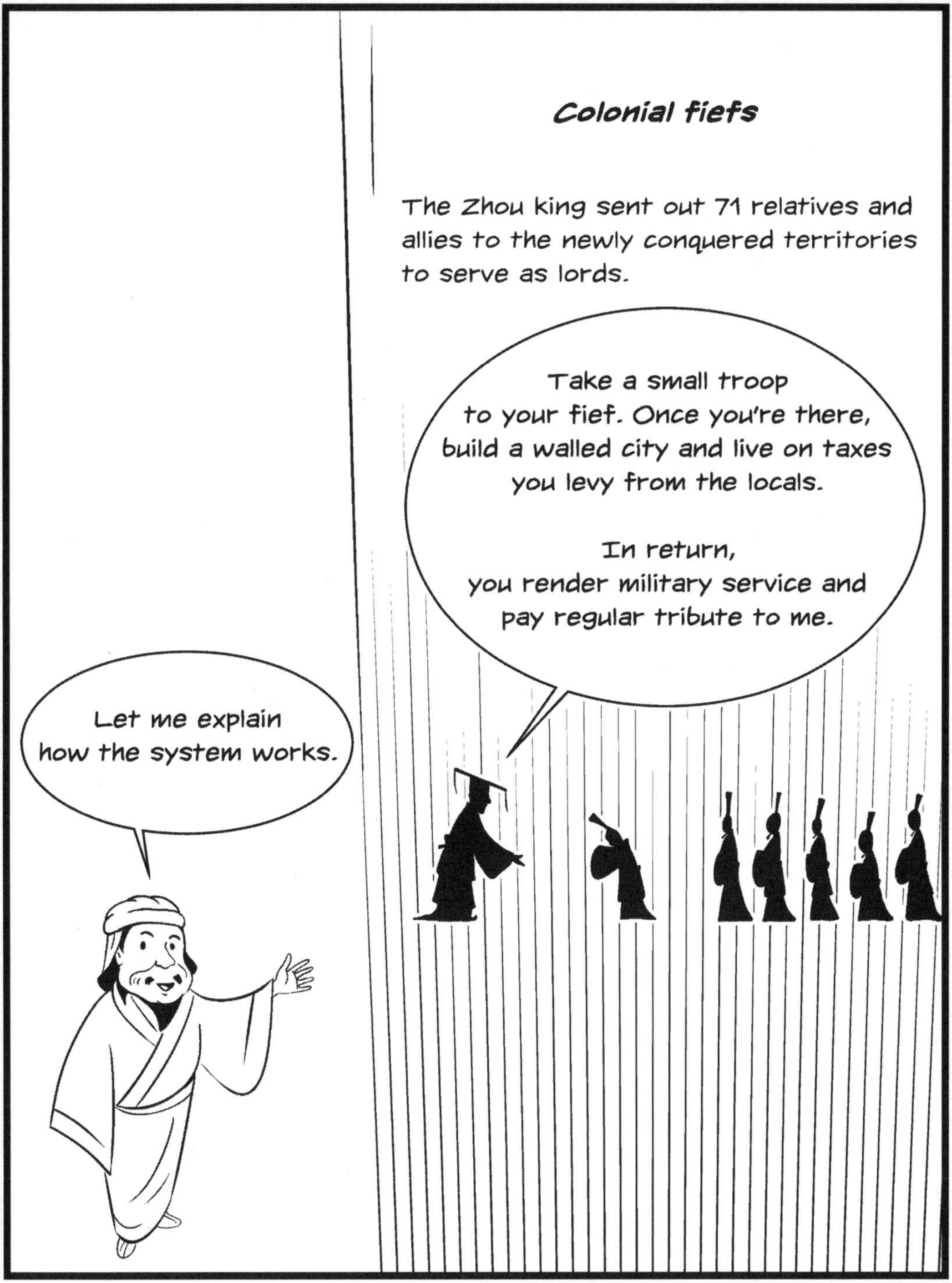
Colonial fiefs
The Zhou king sent out 71 relatives and allies to the newly conquered territories to serve as lords.
Let me explain how the system works.
Take a small troop to your fief. Once you're there, build a walled city and live on taxes you levy from the locals.
In return, you render military service and pay regular tribute to me.

Clan law

This is a system of inheritance and ancestor worship.

Upon death, a lord shall pass his title and land to his primary descendant, usually his eldest son.

The eldest son is responsible for maintaining the clan's ancestral hall, hosting worship ceremonies, and ruling his clan.

In this way, the family ties between the Zhou king and the first fief-holders can be passed on for generations.

The clans of the Zhou dynasty created many surnames.

姚	陈	吴	周	赵	黄	冯	鲁
Yao	Chen	Wu	Zhou	Zhao	Huang	Feng	Lu

Today, 85% of China's population uses only 100 surnames. Many of these surnames come from the Zhou period.

Rites and music

The Duke of Zhou supervised the creation of the earliest books codifying rites and ceremonies.

- **The Rites of Zhou** outlines the basic structure of the Zhou government.

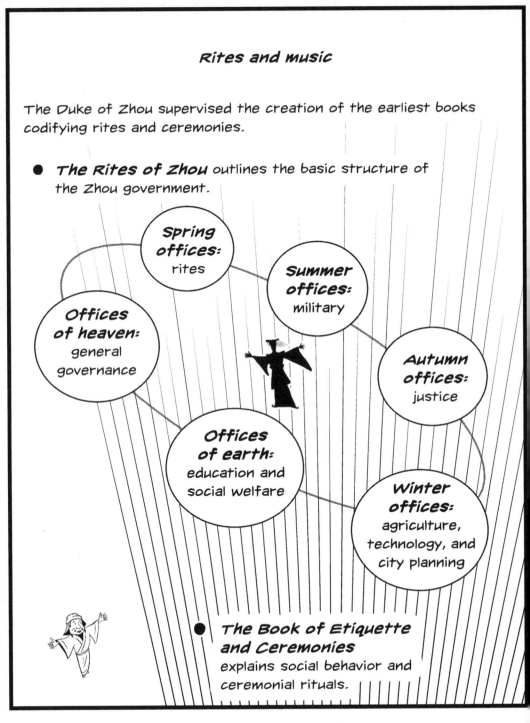

Spring offices: rites

Summer offices: military

Offices of heaven: general governance

Autumn offices: justice

Offices of earth: education and social welfare

Winter offices: agriculture, technology, and city planning

- **The Book of Etiquette and Ceremonies** explains social behavior and ceremonial rituals.

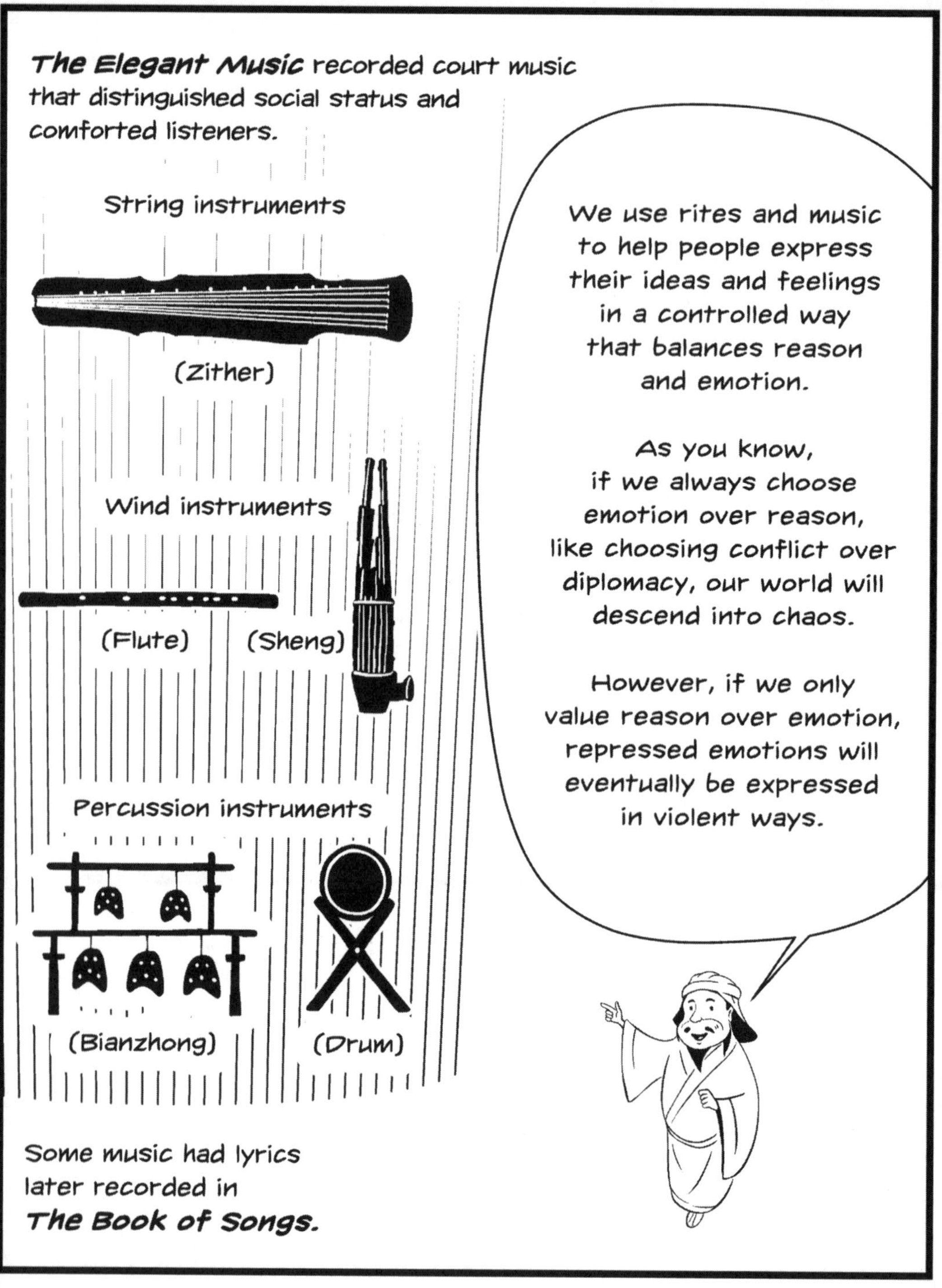

The Elegant Music recorded court music that distinguished social status and comforted listeners.
String instruments
(Zither)
Wind instruments
(Flute)
(Sheng)
Percussion instruments
(Bianzhong)
(Drum)
Some music had lyrics later recorded in ***The Book of Songs.***
We use rites and music to help people express their ideas and feelings in a controlled way that balances reason and emotion.
As you know, if we always choose emotion over reason, like choosing conflict over diplomacy, our world will descend into chaos.
However, if we only value reason over emotion, repressed emotions will eventually be expressed in violent ways.

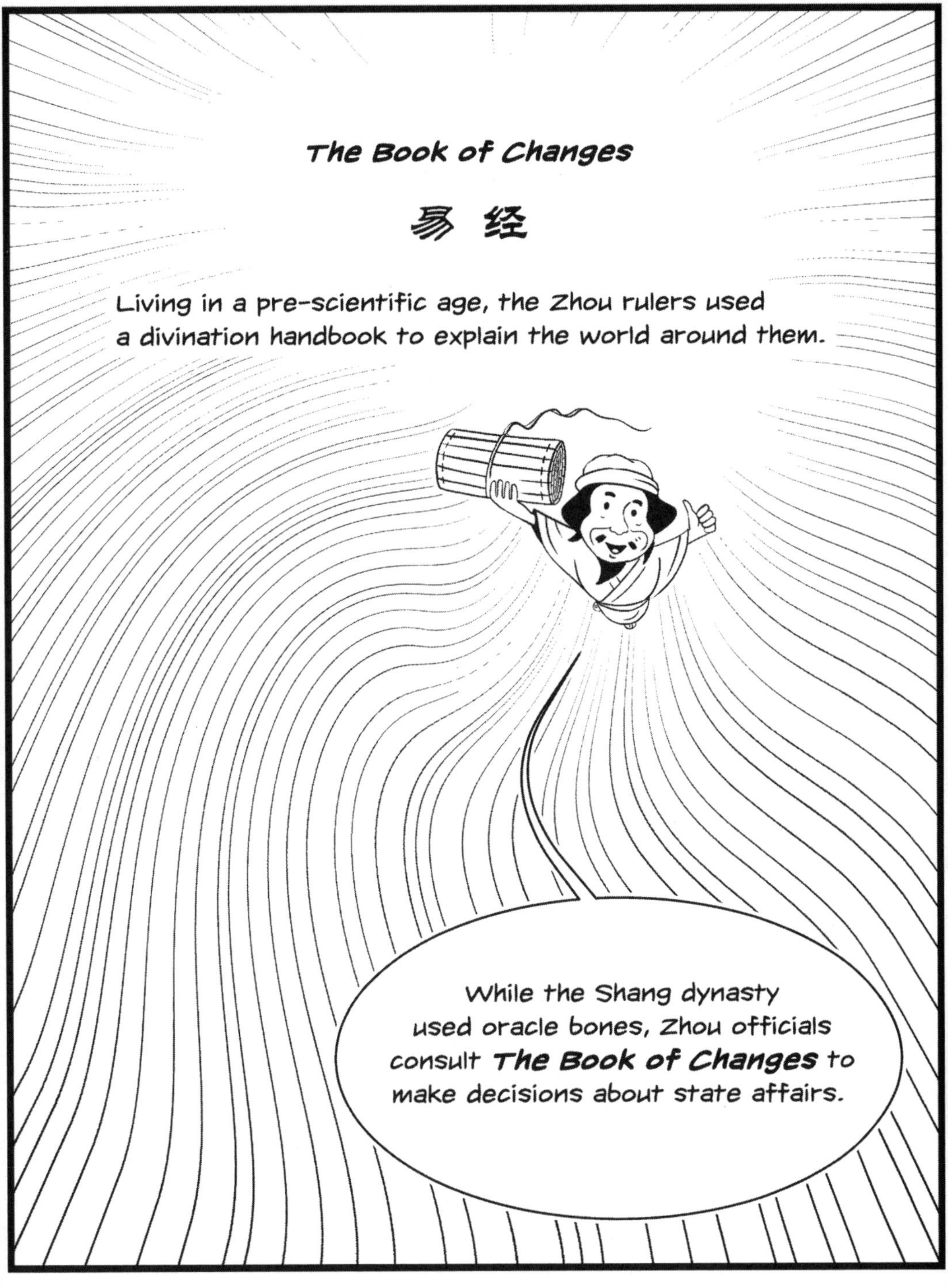
The Book of Changes
易经
Living in a pre-scientific age, the Zhou rulers used a divination handbook to explain the world around them.
While the Shang dynasty used oracle bones, Zhou officials consult *The Book of Changes* to make decisions about state affairs.

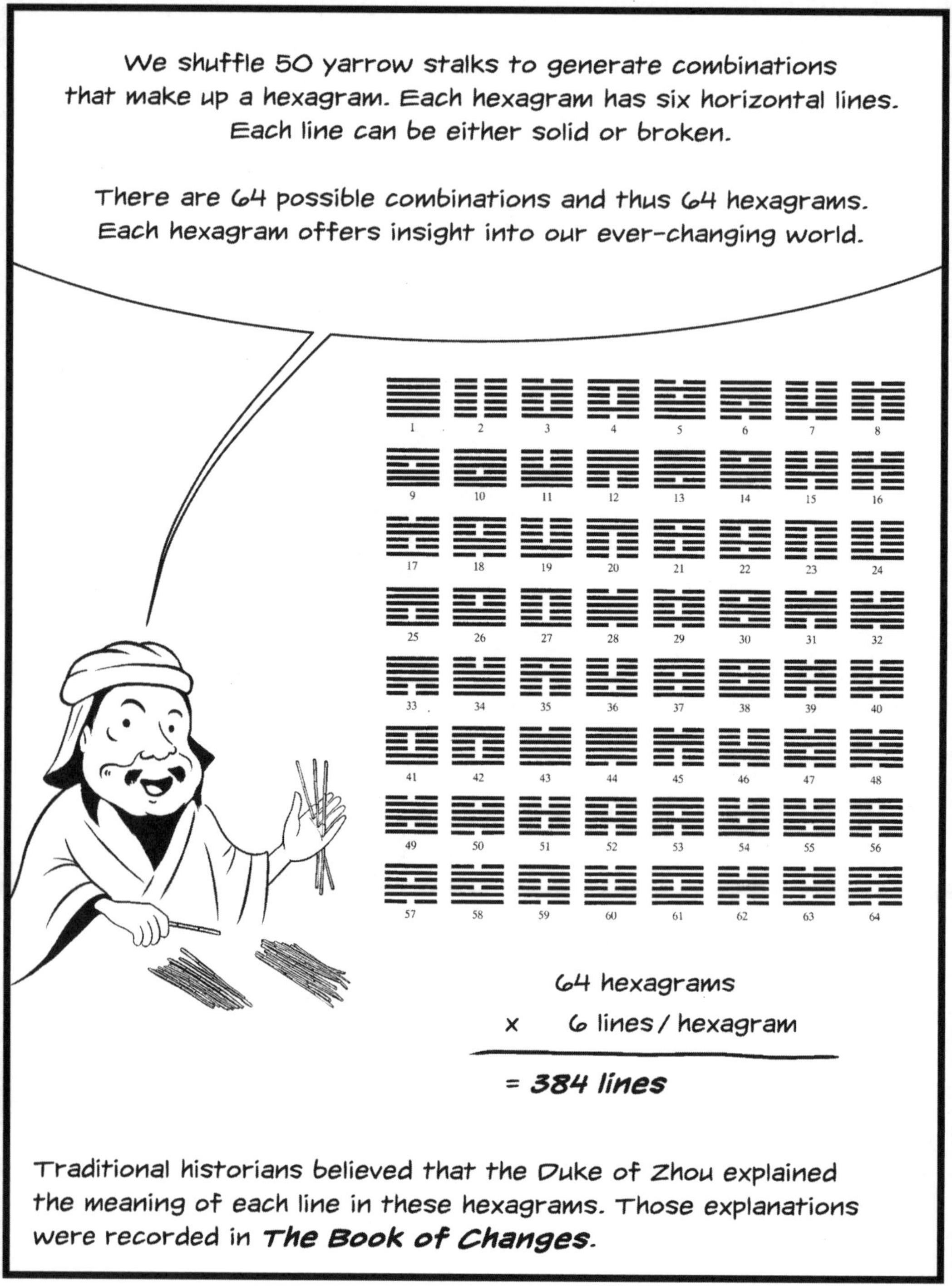
We shuffle 50 yarrow stalks to generate combinations that make up a hexagram. Each hexagram has six horizontal lines. Each line can be either solid or broken.
There are 64 possible combinations and thus 64 hexagrams. Each hexagram offers insight into our ever-changing world.
1 2 3 4 5 6 7 8
9 10 11 12 13 14 15 16
17 18 19 20 21 22 23 24
25 26 27 28 29 30 31 32
33 34 35 36 37 38 39 40
41 42 43 44 45 46 47 48
49 50 51 52 53 54 55 56
57 58 59 60 61 62 63 64
64 hexagrams
x 6 lines / hexagram
= 384 lines
Traditional historians believed that the Duke of Zhou explained the meaning of each line in these hexagrams. Those explanations were recorded in The Book of Changes.

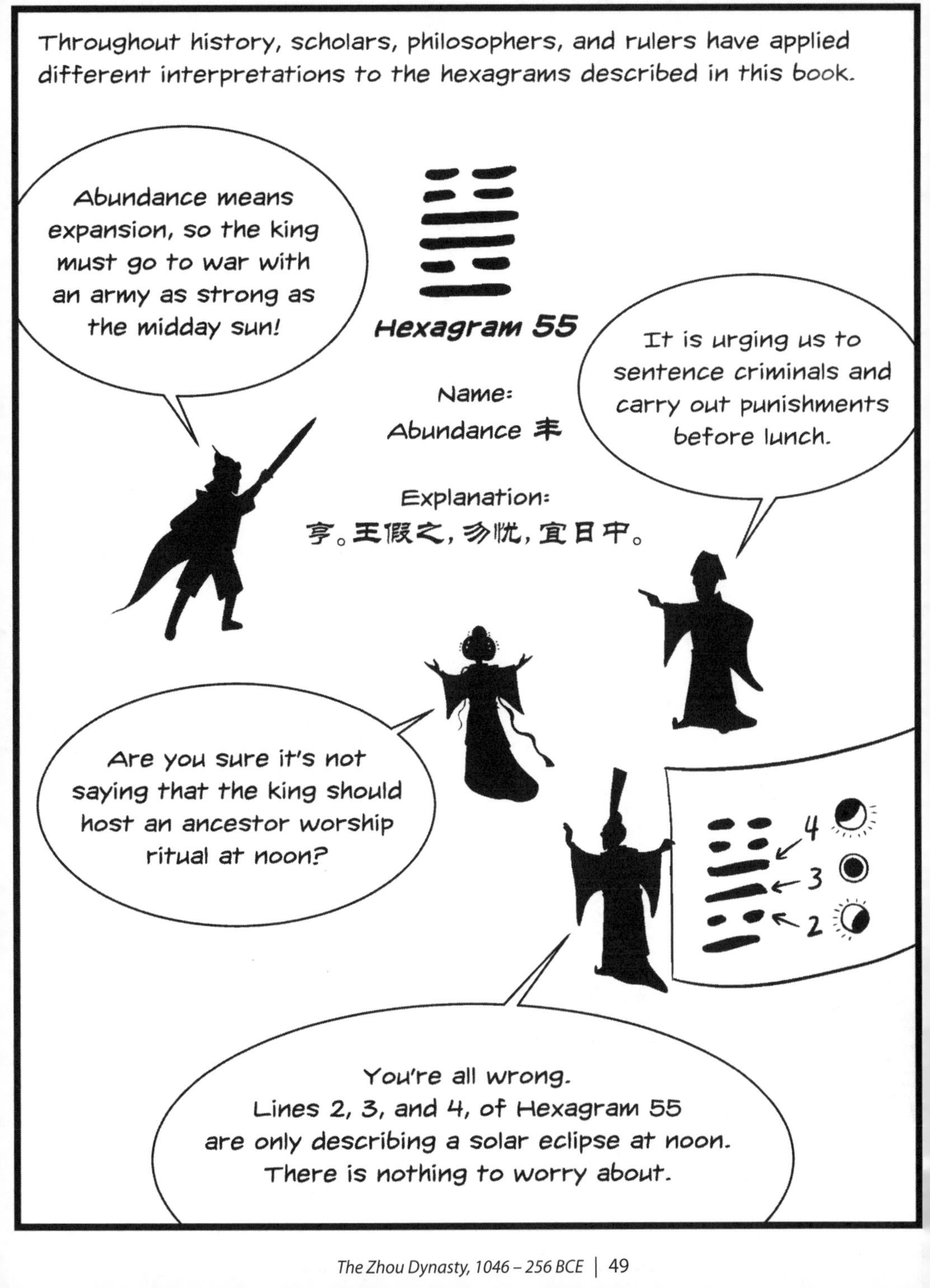
Throughout history, scholars, philosophers, and rulers have applied different interpretations to the hexagrams described in this book.
Abundance means expansion, so the king must go to war with an army as strong as the midday sun!
Hexagram 55
Name:
Abundance 丰
Explanation:
亨。王假之，勿忧，宜日中。
It is urging us to sentence criminals and carry out punishments before lunch.
Are you sure it's not saying that the king should host an ancestor worship ritual at noon?
4
3
2
You're all wrong.
Lines 2, 3, and 4, of Hexagram 55
are only describing a solar eclipse at noon.
There is nothing to worry about.

Mandate of Heaven

The Duke of Zhou left many legacies, the most famous one being the Mandate of Heaven.

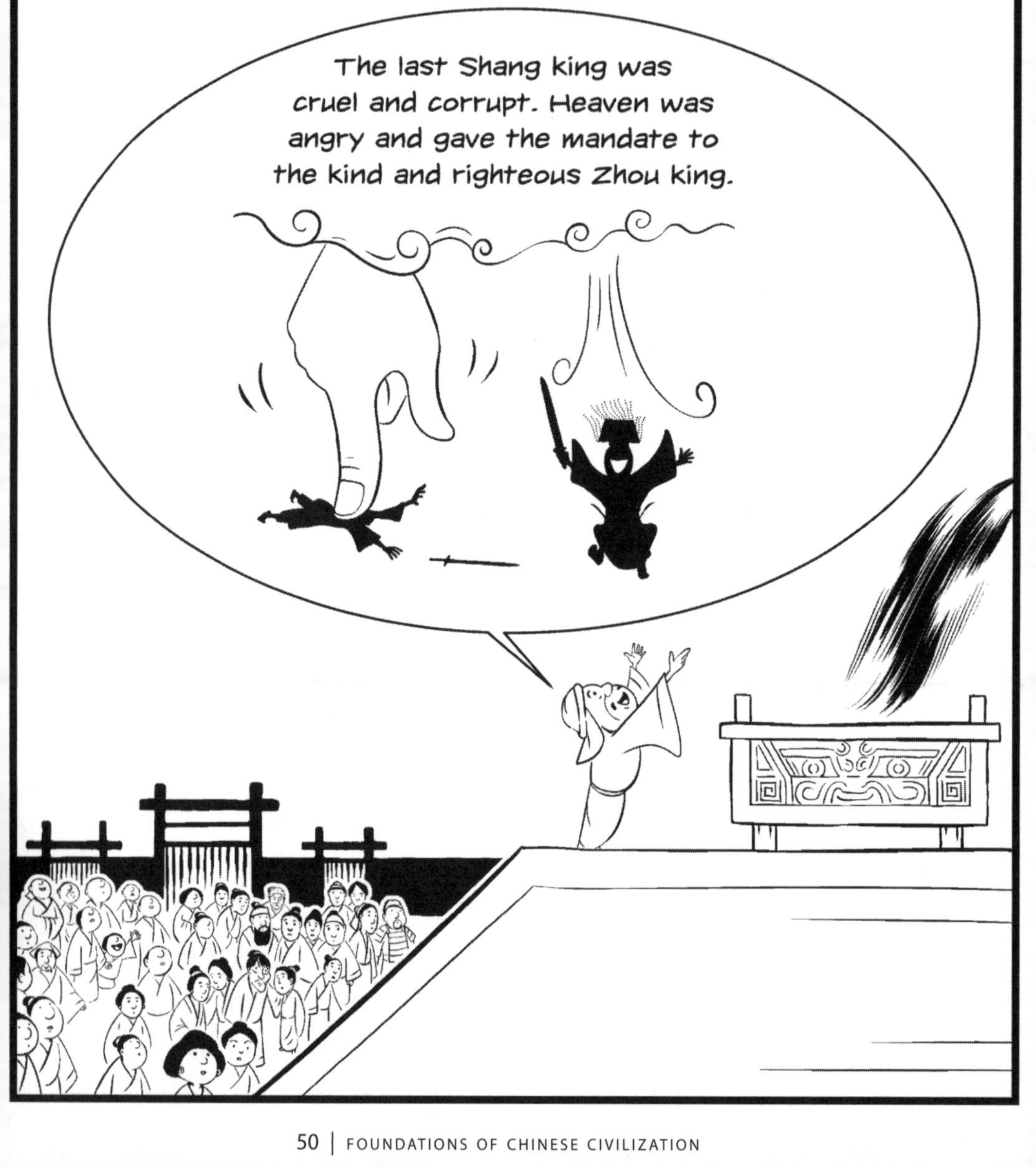
The last Shang king was cruel and corrupt. Heaven was angry and gave the mandate to the kind and righteous Zhou king.

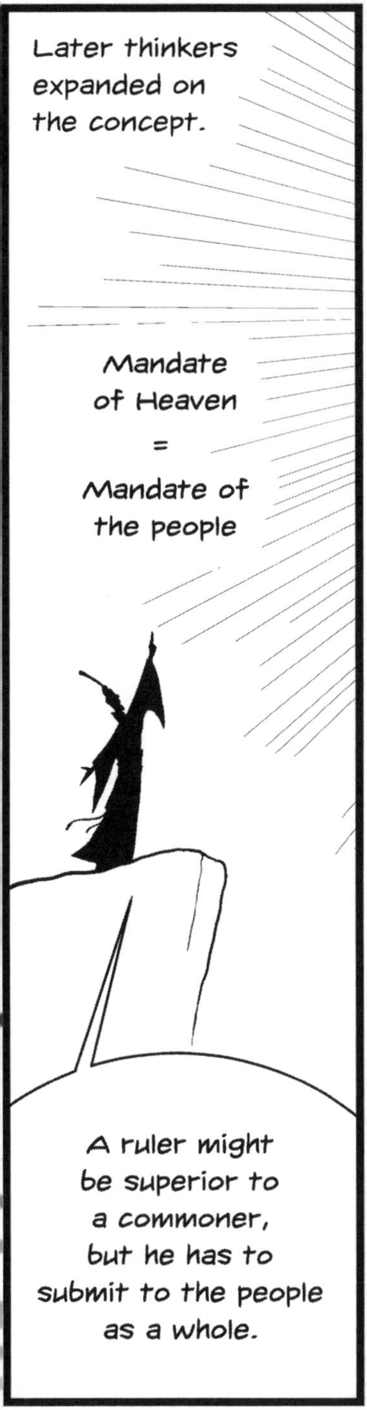
Later thinkers expanded on the concept.
Mandate of Heaven = Mandate of the people
A ruler might be superior to a commoner, but he has to submit to the people as a whole.

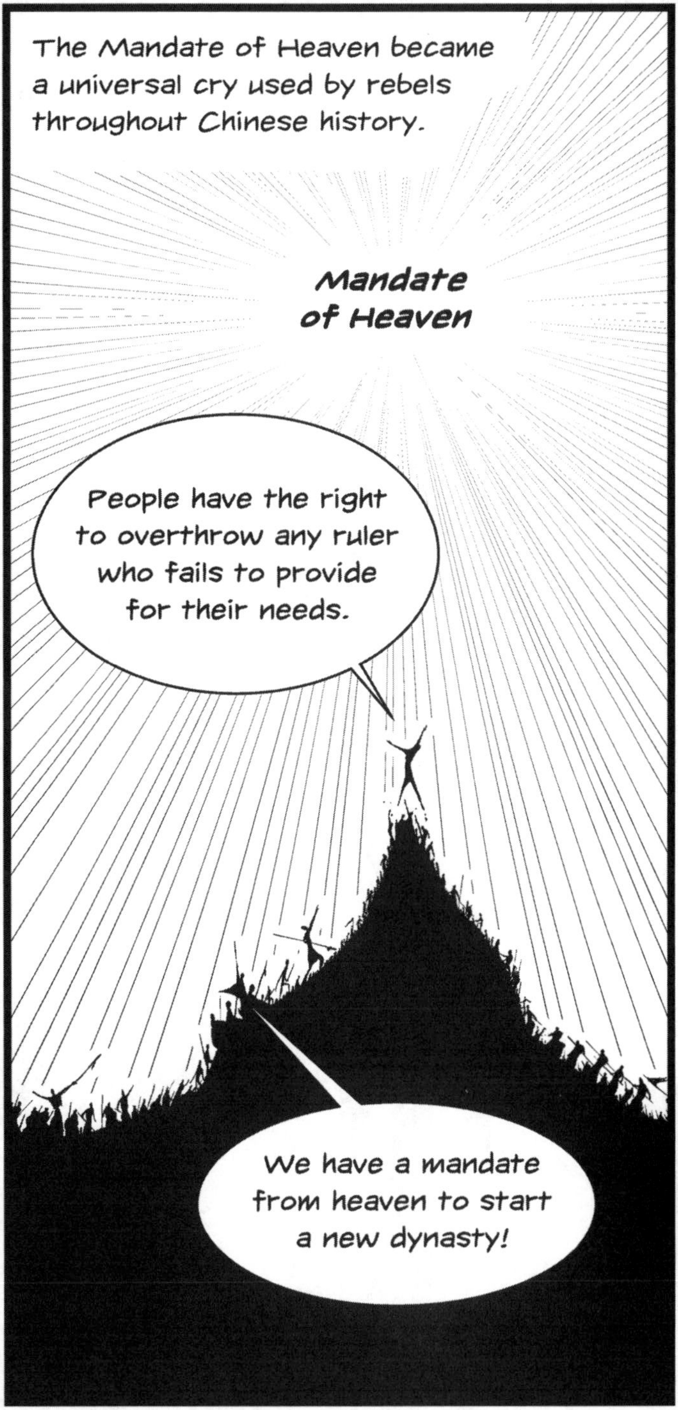
The Mandate of Heaven became a universal cry used by rebels throughout Chinese history.
Mandate of Heaven
People have the right to overthrow any ruler who fails to provide for their needs.
We have a mandate from heaven to start a new dynasty!

Well-field system

The fear of losing the Mandate of Heaven compelled early Zhou rulers to make sure that every family had land to farm and food to eat.

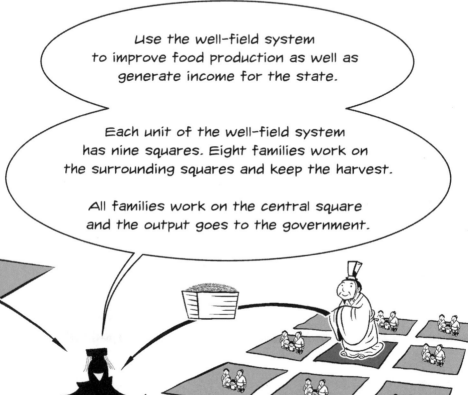

Use the well-field system to improve food production as well as generate income for the state.

Each unit of the well-field system has nine squares. Eight families work on the surrounding squares and keep the harvest.

All families work on the central square and the output goes to the government.

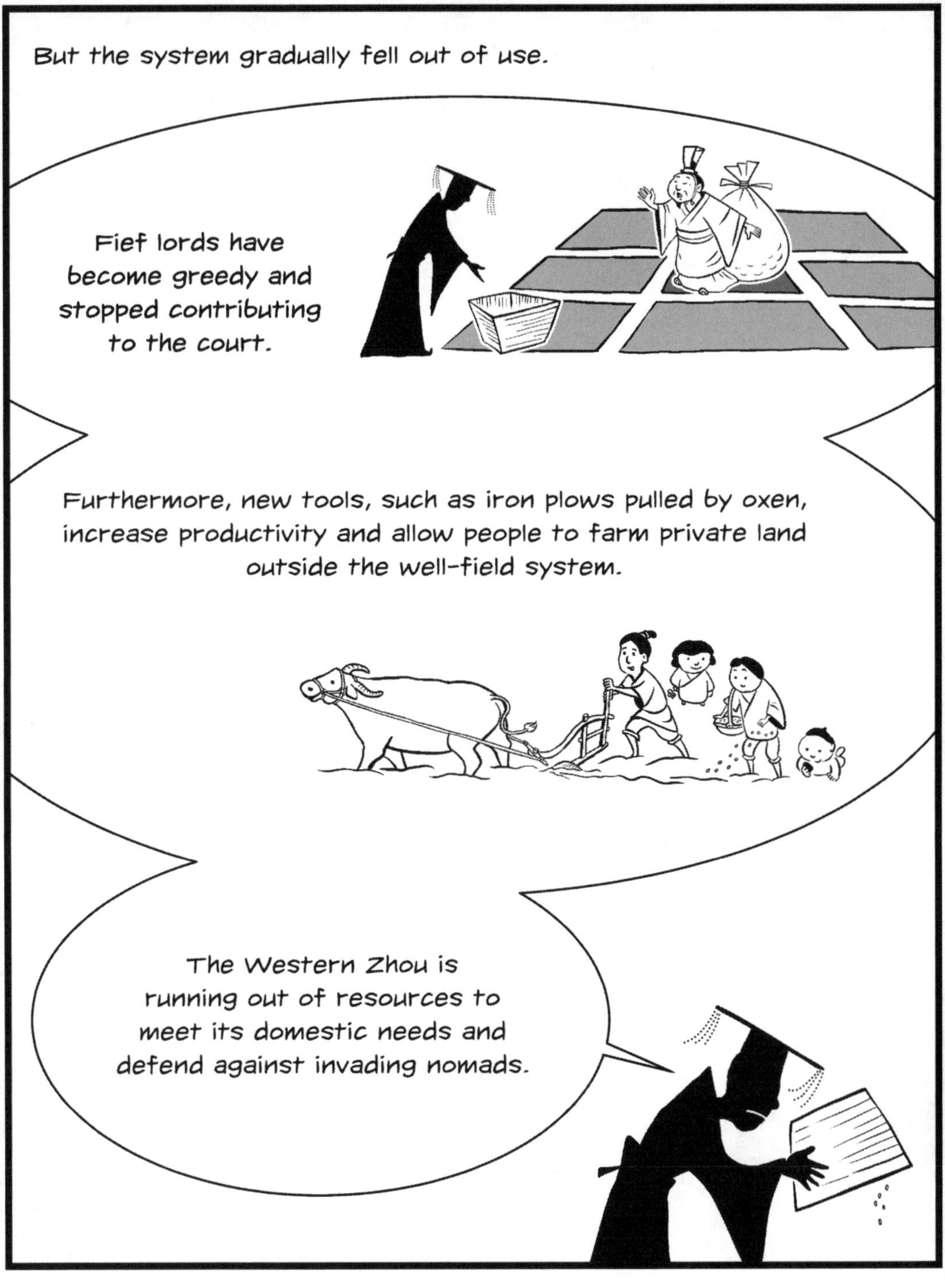
But the system gradually fell out of use.
Fief lords have become greedy and stopped contributing to the court.
Furthermore, new tools, such as iron plows pulled by oxen, increase productivity and allow people to farm private land outside the well-field system.
The Western Zhou is running out of resources to meet its domestic needs and defend against invading nomads.

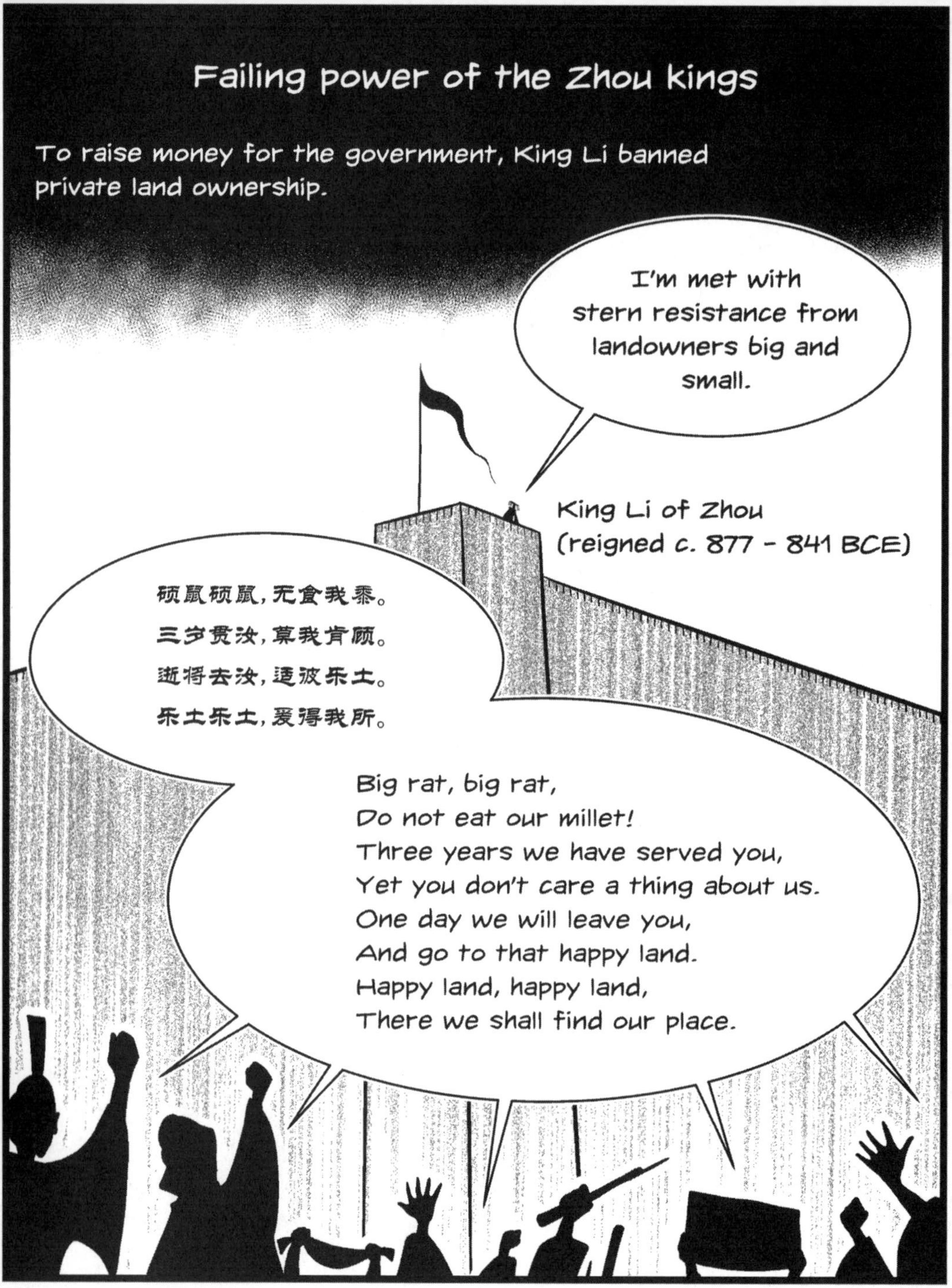

Failing power of the Zhou kings
To raise money for the government, King Li banned private land ownership.
I'm met with stern resistance from landowners big and small.
King Li of Zhou (reigned c. 877 - 841 BCE)
硕鼠硕鼠，无食我黍。
三岁贯汝，莫我肯顾。
逝将去汝，适彼乐土。
乐土乐土，爰得我所。
Big rat, big rat,
Do not eat our millet!
Three years we have served you,
Yet you don't care a thing about us.
One day we will leave you,
And go to that happy land.
Happy land, happy land,
There we shall find our place.

King Li was determined to silence any opposition.

Strike down anyone who is against my policy.

To block peoples' mouths is worse than blocking a river. When a blocked river bursts its banks, it will hurt many people.

And burst the river did. In 841 BCE, a major riot broke out among residents of the capital Haojing.

King Li escaped.

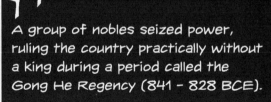

A group of nobles seized power, ruling the country practically without a king during a period called the Gong He Regency (841 – 828 BCE).

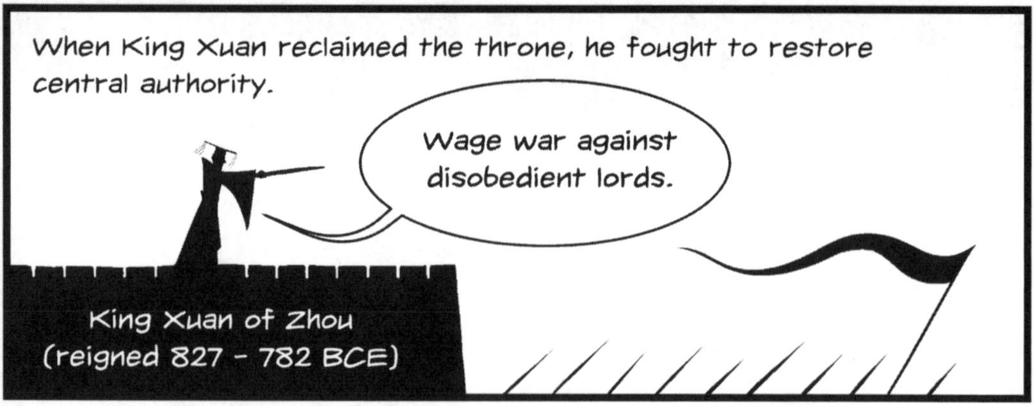
When King Xuan reclaimed the throne, he fought to restore central authority.
Wage war against disobedient lords.
King Xuan of Zhou
(reigned 827 - 782 BCE)

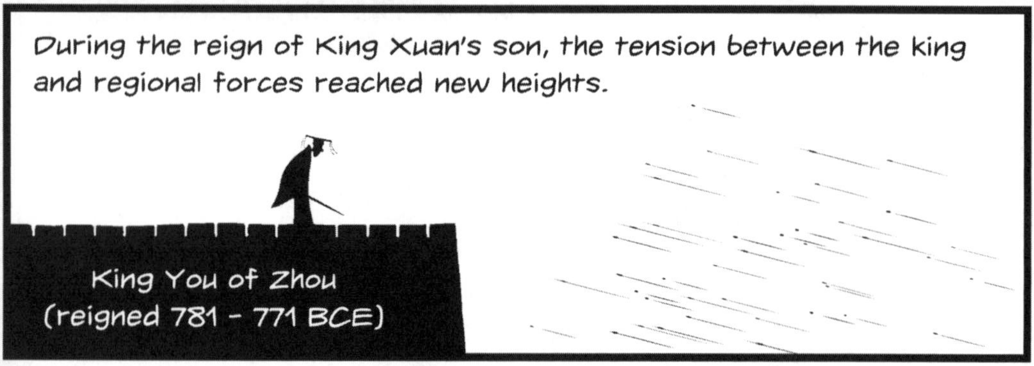
During the reign of King Xuan's son, the tension between the king and regional forces reached new heights.
King You of Zhou
(reigned 781 - 771 BCE)

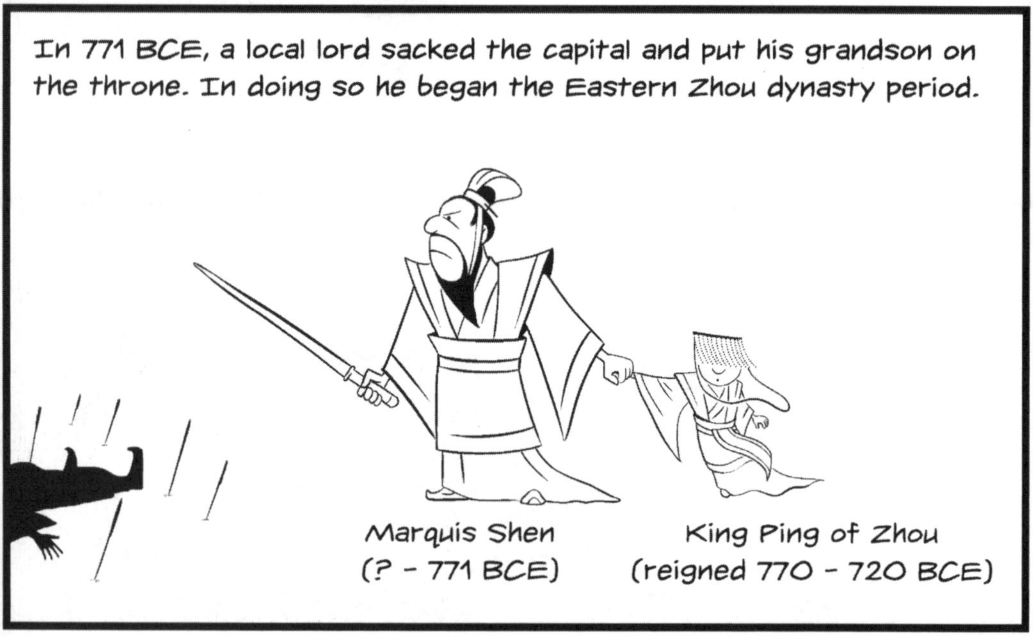
In 771 BCE, a local lord sacked the capital and put his grandson on the throne. In doing so he began the Eastern Zhou dynasty period.
Marquis Shen
(? - 771 BCE)
King Ping of Zhou
(reigned 770 - 720 BCE)

Eastern Zhou

During the Eastern Zhou (770 – 256 BCE), Zhou kings ruled in name only and regional lords had the real power.

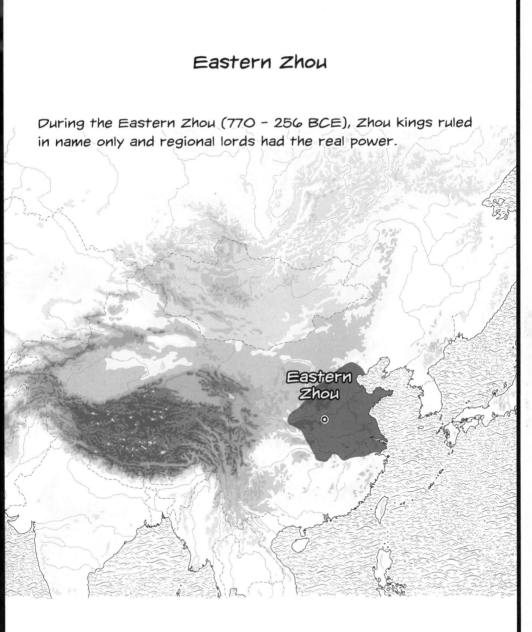

Eastern
Zhou

◎ Capital Luoyi (Luoyang)

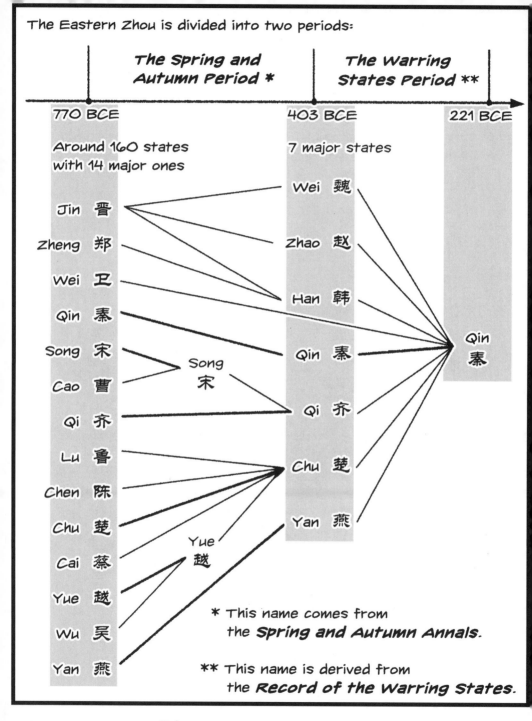

The Eastern Zhou is divided into two periods:

The Spring and Autumn Period *

The Warring States Period **

770 BCE

403 BCE

221 BCE

Around 160 states with 14 major ones

7 major states

Jin 晋
Zheng 郑
Wei 卫
Qin 秦
Song 宋
Cao 曹
Qi 齐
Lu 鲁
Chen 陈
Chu 楚
Cai 蔡
Yue 越
Wu 吴
Yan 燕

Song 宋

Yue 越

Wei 魏
Zhao 赵
Han 韩
Qin 秦
Qi 齐
Chu 楚
Yan 燕

Qin 秦

* This name comes from the **Spring and Autumn Annals**.

** This name is derived from the **Record of the Warring States**.

Changing warfare

Powerful states often preyed upon weak ones. Military conflict increased dramatically.

	The Spring and Autumn Period	The Warring States Period
Duration of wars	1 – 10 days	From a few months to 5 years
Soldiers	20,000 – 100,000 men	300,000 – 1 million men
Weapons	• Sophisticated bronze weapons • Chariots • Bows used by highly skilled archers	• Crude but readily available iron weapons • Cavalries • Crossbows that required little training
Battle locations	Wide-open spaces	Anywhere

Emergence of trade and money

Few states had all the resources they needed. Extensive interstate trade began in the Spring and Autumn Period.

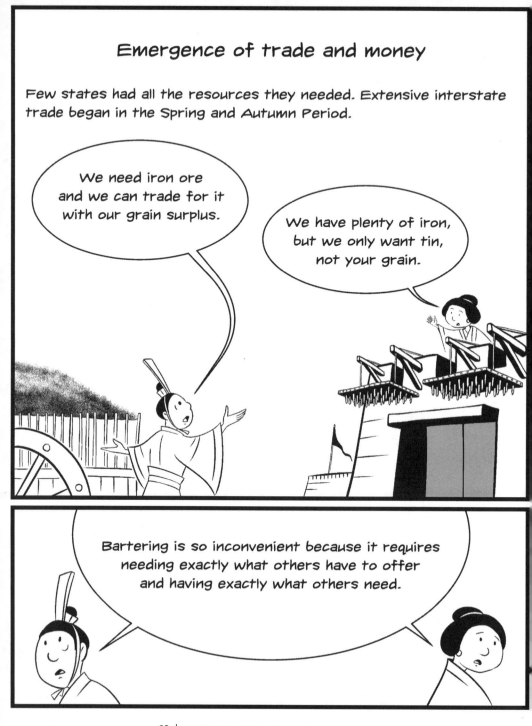

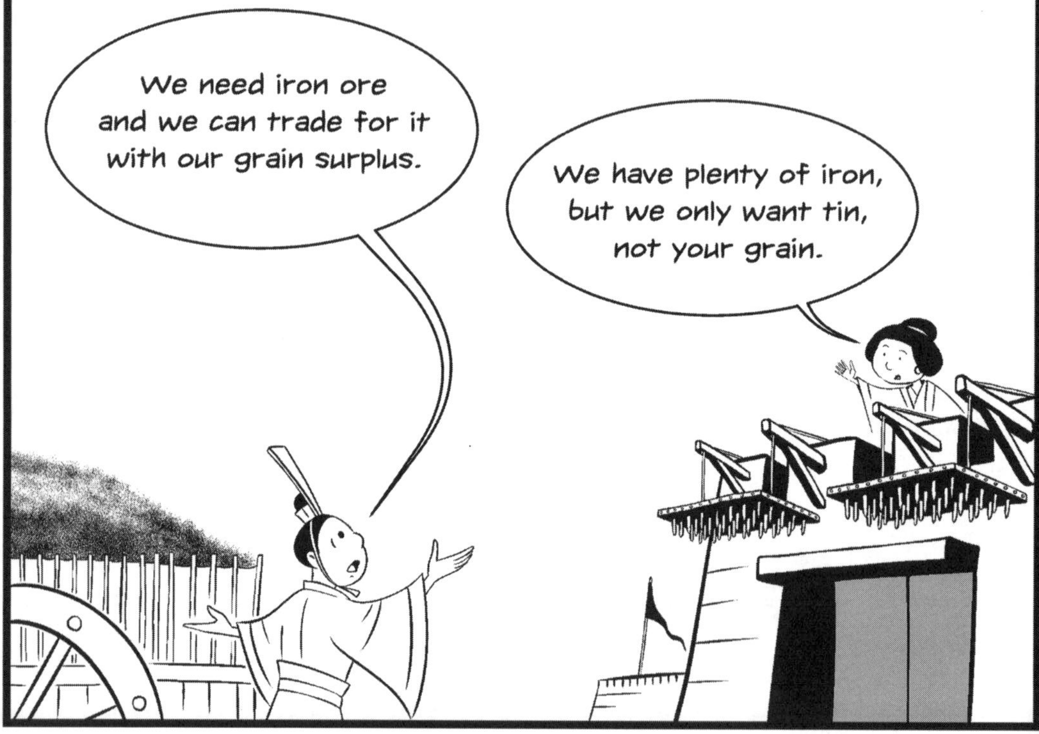
We need iron ore and we can trade for it with our grain surplus.
We have plenty of iron, but we only want tin, not your grain.

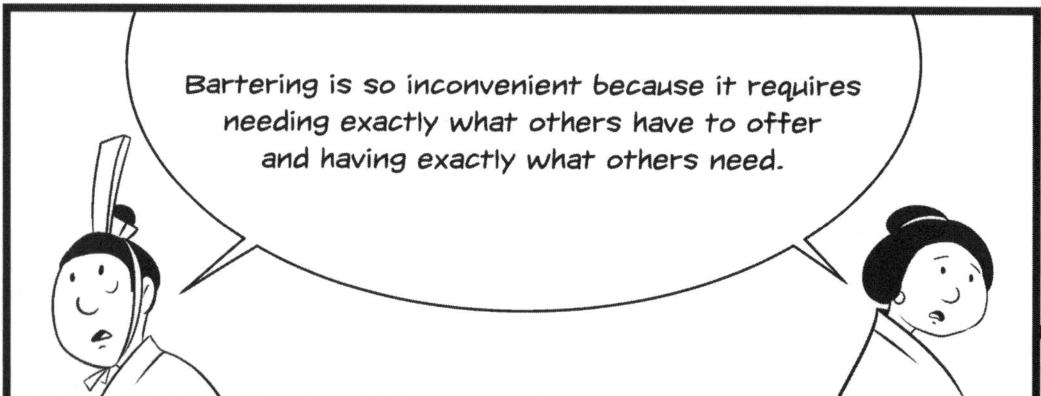
Bartering is so inconvenient because it requires needing exactly what others have to offer and having exactly what others need.

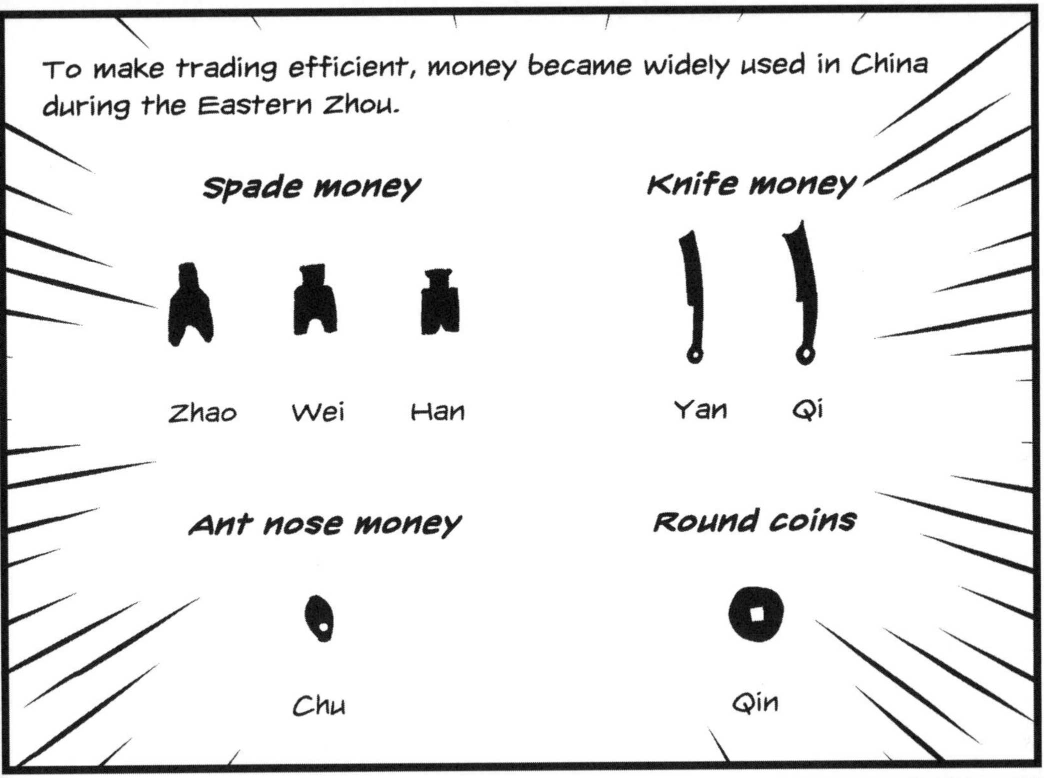
To make trading efficient, money became widely used in China during the Eastern Zhou.
Spade money
Knife money
Zhao
Wei
Han
Yan
Qi
Ant nose money
Round coins
Chu
Qin

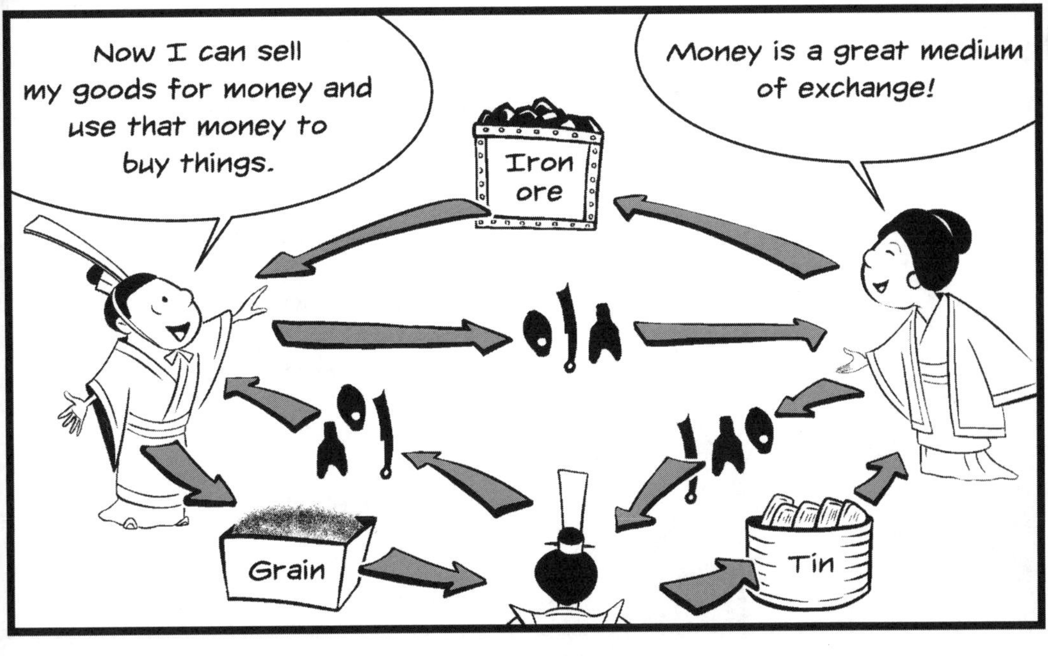
Now I can sell my goods for money and use that money to buy things.
Money is a great medium of exchange!
Iron ore
Grain
Tin

A hundred schools of thought

While some amassed great fortune and power during the turbulent times of the Eastern Zhou, many fell on hard times, among them nobles and officials.

One possible livelihood for once-powerful elites was teaching. These private teachers sowed the seeds of great intellectual expansion. Their collective philosophies later became known as the Hundred Schools of Thought.

Confucianism

Taoism

Legalism

Mohism

School of Yin & Yang

School of Names

School of Agriculture

School of Diplomacy

School of "Minor-talks"

School of the Military

The Miscellaneous School

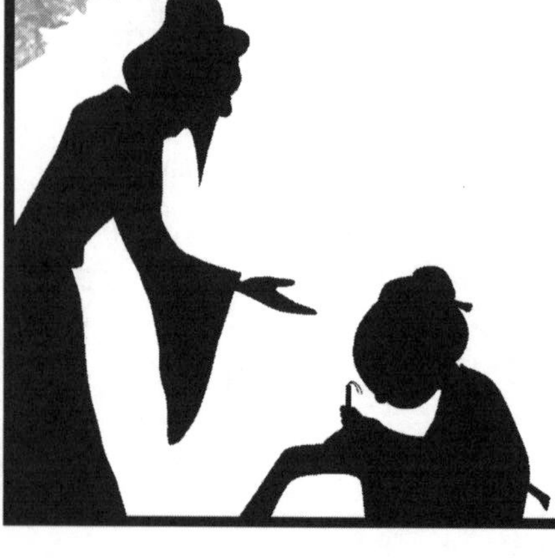

There were six major schools.

School of thought	Origin
Confucianism 儒家	Experts in the classics, rites, and music
Taoism 道家	Officials-turned-hermits living in seclusion from society and pursuing knowledge and self-improvement
Legalism 法家	Legal and political advisors
Mohism 墨家	Military officers
School of Yin & Yang 阴阳家	Alchemists, diviners, doctors
School of Names 名家	Public speakers, debaters

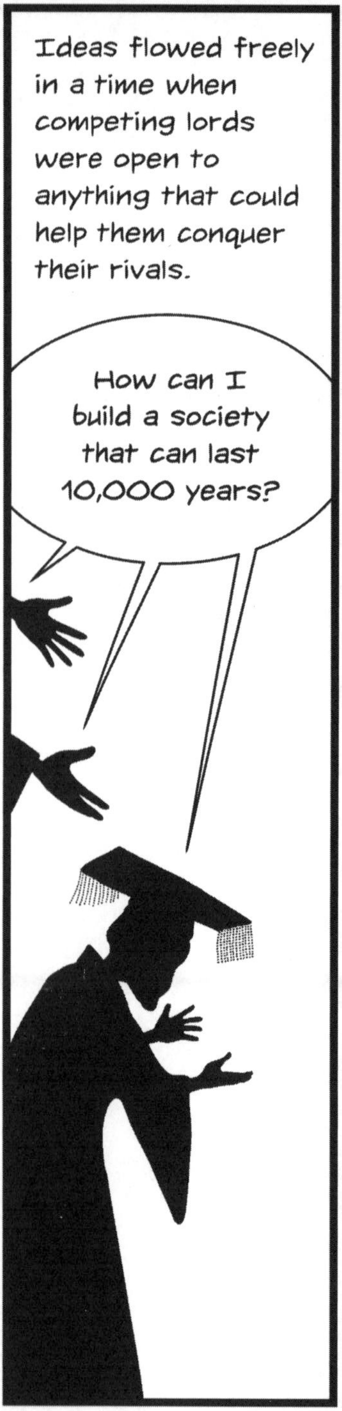
Ideas flowed freely in a time when competing lords were open to anything that could help them conquer their rivals.
How can I build a society that can last 10,000 years?

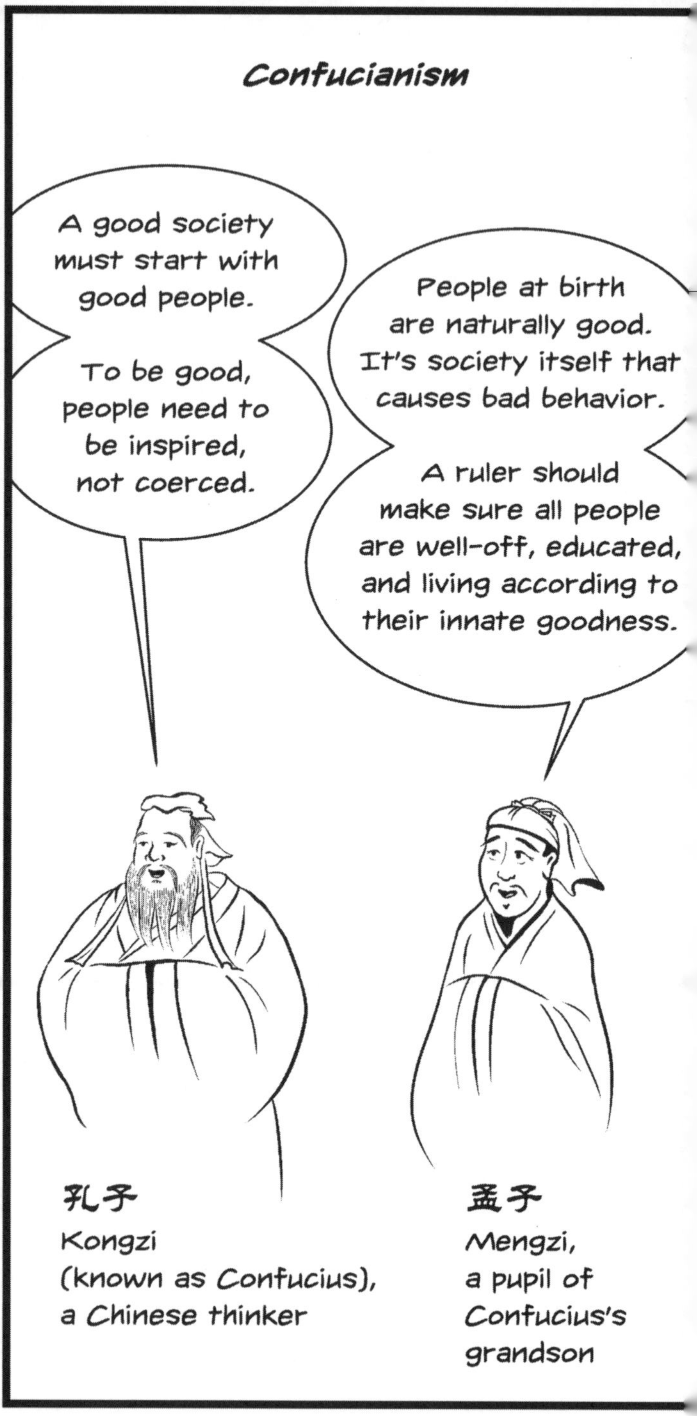
Confucianism
A good society must start with good people.
To be good, people need to be inspired, not coerced.
People at birth are naturally good. It's society itself that causes bad behavior.
A ruler should make sure all people are well-off, educated, and living according to their innate goodness.
孔子
Kongzi
(known as Confucius),
a Chinese thinker
孟子
Mengzi,
a pupil of
Confucius's
grandson

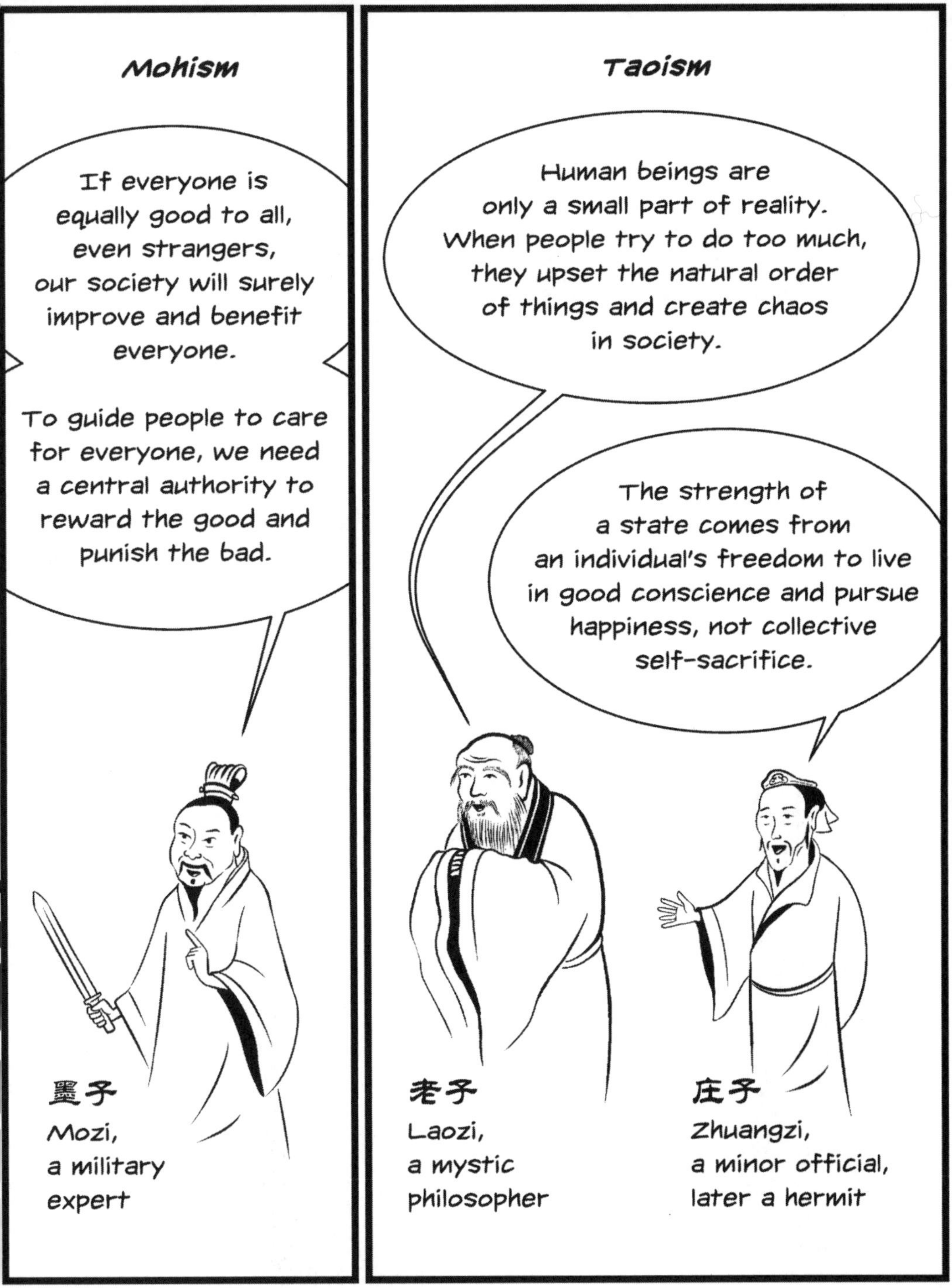
Mohism
If everyone is equally good to all, even strangers, our society will surely improve and benefit everyone.
To guide people to care for everyone, we need a central authority to reward the good and punish the bad.
墨子
Mozi, a military expert
Taoism
Human beings are only a small part of reality. When people try to do too much, they upset the natural order of things and create chaos in society.
The strength of a state comes from an individual's freedom to live in good conscience and pursue happiness, not collective self-sacrifice.
老子
Laozi, a mystic philosopher
庄子
Zhuangzi, a minor official, later a hermit

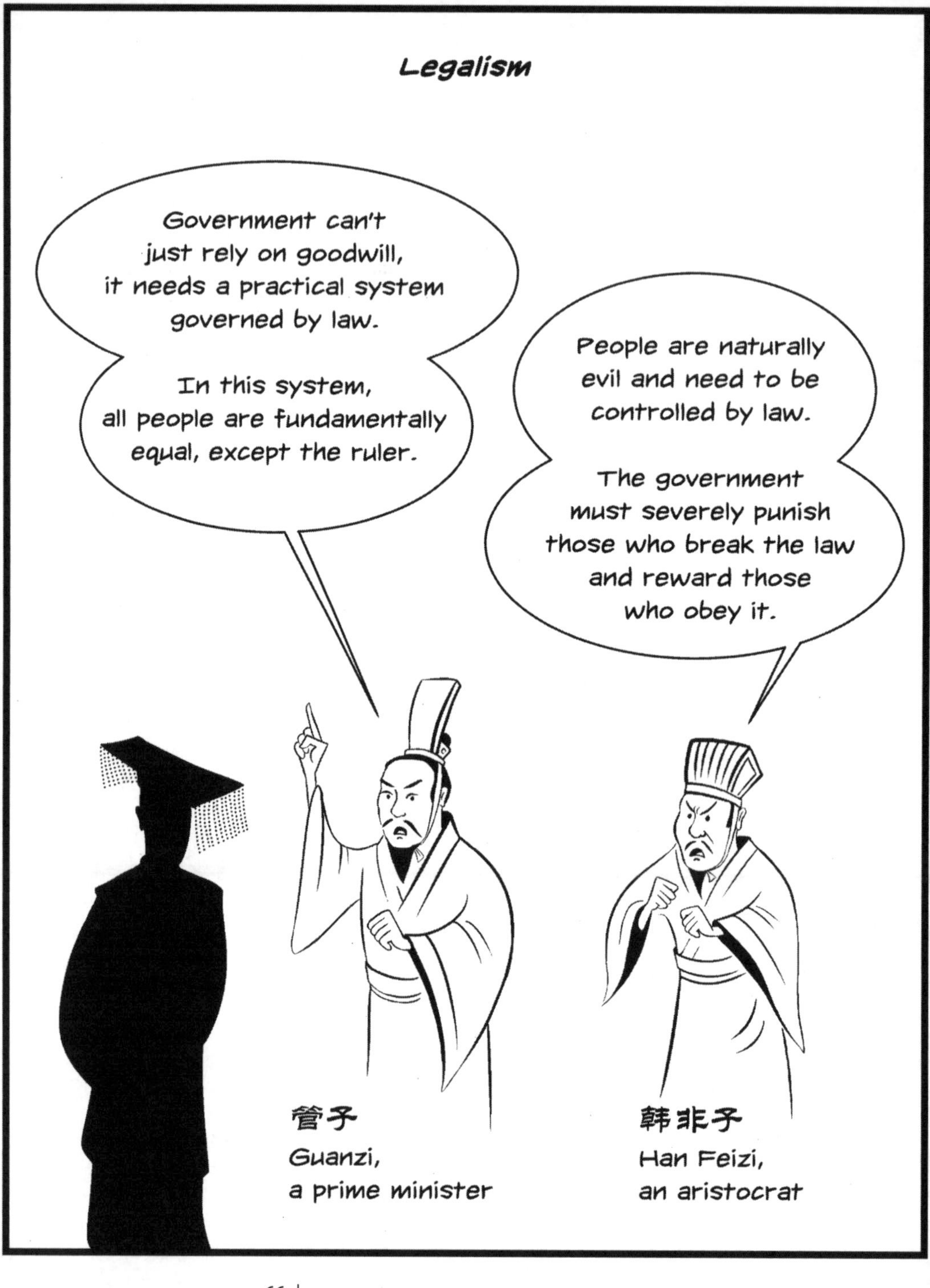
Legalism
Government can't just rely on goodwill, it needs a practical system governed by law.
In this system, all people are fundamentally equal, except the ruler.
People are naturally evil and need to be controlled by law.
The government must severely punish those who break the law and reward those who obey it.
管子
Guanzi, a prime minister
韩非子
Han Feizi, an aristocrat

A minor school of thought at the time, the School of the Military is very popular today.

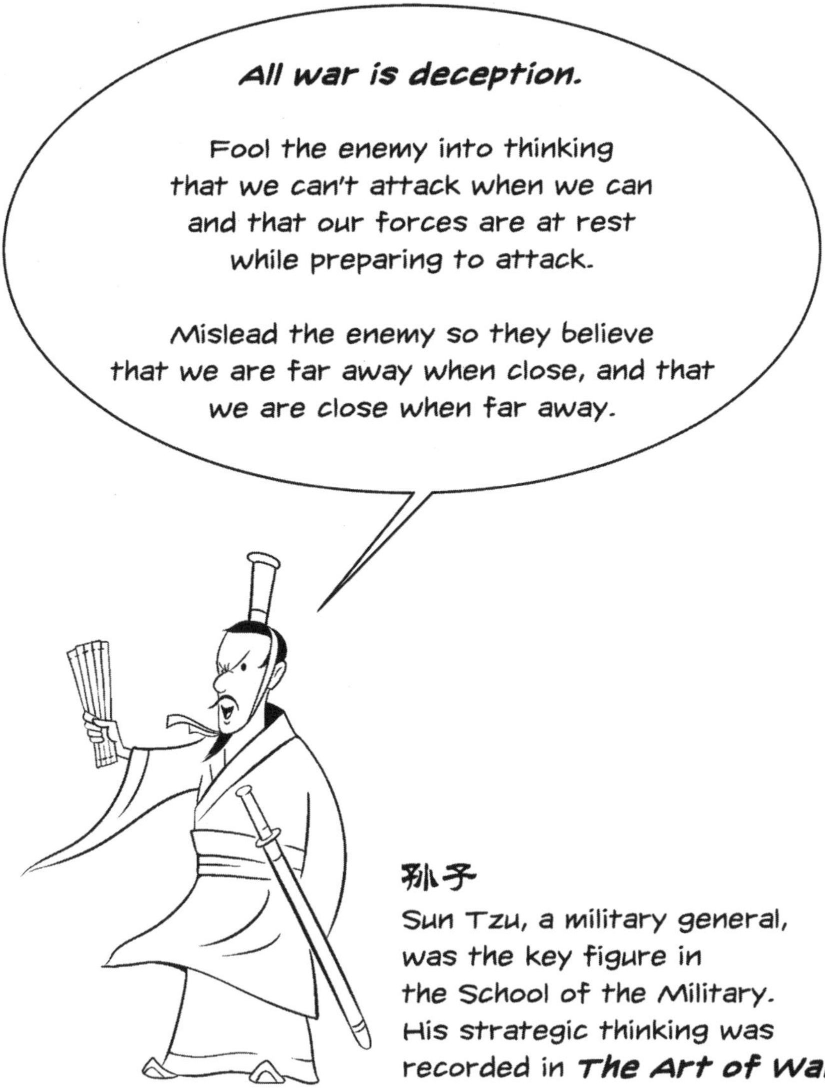
All war is deception.
Fool the enemy into thinking that we can't attack when we can and that our forces are at rest while preparing to attack.
Mislead the enemy so they believe that we are far away when close, and that we are close when far away.

孙子

Sun Tzu, a military general, was the key figure in the School of the Military. His strategic thinking was recorded in ***The Art of War.***

Among all the Eastern Zhou thinkers, Confucius is best-known. He is probably the most influential person in the entire history of China.

Confucius
(551 – 479 BCE)

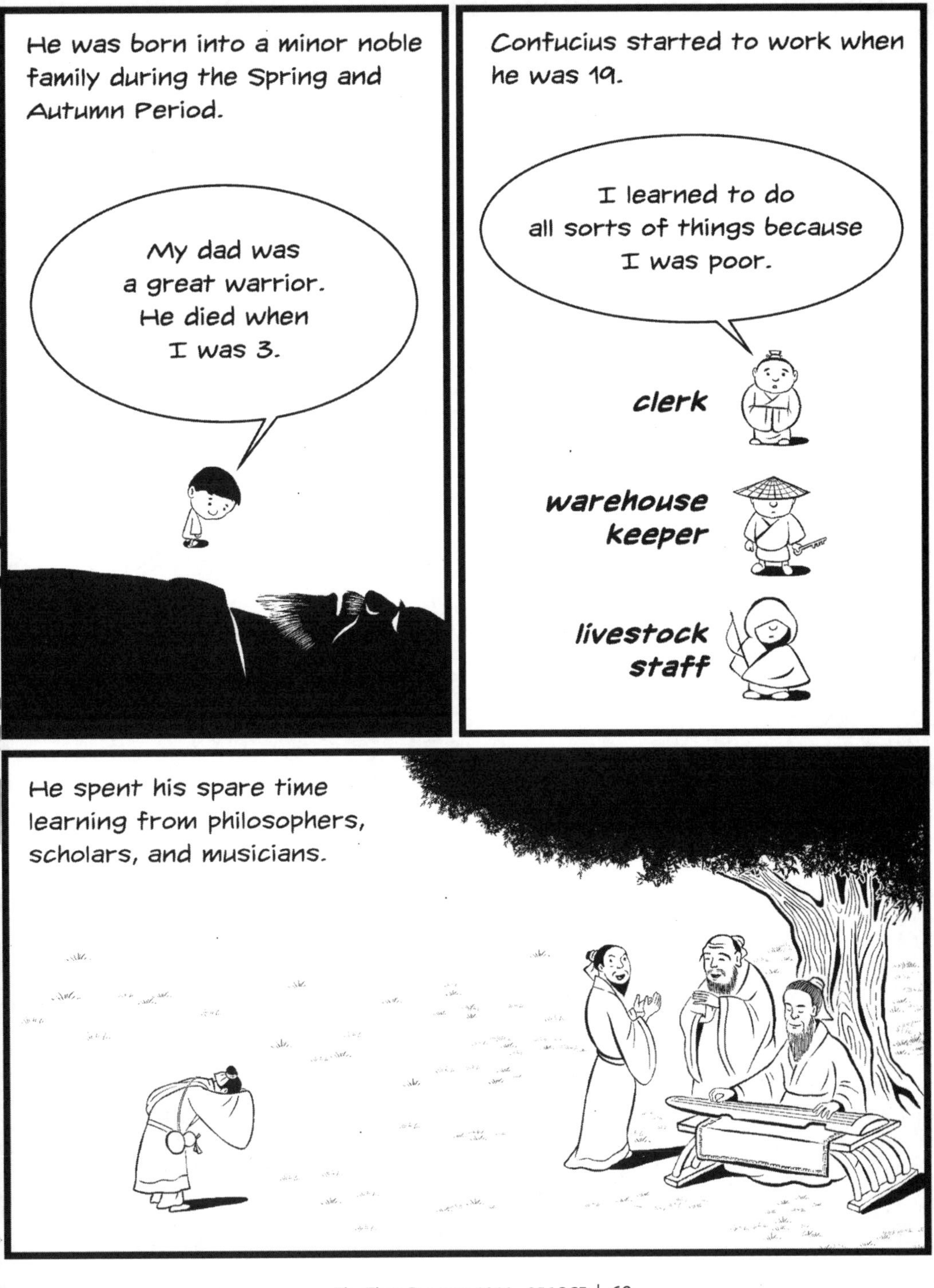
He was born into a minor noble family during the Spring and Autumn Period.
My dad was a great warrior. He died when I was 3.
Confucius started to work when he was 19.
I learned to do all sorts of things because I was poor.
clerk
warehouse keeper
livestock staff
He spent his spare time learning from philosophers, scholars, and musicians.

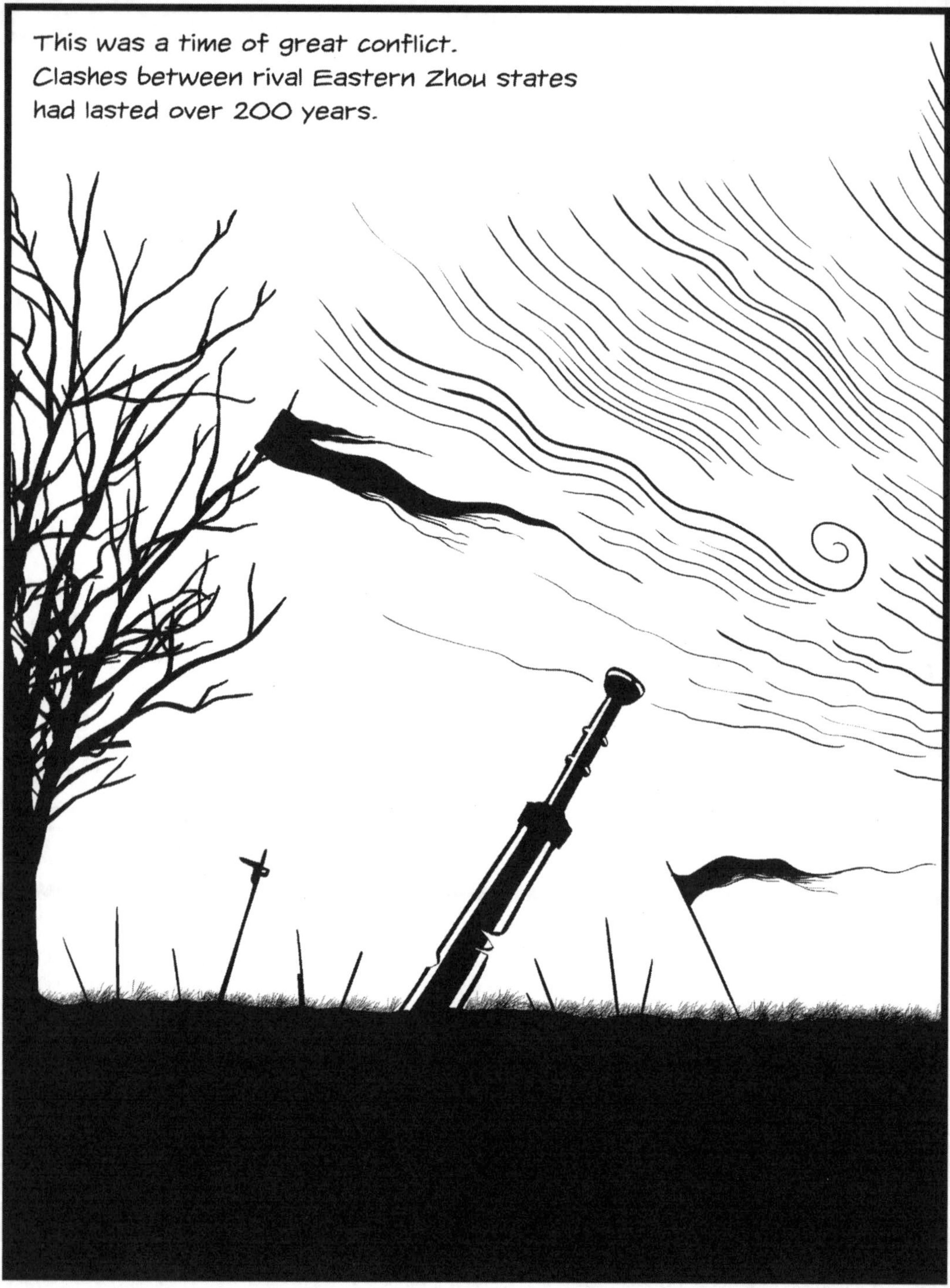
This was a time of great conflict. Clashes between rival Eastern Zhou states had lasted over 200 years.

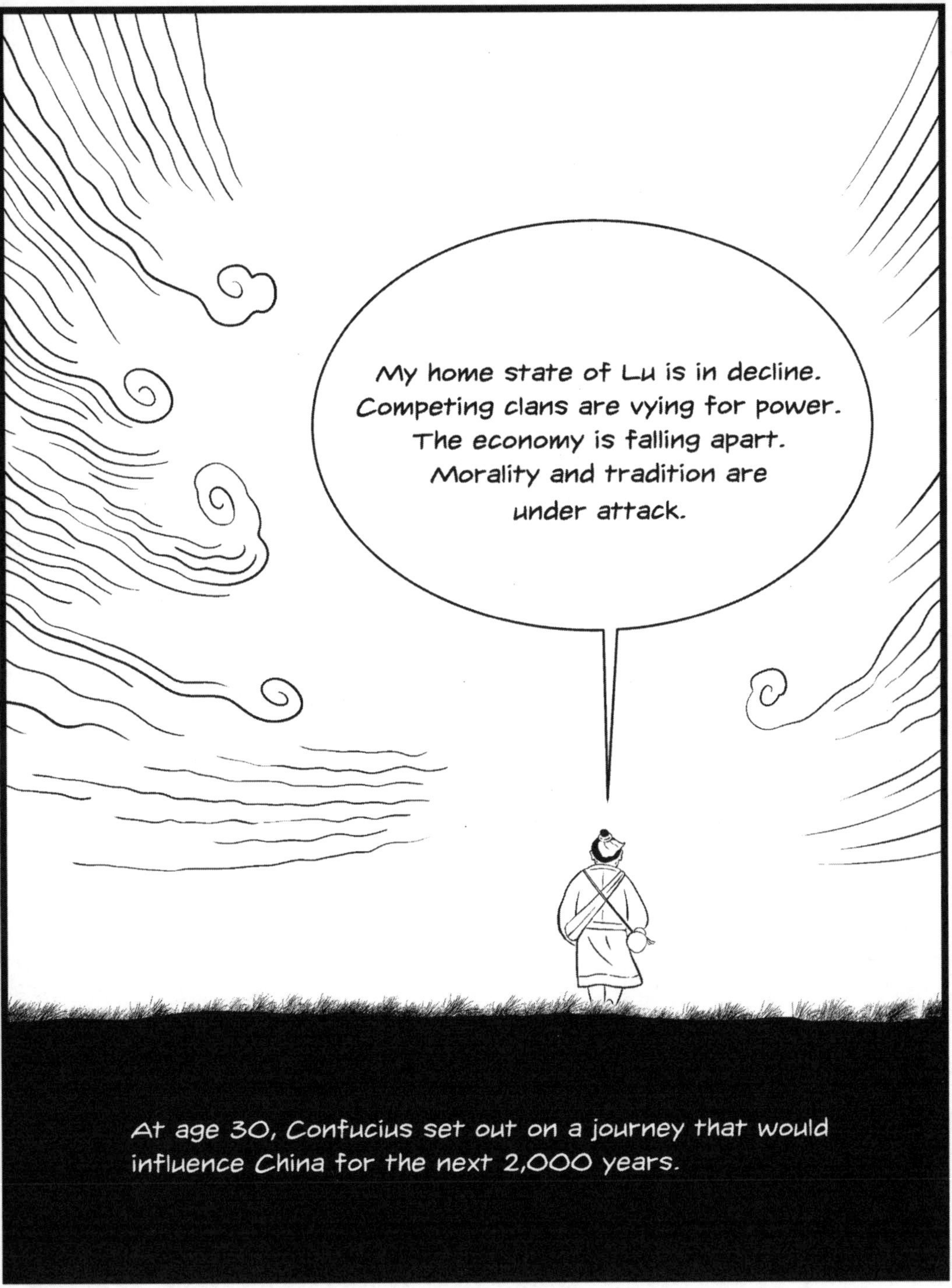
My home state of Lu is in decline. Competing clans are vying for power. The economy is falling apart. Morality and tradition are under attack.
At age 30, Confucius set out on a journey that would influence China for the next 2,000 years.

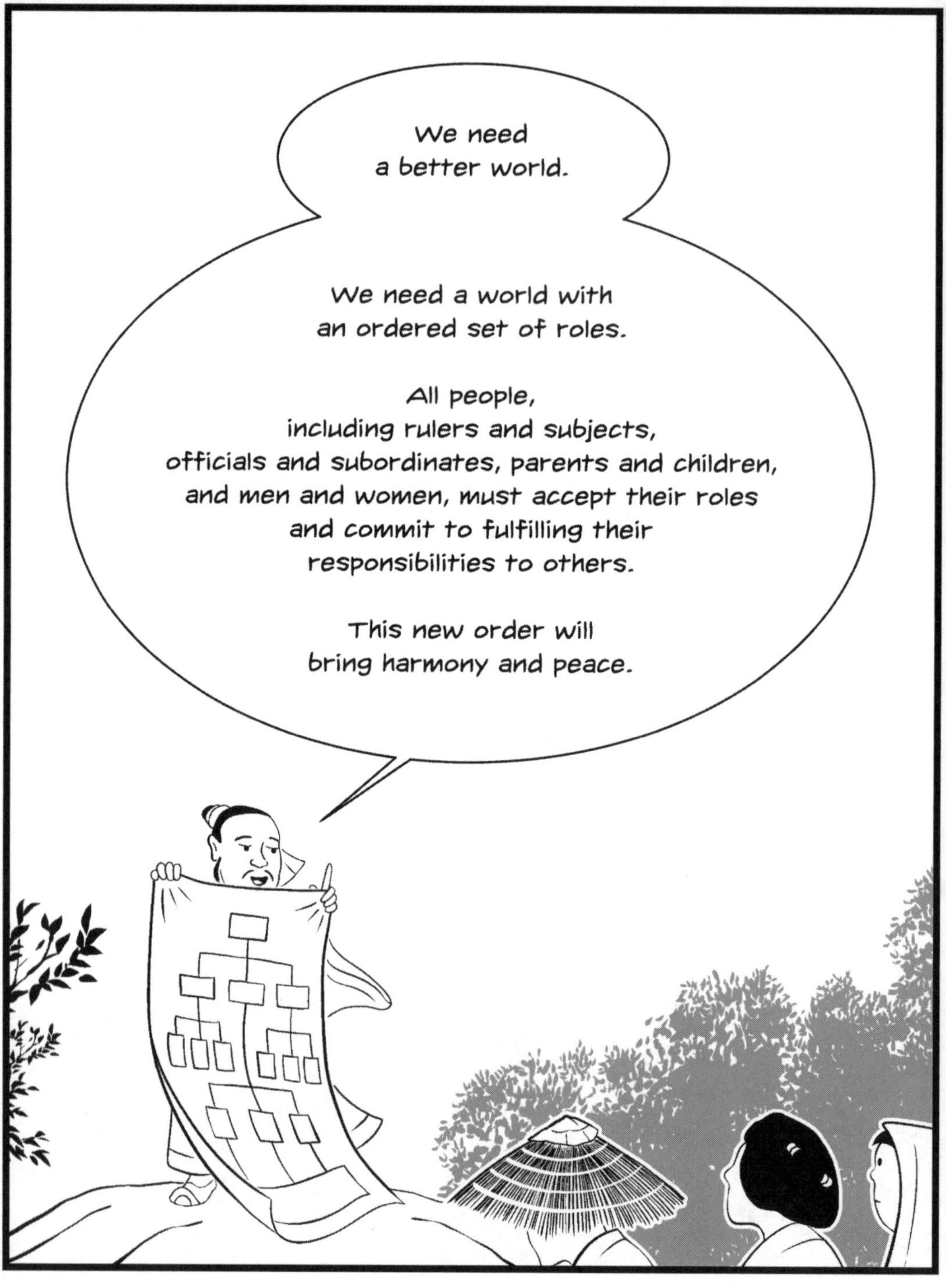
We need a better world.
We need a world with an ordered set of roles.
All people, including rulers and subjects, officials and subordinates, parents and children, and men and women, must accept their roles and commit to fulfilling their responsibilities to others.
This new order will bring harmony and peace.

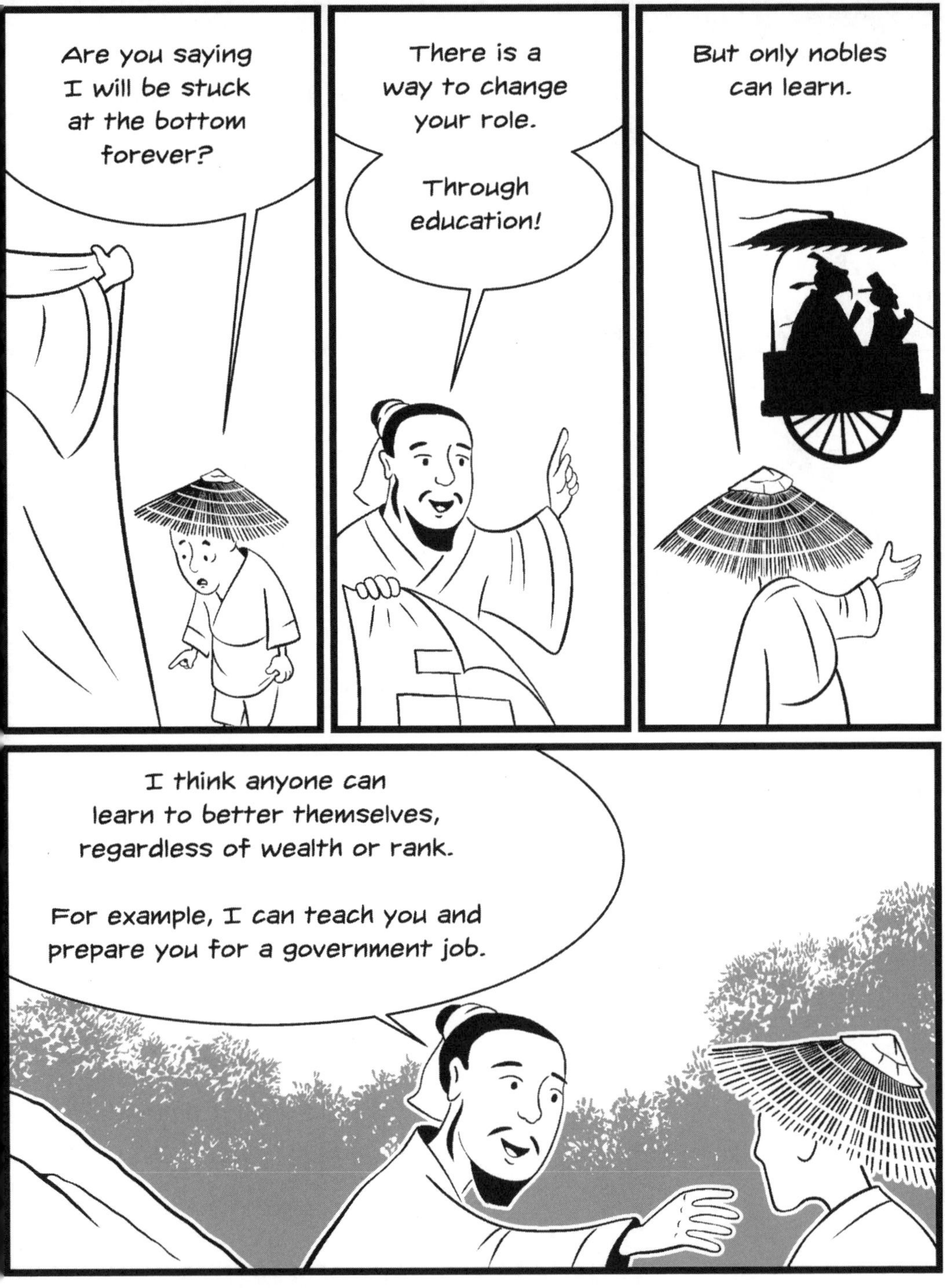
Are you saying I will be stuck at the bottom forever?
There is a way to change your role.
Through education!
But only nobles can learn.
I think anyone can learn to better themselves, regardless of wealth or rank.
For example, I can teach you and prepare you for a government job.

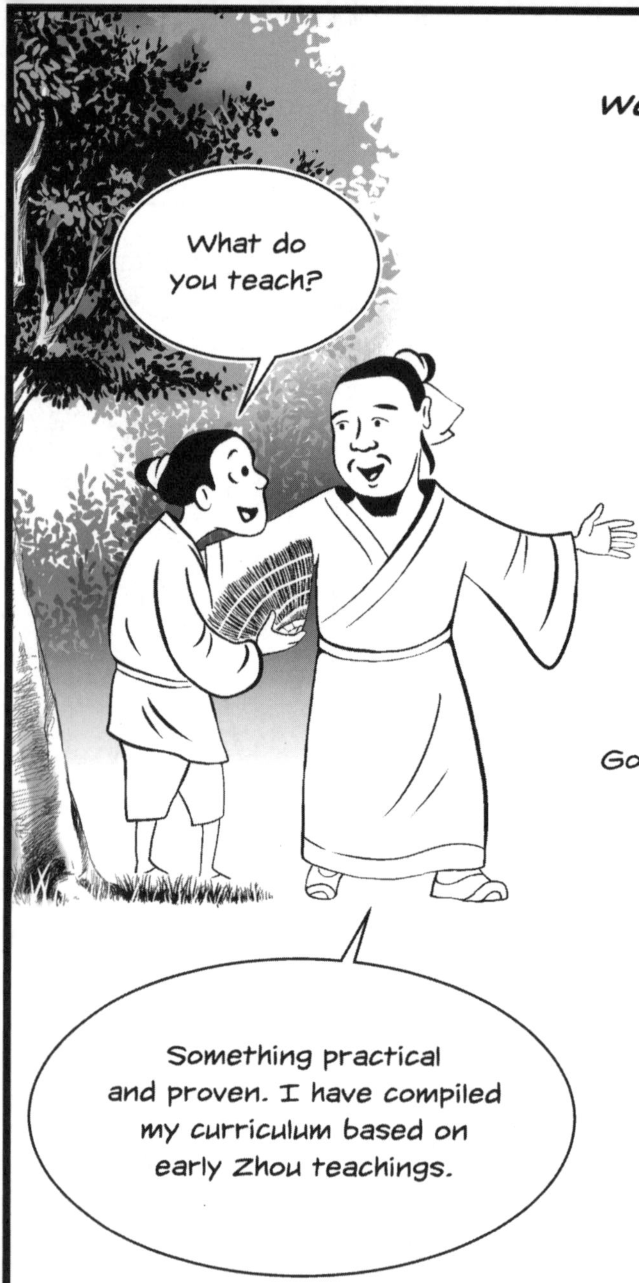
What do you teach?
Something practical and proven. I have compiled my curriculum based on early Zhou teachings.

Western Zhou teaching:

Six virtues: 六德:

Knowledge	知
Benevolence	仁
Dignity	圣
Righteousness	义
Loyalty	忠
Kindness	和

Six elements: 六行:

Filial piety	孝
Friendship	友
Good neighborliness	睦
Elegance	姻
Responsibility	任
Sympathy	恤

Six arts: 六艺:

Rites	礼
Music	乐
Archery	射
Horseback riding	御
Writing	书
Mathematics	数

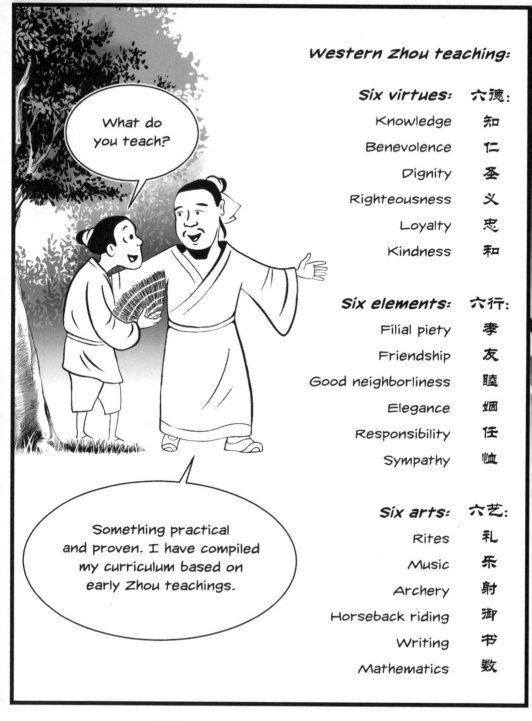

Confucian teaching:

五常: *Five virtues:*

仁 Benevolence

义 Righteousness,

礼 Ritual

知 Knowledge

信 Integrity

四德: *Four elements:*

忠 Loyalty

孝 Filial piety

节 Self-restraint

义 Devotion to principle

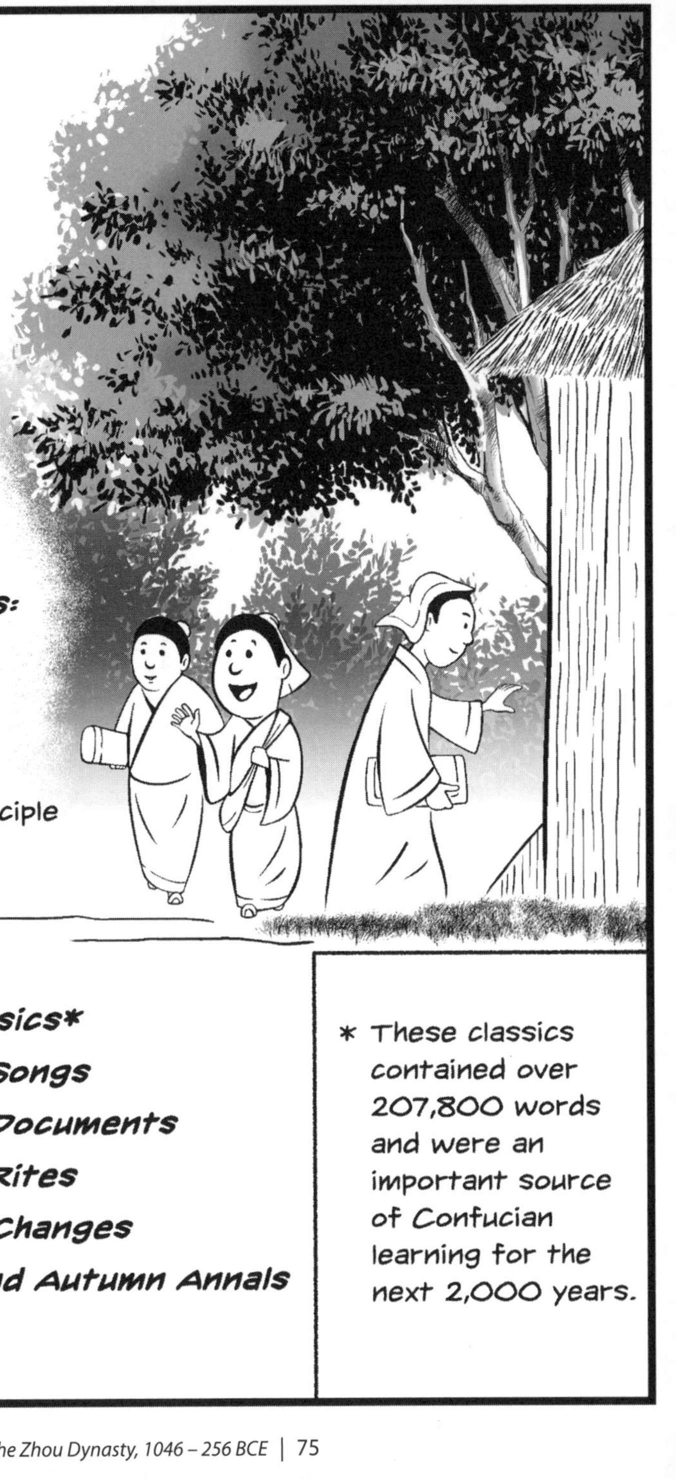

五经: *The Five Classics**

诗经 *The Book of Songs*

尚书 *The Book of Documents*

礼记 *The Book of Rites*

易经 *The Book of Changes*

春秋 *The Spring and Autumn Annals*

* These classics contained over 207,800 words and were an important source of Confucian learning for the next 2,000 years.

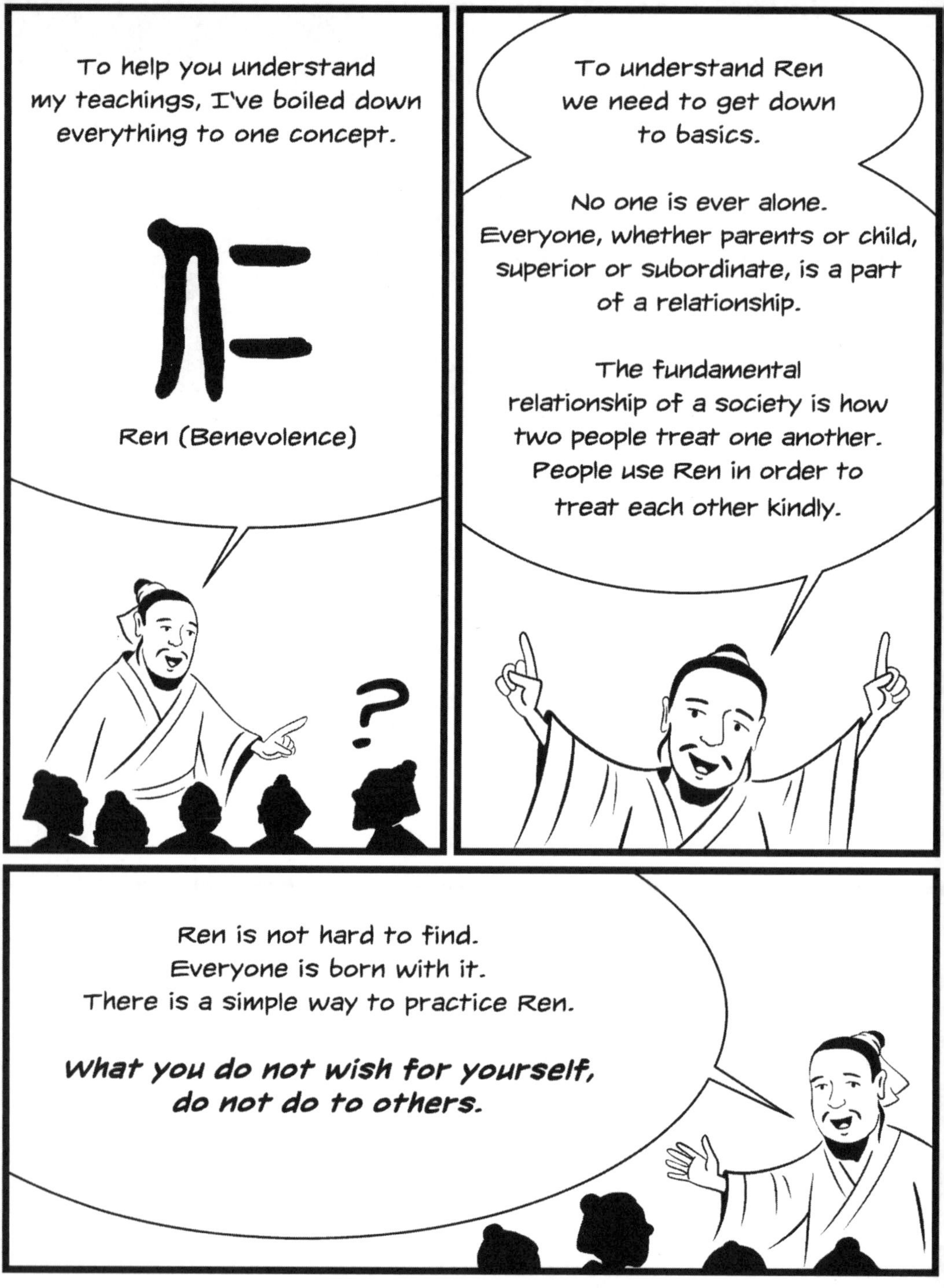
To help you understand my teachings, I've boiled down everything to one concept.
仁
Ren (Benevolence)
?
To understand Ren we need to get down to basics.
No one is ever alone. Everyone, whether parents or child, superior or subordinate, is a part of a relationship.
The fundamental relationship of a society is how two people treat one another. People use Ren in order to treat each other kindly.
Ren is not hard to find. Everyone is born with it. There is a simple way to practice Ren.
What you do not wish for yourself, do not do to others.

Confucius taught over 3,000 students.
In his books, he laid out a roadmap
for his followers:

格物

If you study, you know.

致知

If you know, you are wise.

诚意

If you are wise, you are fair.

正心

If you are fair, you grow.

修身

If you grow, you can manage your family well.

齐家

If you can manage your family well, you can serve the country.

治国

If you can serve the country, you can improve the world.

平天下

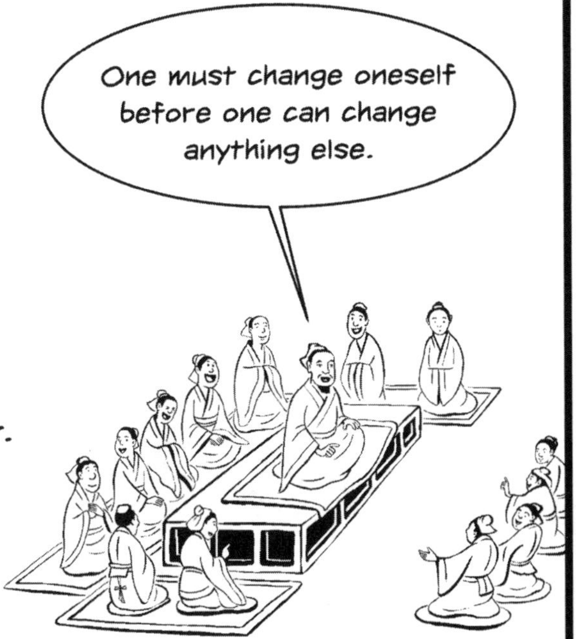
One must change oneself before one can change anything else.

Confucius created an educational system that could:

Provide a government with knowledgeable candidates for official posts

Motivate commoners to better themselves and achieve a higher social status through learning

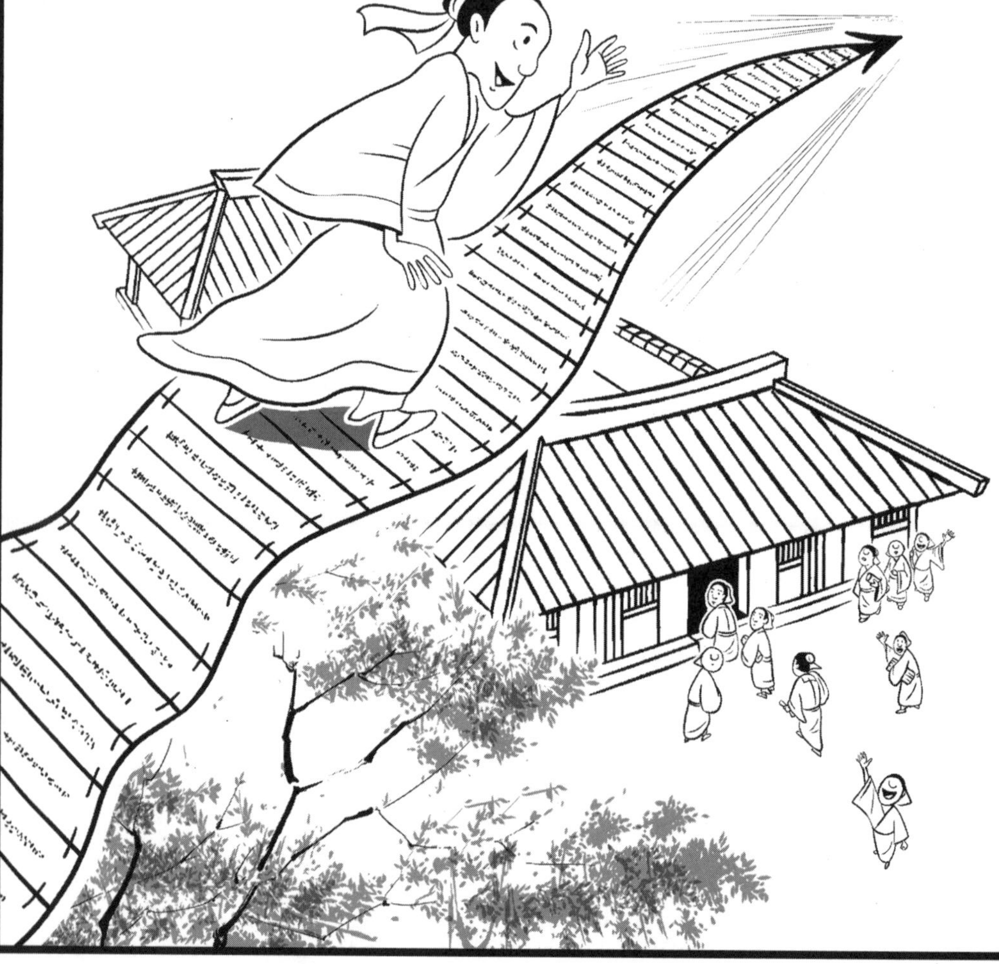

His values eventually formed the ethical core of traditional Chinese society. Today, many Chinese still measure their lives according to the roadmap Confucius used to describe his own life's journey.

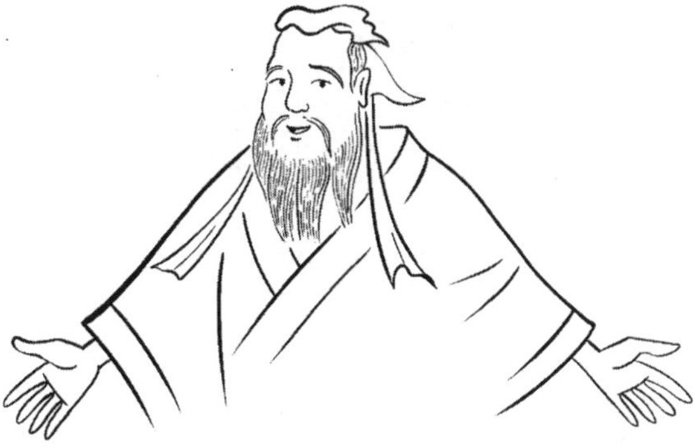

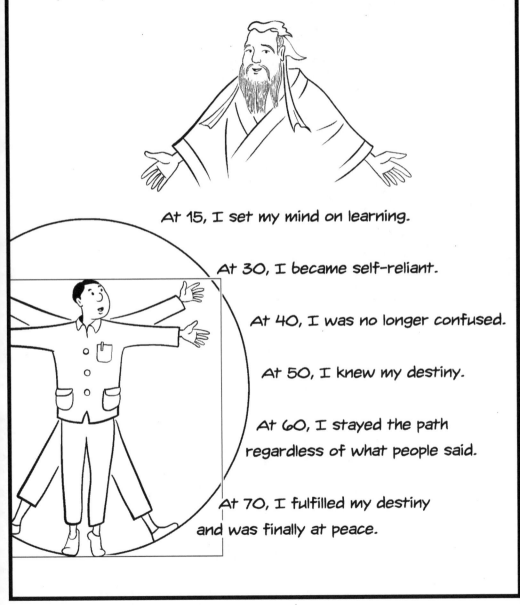

At 15, I set my mind on learning.

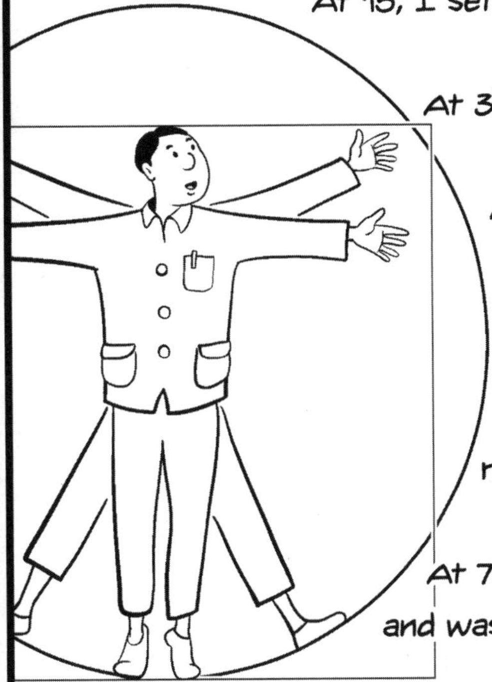

At 30, I became self-reliant.

At 40, I was no longer confused.

At 50, I knew my destiny.

At 60, I stayed the path regardless of what people said.

At 70, I fulfilled my destiny and was finally at peace.

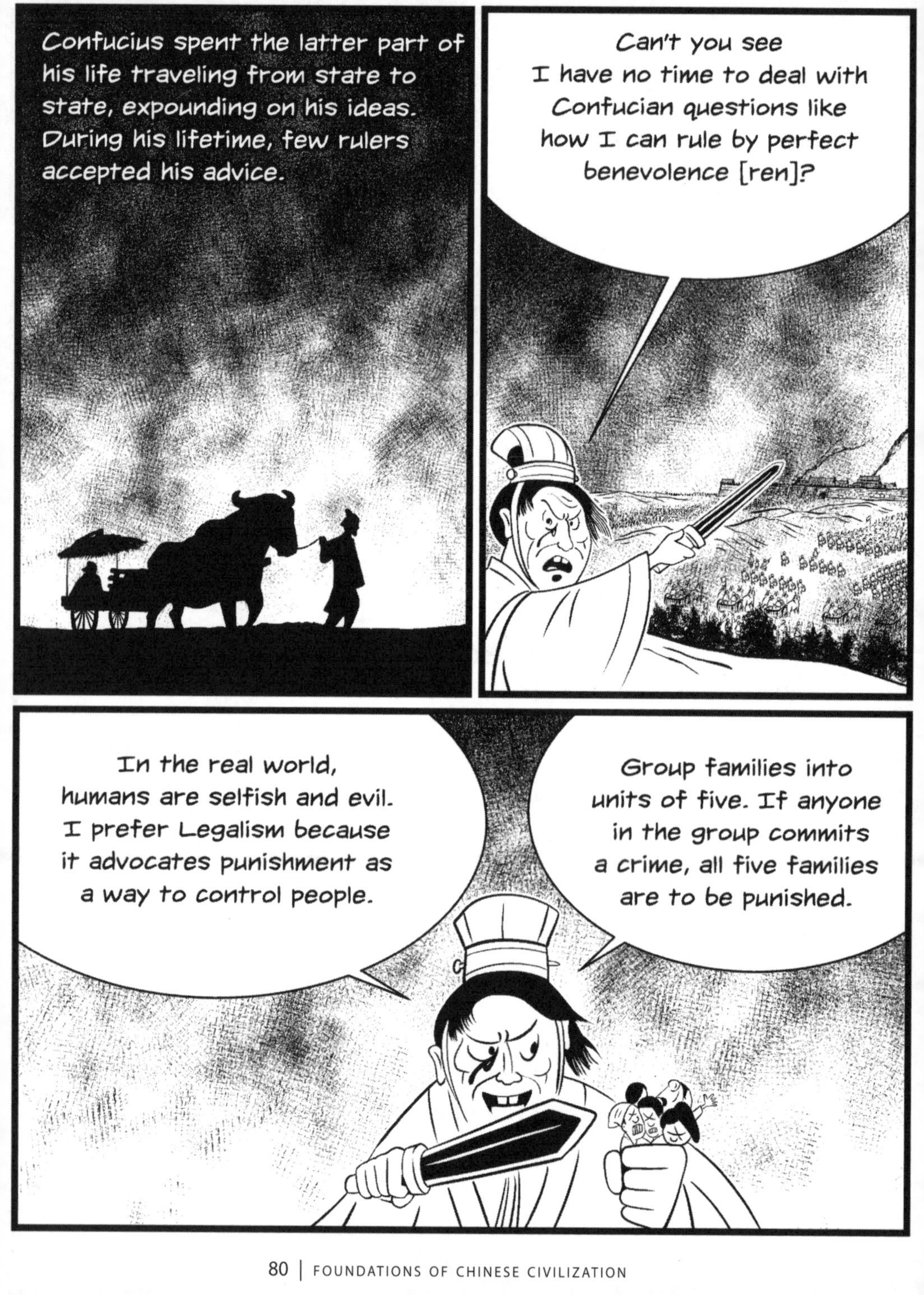
Confucius spent the latter part of his life traveling from state to state, expounding on his ideas. During his lifetime, few rulers accepted his advice.
Can't you see I have no time to deal with Confucian questions like how I can rule by perfect benevolence [ren]?
In the real world, humans are selfish and evil. I prefer Legalism because it advocates punishment as a way to control people.
Group families into units of five. If anyone in the group commits a crime, all five families are to be punished.

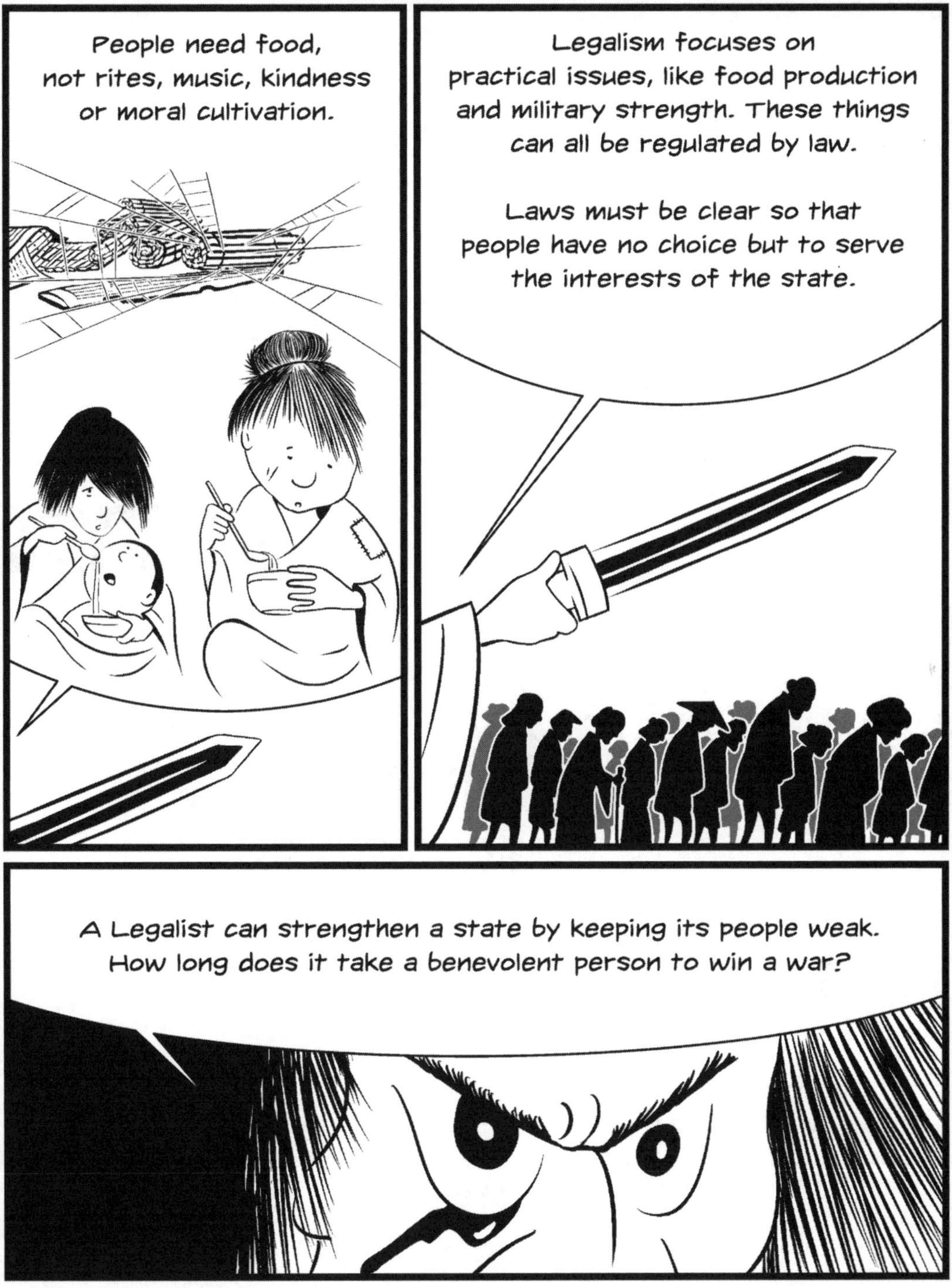
People need food, not rites, music, kindness or moral cultivation.
Legalism focuses on practical issues, like food production and military strength. These things can all be regulated by law.
Laws must be clear so that people have no choice but to serve the interests of the state.
A Legalist can strengthen a state by keeping its people weak. How long does it take a benevolent person to win a war?

Advantages of the Qin

Most warring states used Legalism to centralize power and maximize military might. But the Qin state had unique advantages. As a border state of the Eastern Zhou, the Qin occupied a fertile plain surrounded by mountains.

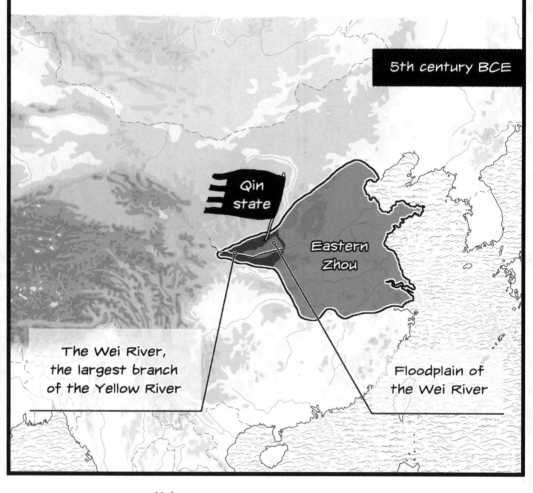

5th century BCE

Qin state

Eastern Zhou

The Wei River, the largest branch of the Yellow River

Floodplain of the Wei River

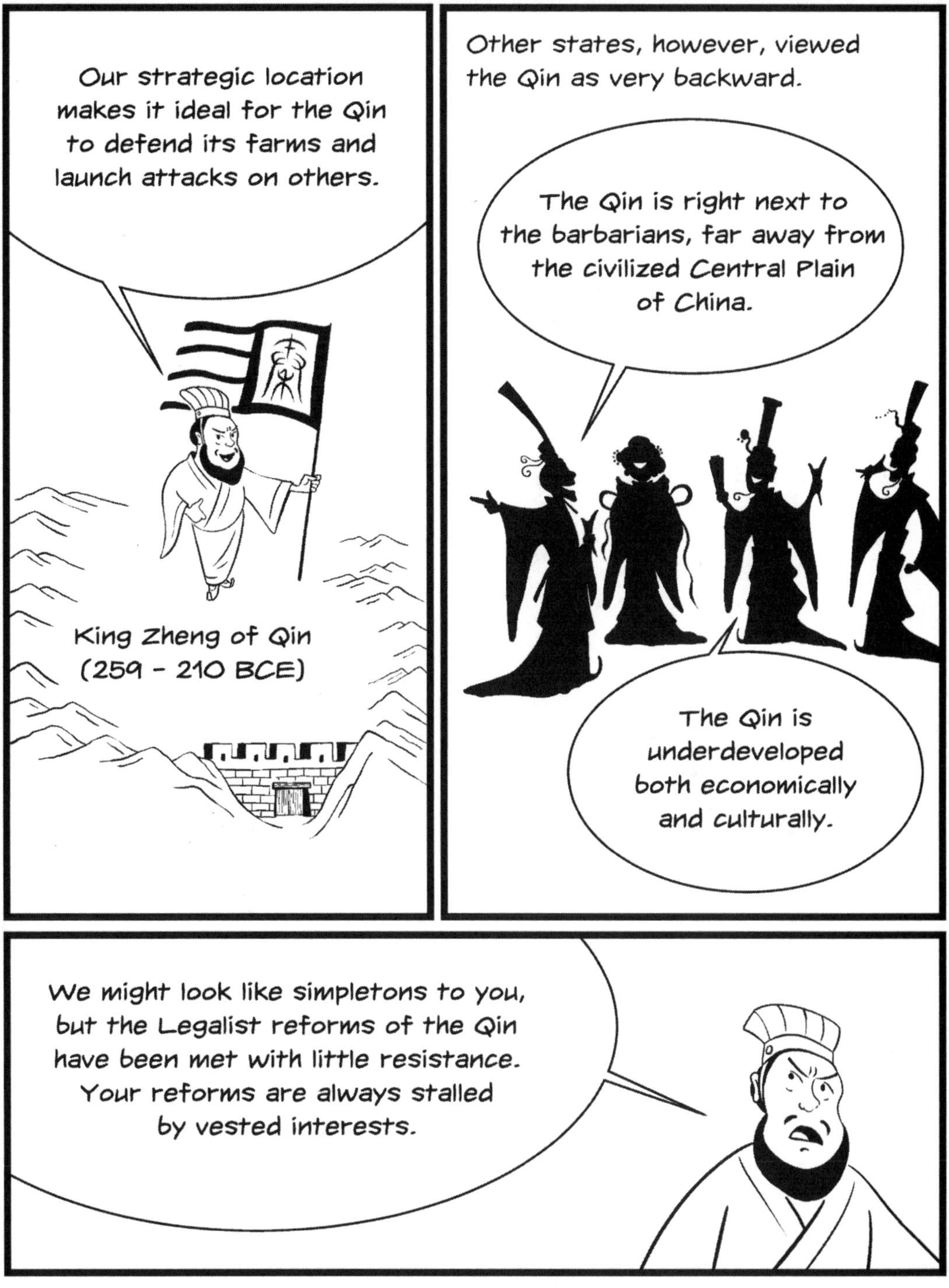
Our strategic location makes it ideal for the Qin to defend its farms and launch attacks on others.
King Zheng of Qin (259 – 210 BCE)
Other states, however, viewed the Qin as very backward.
The Qin is right next to the barbarians, far away from the civilized Central Plain of China.
The Qin is underdeveloped both economically and culturally.
We might look like simpletons to you, but the Legalist reforms of the Qin have been met with little resistance. Your reforms are always stalled by vested interests.

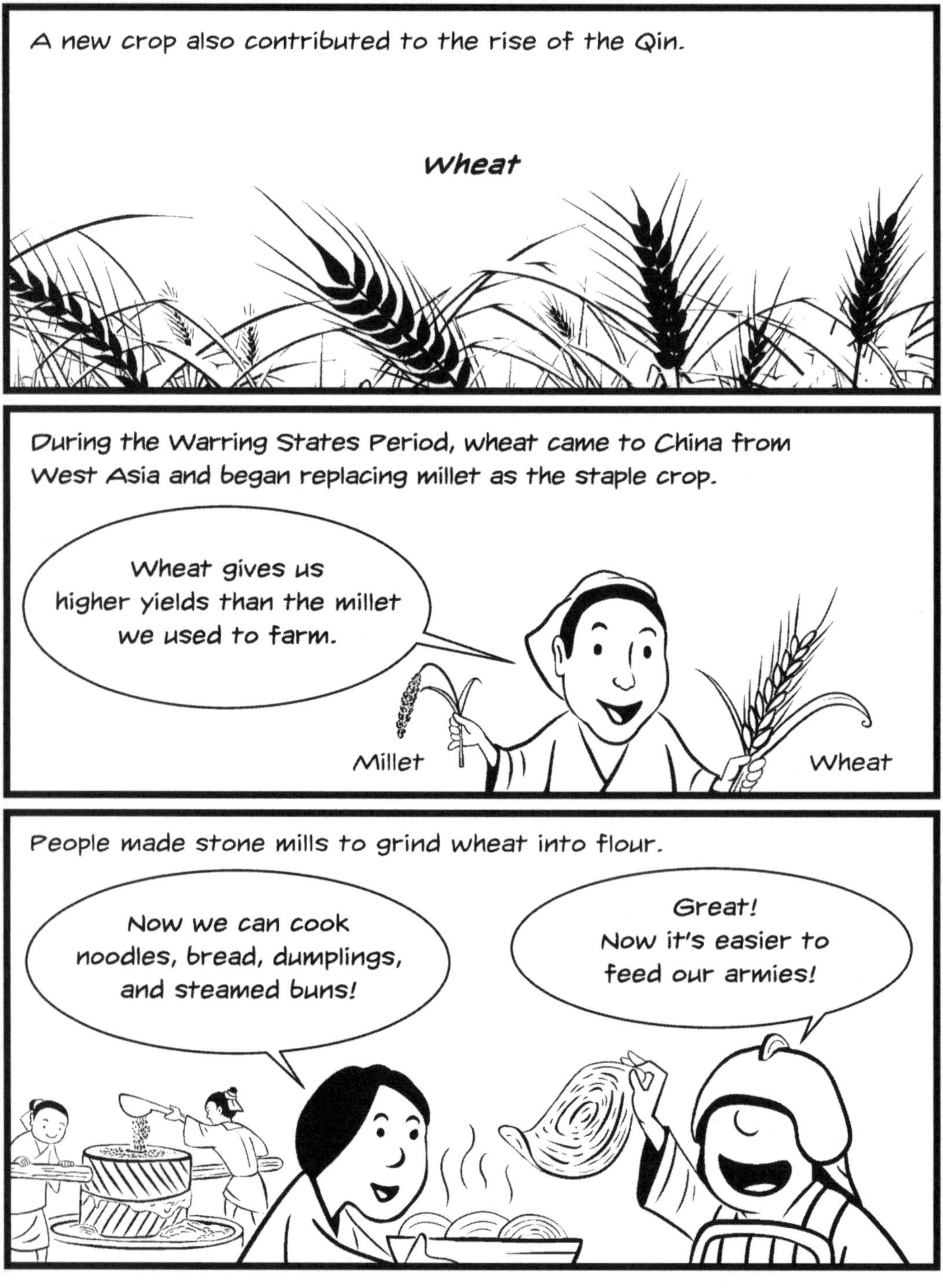
A new crop also contributed to the rise of the Qin.
Wheat
During the Warring States Period, wheat came to China from West Asia and began replacing millet as the staple crop.
Wheat gives us higher yields than the millet we used to farm.
Millet
Wheat
People made stone mills to grind wheat into flour.
Now we can cook noodles, bread, dumplings, and steamed buns!
Great! Now it's easier to feed our armies!

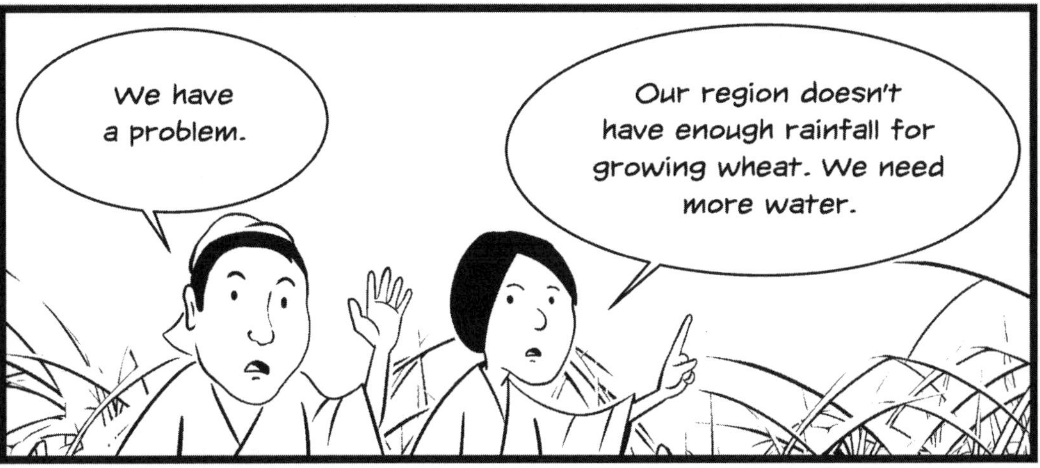
We have a problem.
Our region doesn't have enough rainfall for growing wheat. We need more water.

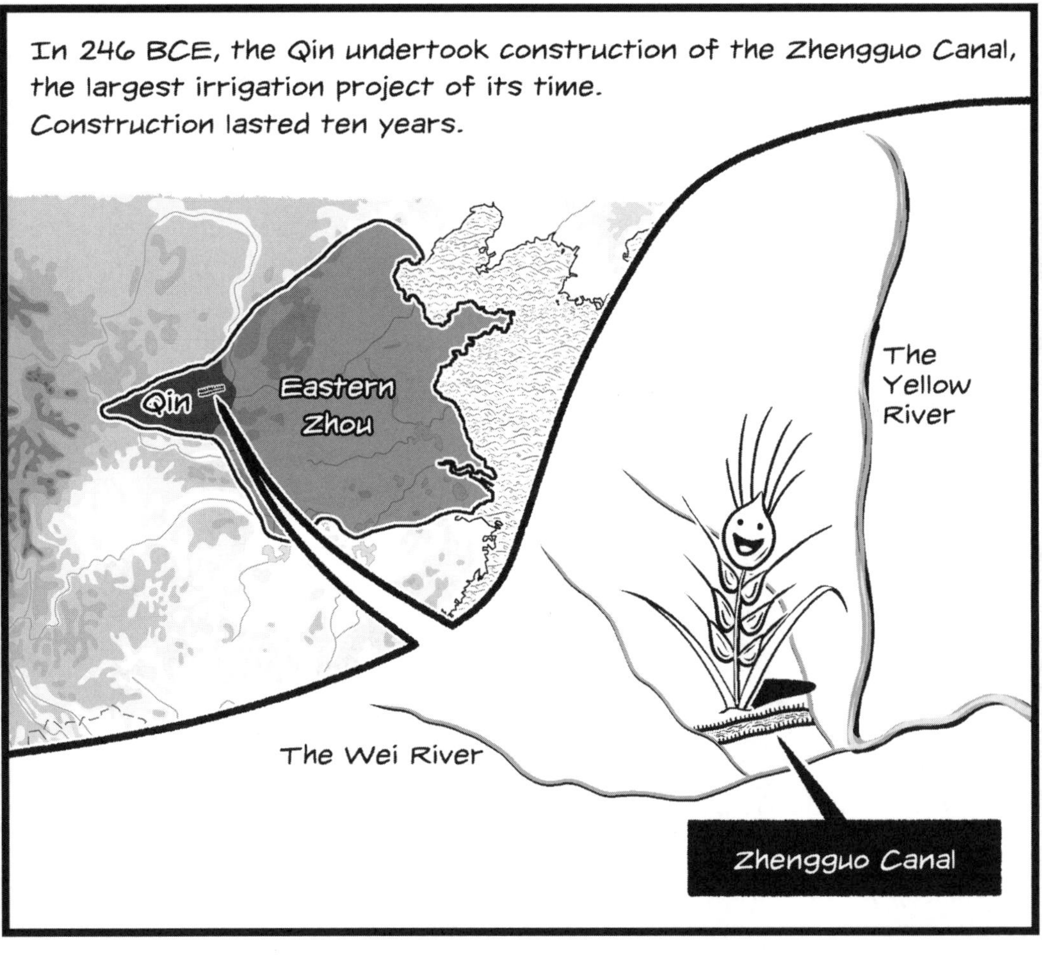
In 246 BCE, the Qin undertook construction of the Zhengguo Canal, the largest irrigation project of its time. Construction lasted ten years.
Qin
Eastern Zhou
The Yellow River
The Wei River
Zhengguo Canal

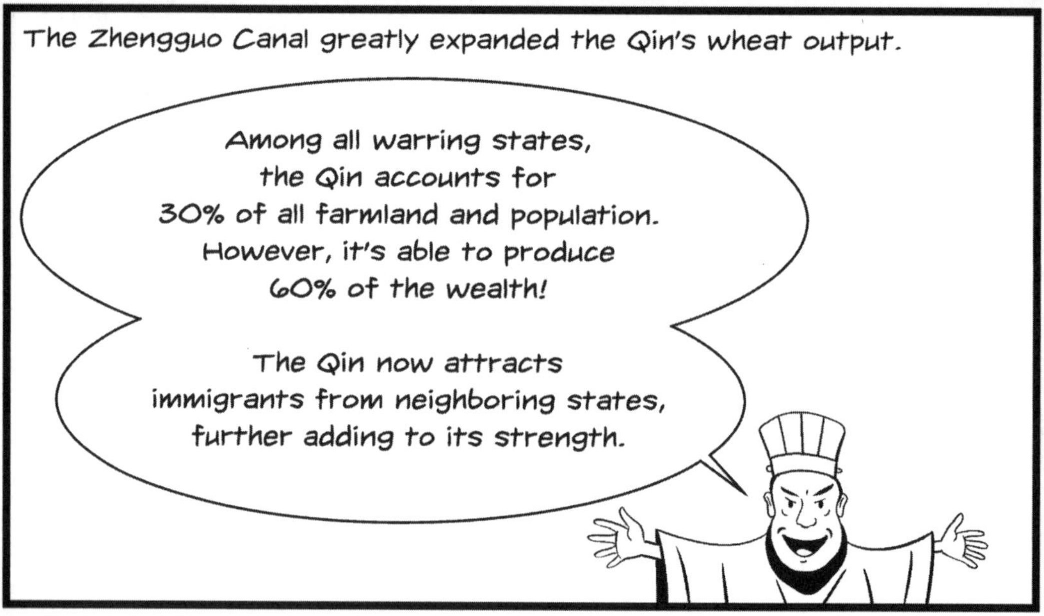
The Zhengguo Canal greatly expanded the Qin's wheat output.
Among all warring states, the Qin accounts for 30% of all farmland and population. However, it's able to produce 60% of the wealth!
The Qin now attracts immigrants from neighboring states, further adding to its strength.

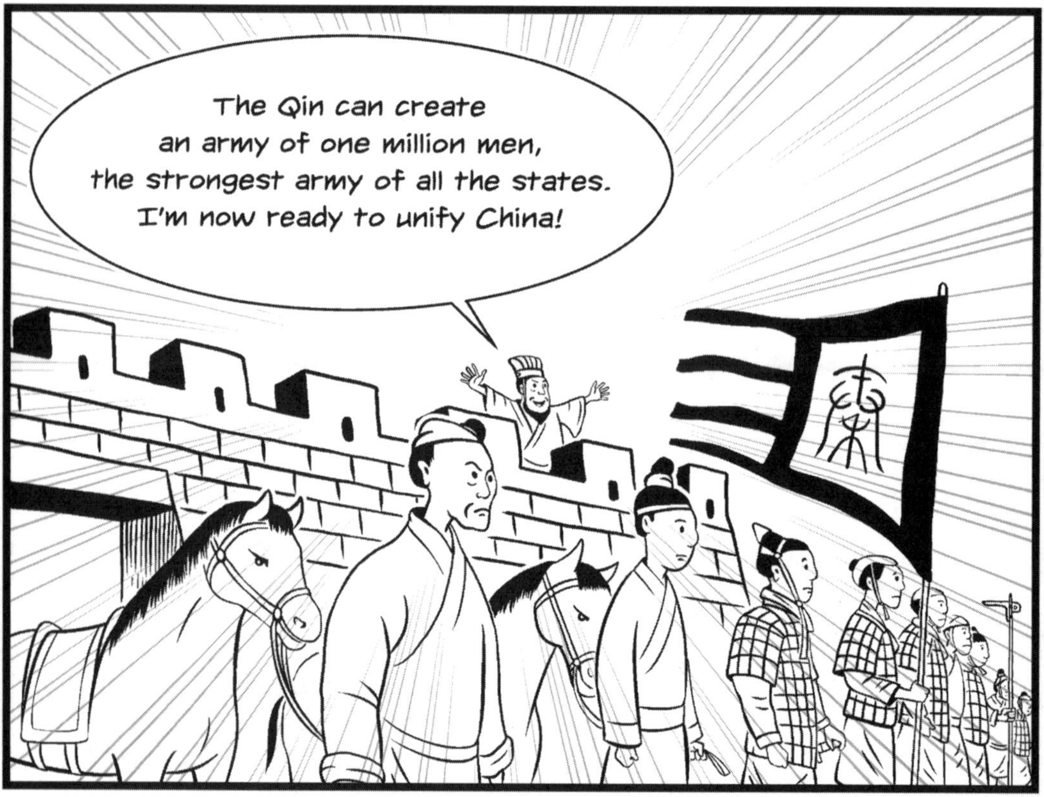
The Qin can create an army of one million men, the strongest army of all the states. I'm now ready to unify China!

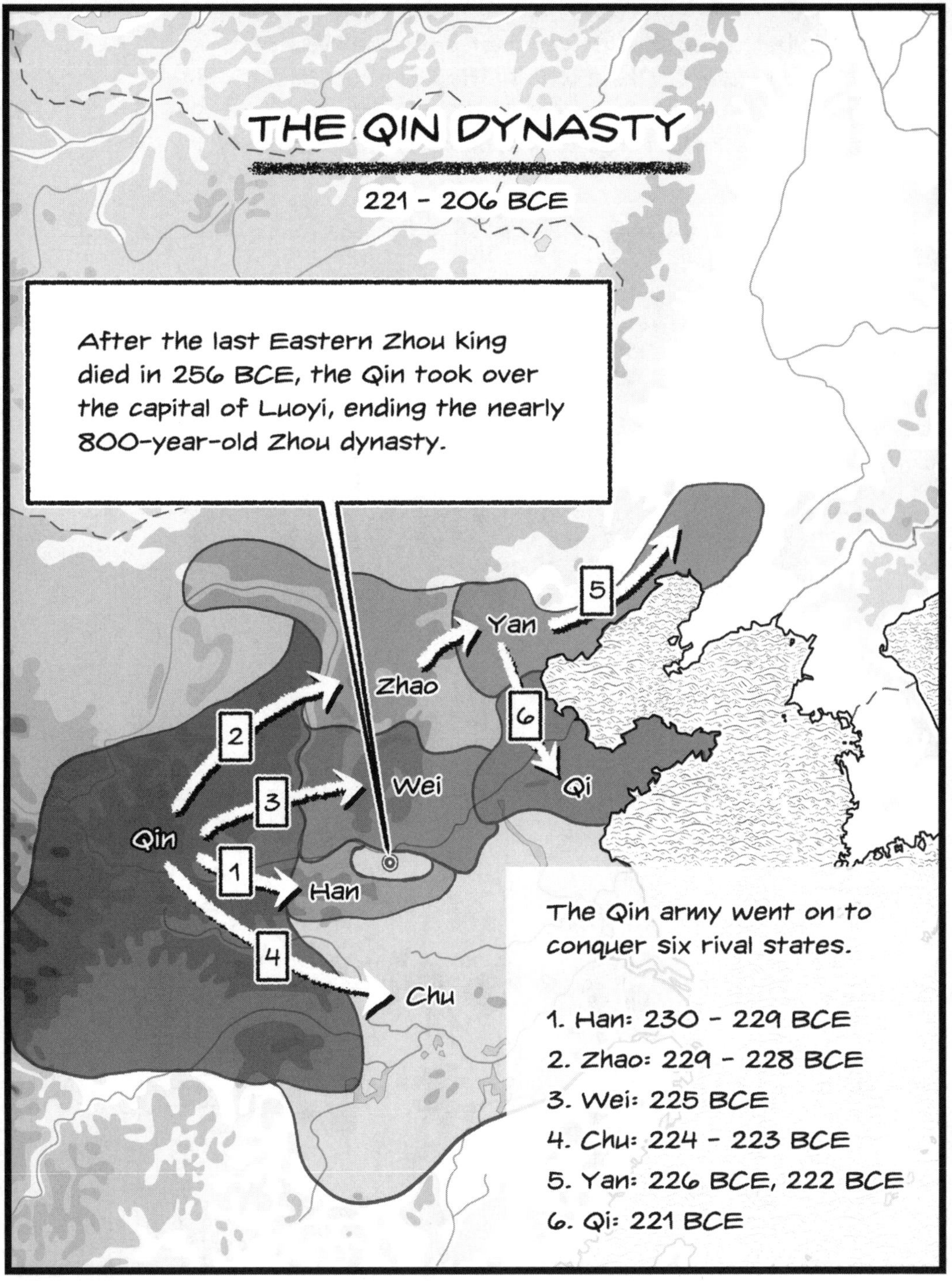
THE QIN DYNASTY
221 - 206 BCE
After the last Eastern Zhou king died in 256 BCE, the Qin took over the capital of Luoyi, ending the nearly 800-year-old Zhou dynasty.
Qin
Han
Chu
Wei
Zhao
Yan
Qi
1
2
3
4
5
6
The Qin army went on to conquer six rival states.
1. Han: 230 - 229 BCE
2. Zhao: 229 - 228 BCE
3. Wei: 225 BCE
4. Chu: 224 - 223 BCE
5. Yan: 226 BCE, 222 BCE
6. Qi: 221 BCE

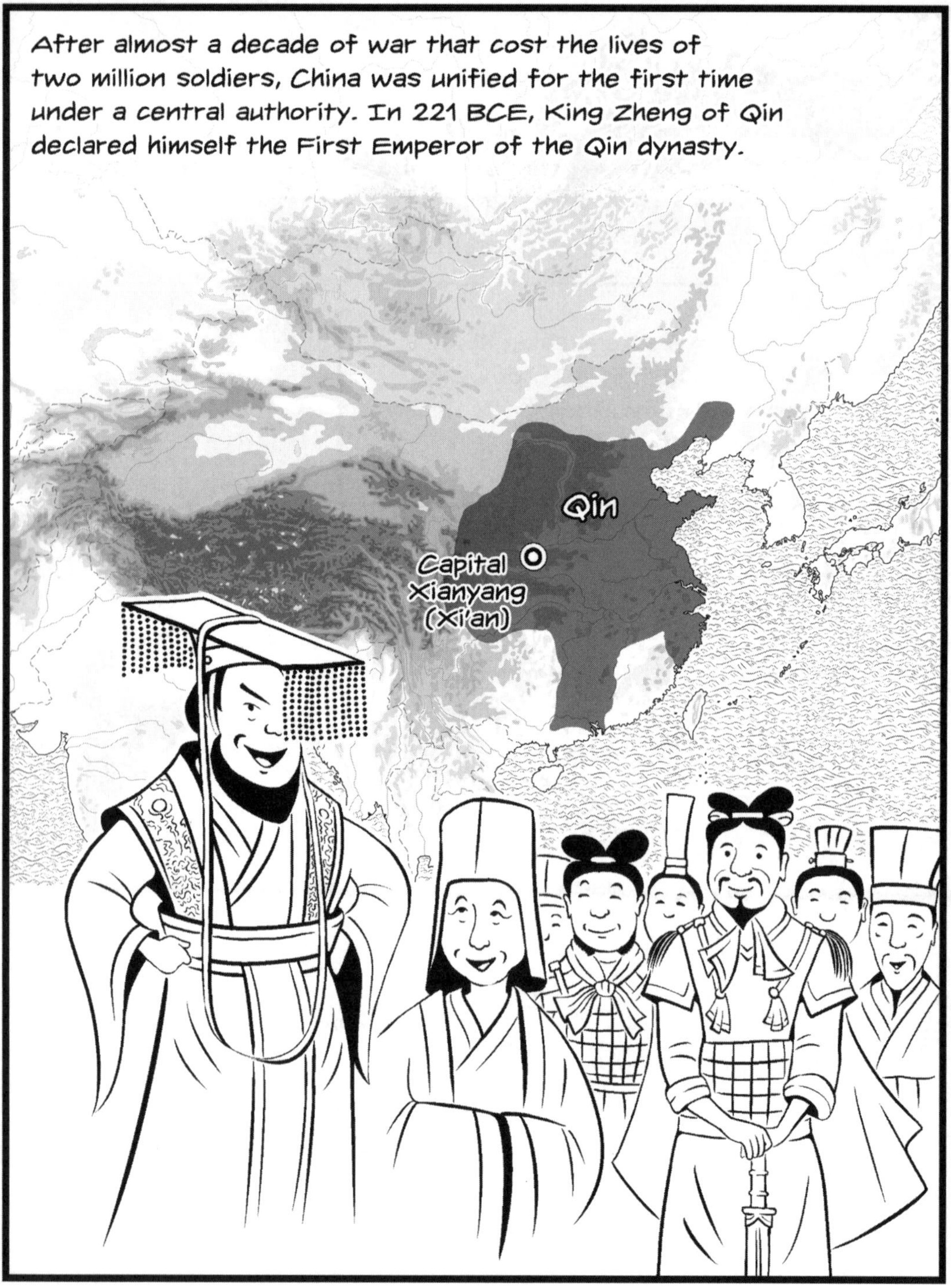
After almost a decade of war that cost the lives of two million soldiers, China was unified for the first time under a central authority. In 221 BCE, King Zheng of Qin declared himself the First Emperor of the Qin dynasty.
Qin
Capital Xianyang (Xi'an)

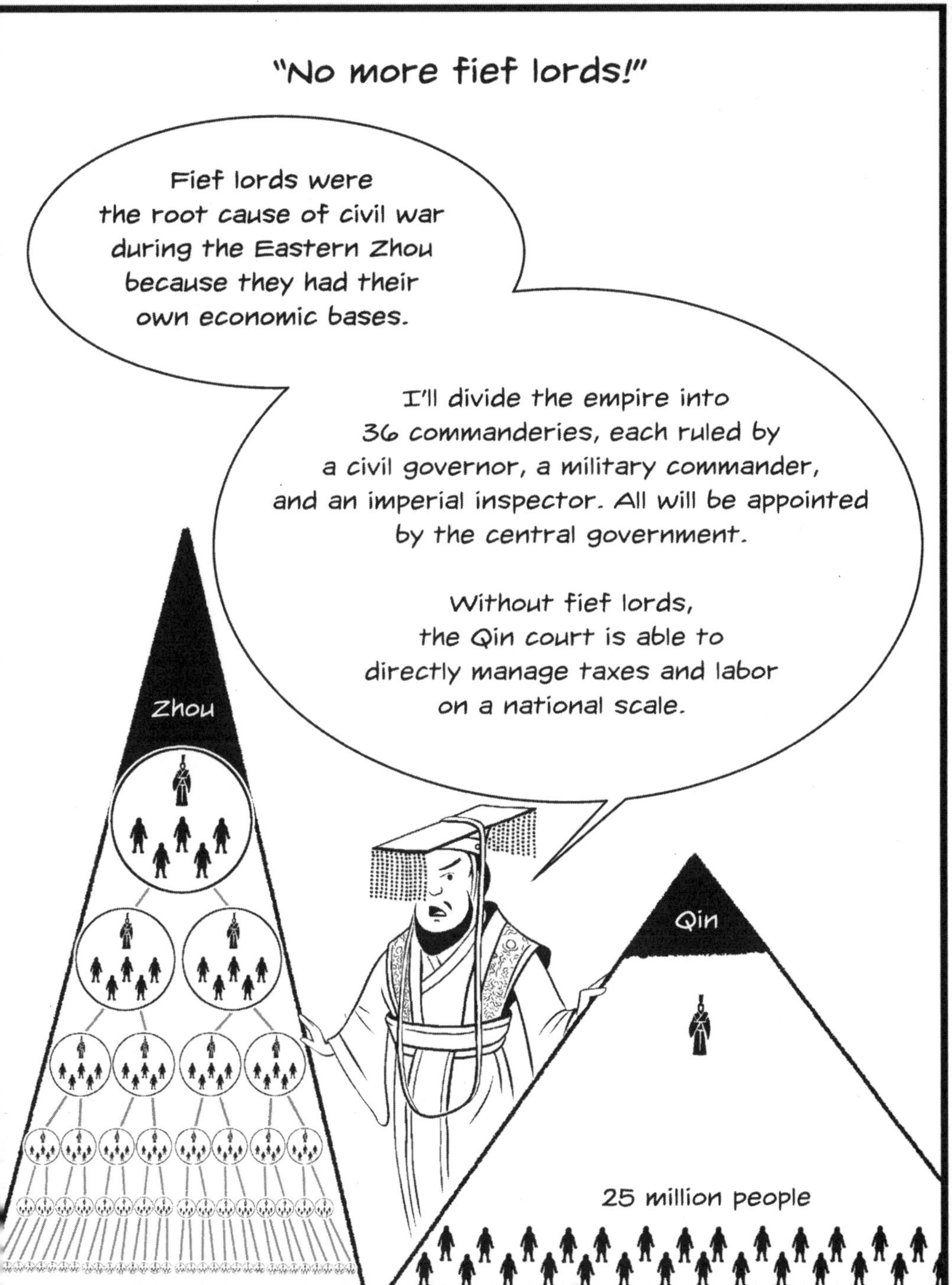
"No more fief lords!"
Fief lords were the root cause of civil war during the Eastern Zhou because they had their own economic bases.
I'll divide the empire into 36 commanderies, each ruled by a civil governor, a military commander, and an imperial inspector. All will be appointed by the central government.
Without fief lords, the Qin court is able to directly manage taxes and labor on a national scale.
Zhou
Qin
25 million people

A more efficient empire

To increase efficiency, the Qin government standardized many aspects of Chinese life.

Writing:

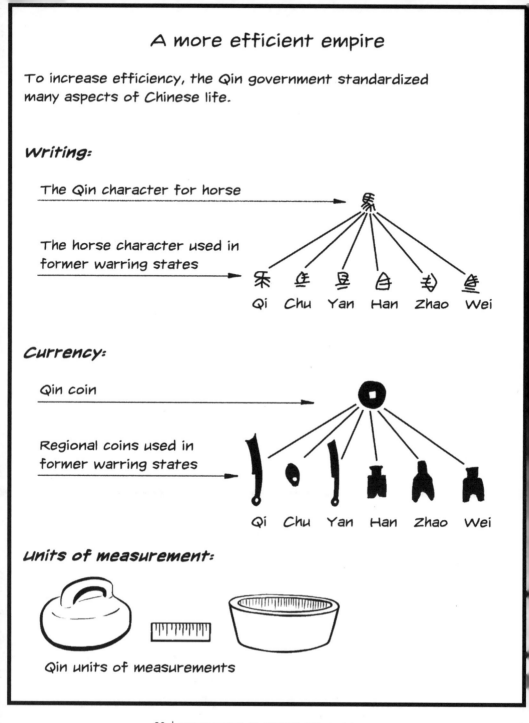

The Qin character for horse

The horse character used in former warring states

Qi Chu Yan Han Zhao Wei

Currency:

Qin coin

Regional coins used in former warring states

Qi Chu Yan Han Zhao Wei

Units of measurement:

Qin units of measurements

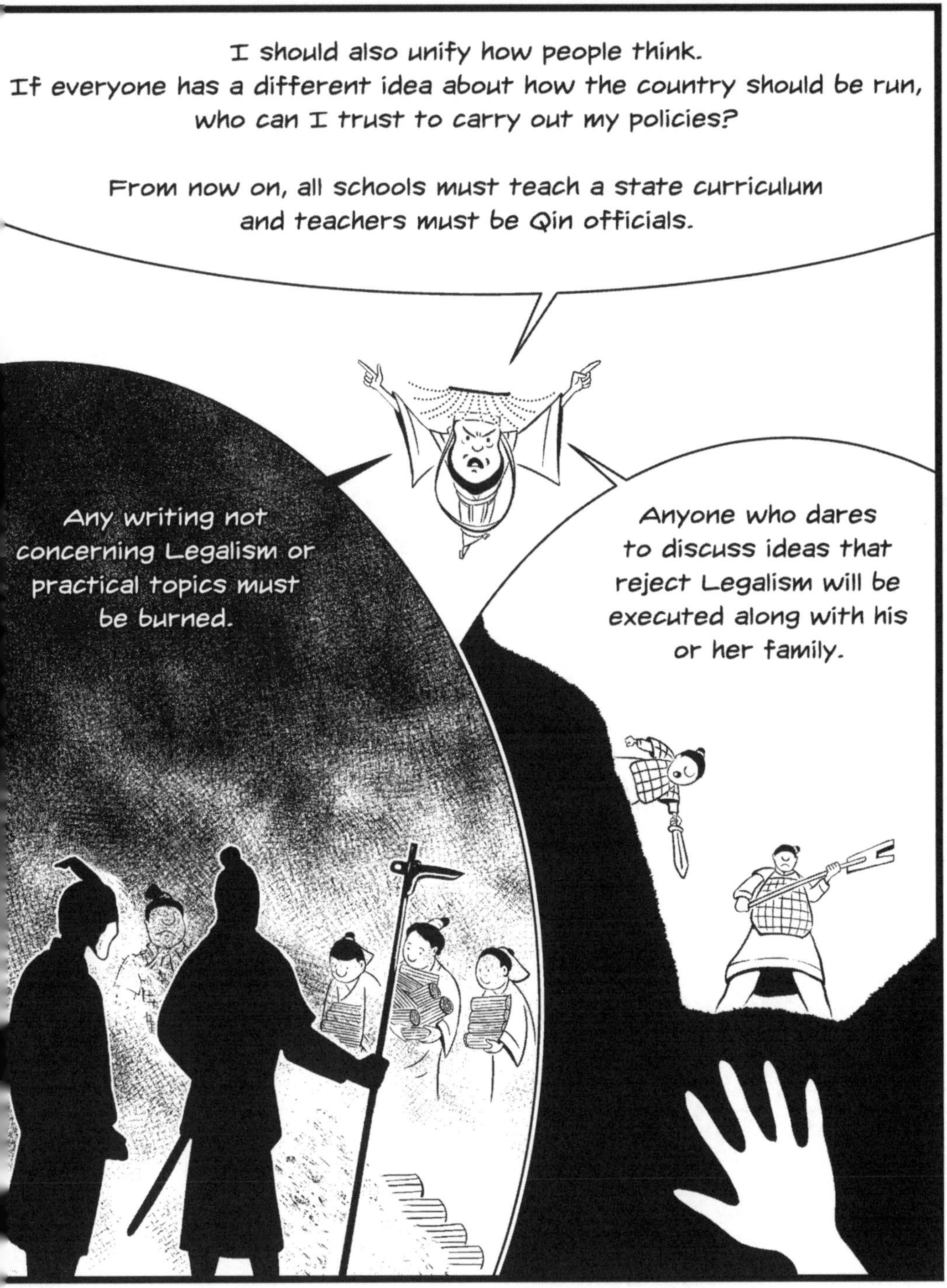
I should also unify how people think.
If everyone has a different idea about how the country should be run, who can I trust to carry out my policies?
From now on, all schools must teach a state curriculum and teachers must be Qin officials.
Any writing not concerning Legalism or practical topics must be burned.
Anyone who dares to discuss ideas that reject Legalism will be executed along with his or her family.

National projects

With strict rules and harsh punishment, the Qin was able to carry out many grand projects.

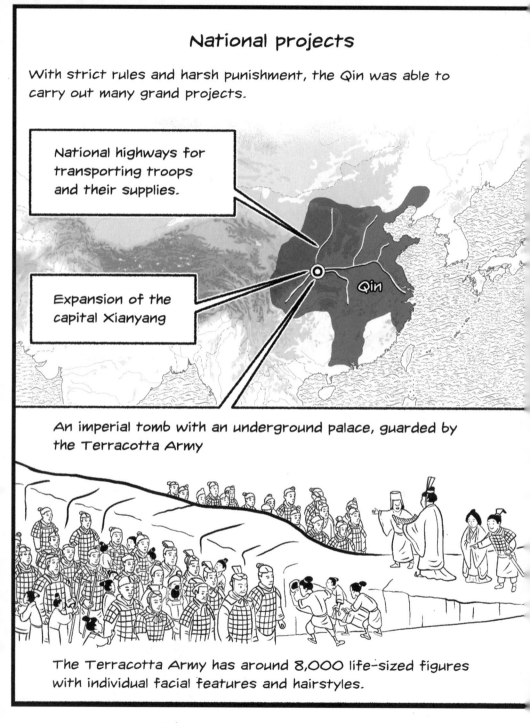

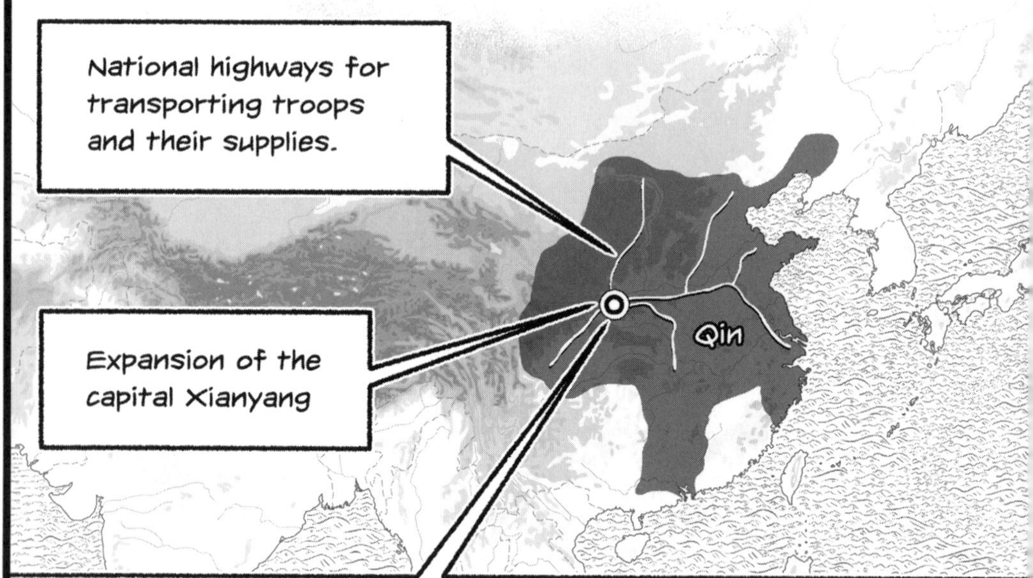
National highways for transporting troops and their supplies.
Expansion of the capital Xianyang
Qin

An imperial tomb with an underground palace, guarded by the Terracotta Army

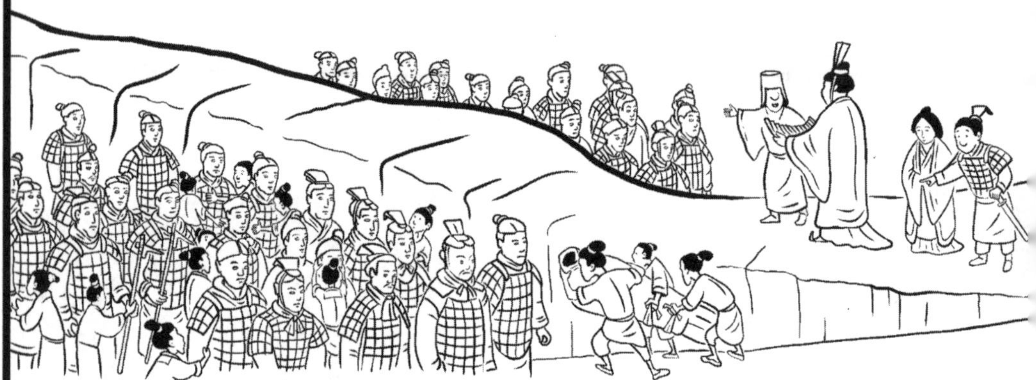

The Terracotta Army has around 8,000 life-sized figures with individual facial features and hairstyles.

Xiongnu threat and the Great Wall

The biggest headache for the Qin was defending its borders against a threat from the north - the Xiongnu tribes.

The early Xiongnu tribes were scattered throughout the upper reaches of the Yellow River. Some historians believe the Xiongnu were of Turkic and Mongol origin.

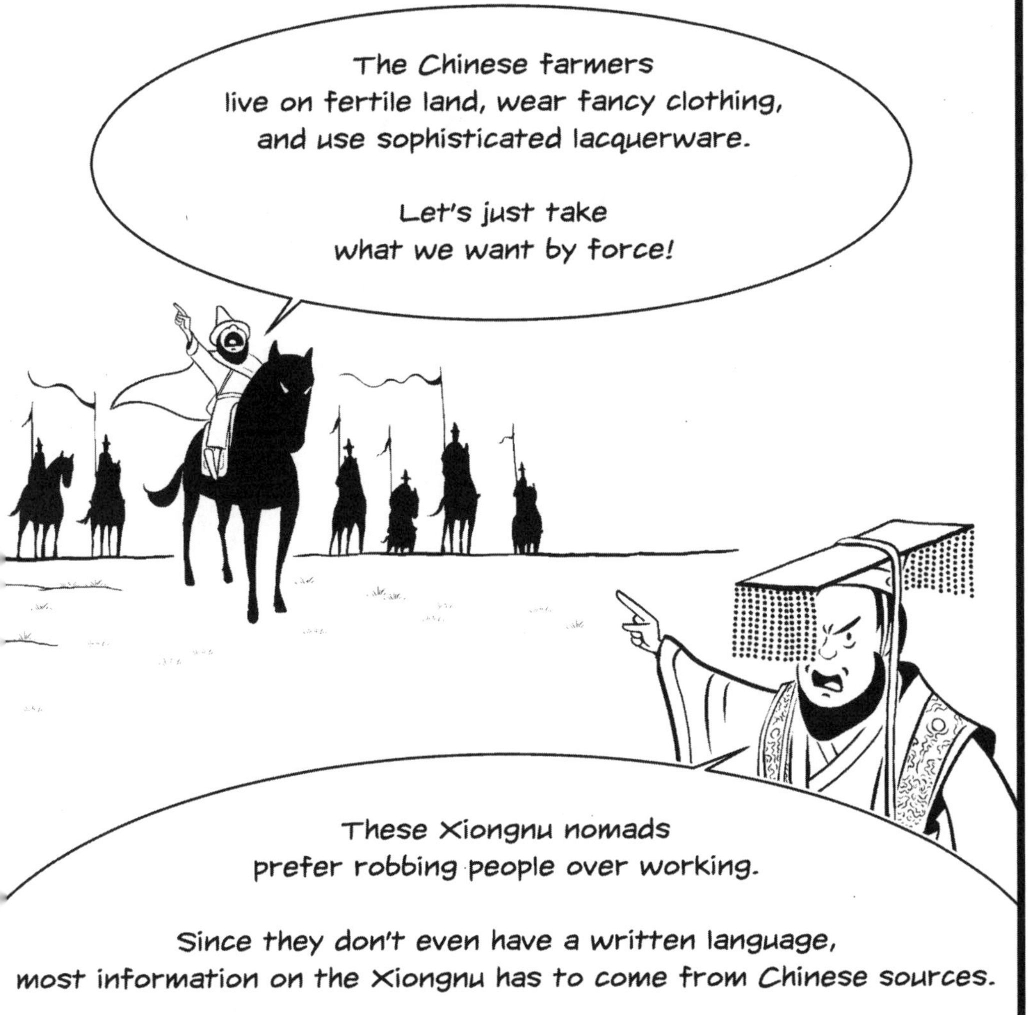

The Chinese farmers live on fertile land, wear fancy clothing, and use sophisticated lacquerware.
Let's just take what we want by force!
These Xiongnu nomads prefer robbing people over working.
Since they don't even have a written language, most information on the Xiongnu has to come from Chinese sources.

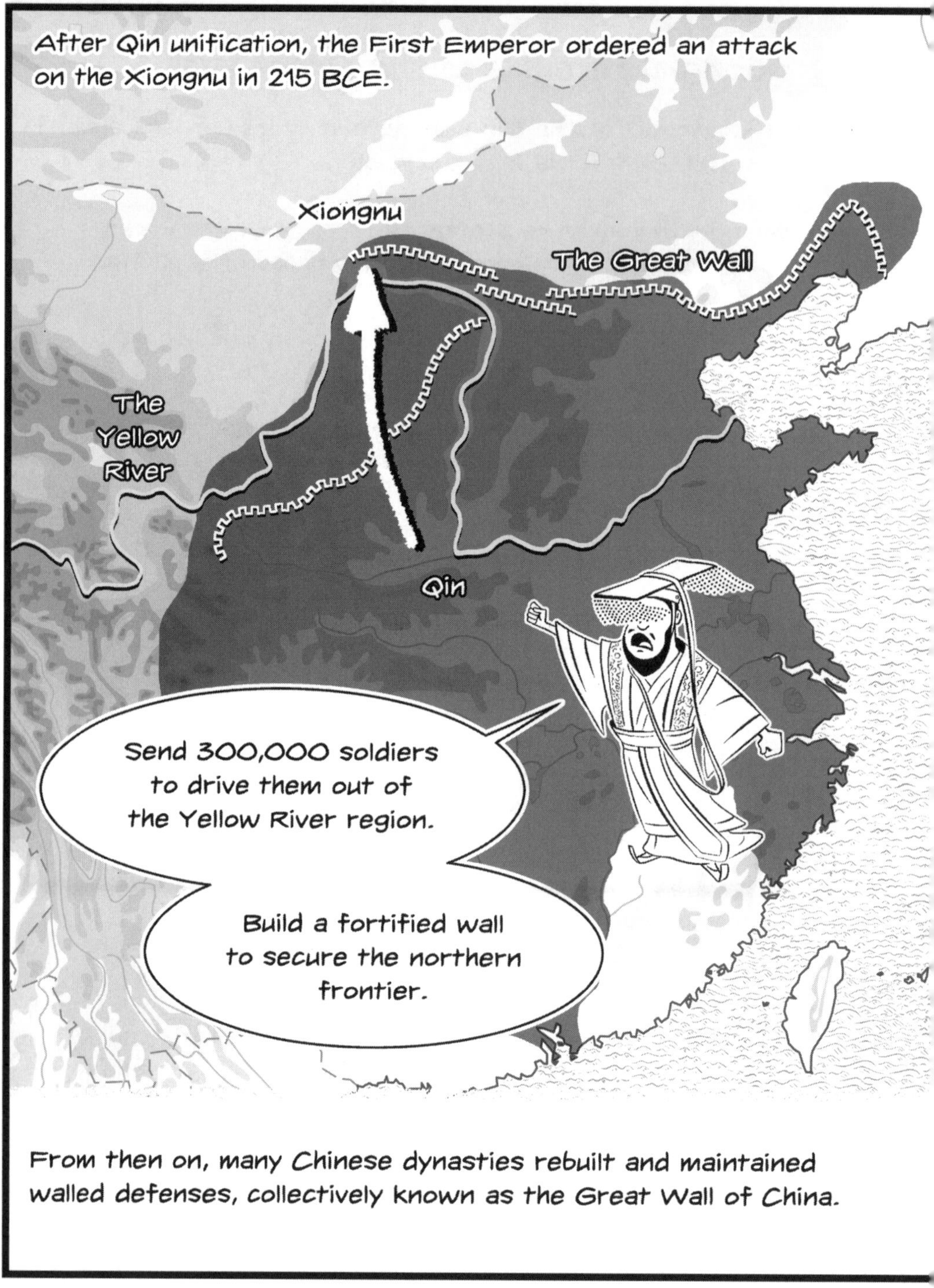
After Qin unification, the First Emperor ordered an attack on the Xiongnu in 215 BCE.
Xiongnu
The Great Wall
The Yellow River
Qin
Send 300,000 soldiers to drive them out of the Yellow River region.
Build a fortified wall to secure the northern frontier.

From then on, many Chinese dynasties rebuilt and maintained walled defenses, collectively known as the Great Wall of China.

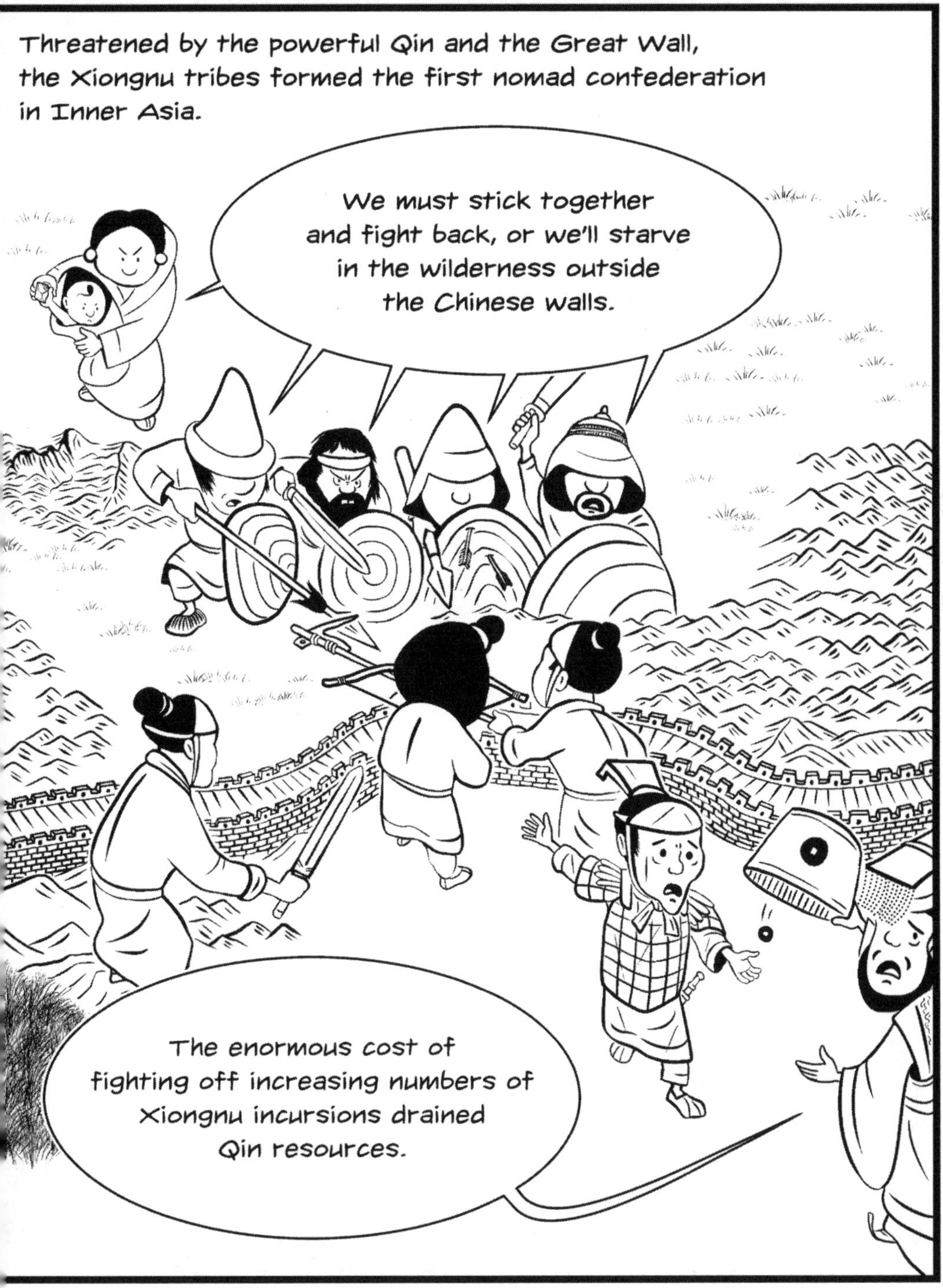
Threatened by the powerful Qin and the Great Wall, the Xiongnu tribes formed the first nomad confederation in Inner Asia.
We must stick together and fight back, or we'll starve in the wilderness outside the Chinese walls.
The enormous cost of fighting off increasing numbers of Xiongnu incursions drained Qin resources.

"It's suicide to fight the entire empire"

Before finding a solution to the Xiongnu problem, the First Emperor died in 210 BCE.

The court was immediately plunged into chaos. The next year riots broke out.

Three years after the emperor's death, the mighty Qin dynasty collapsed.

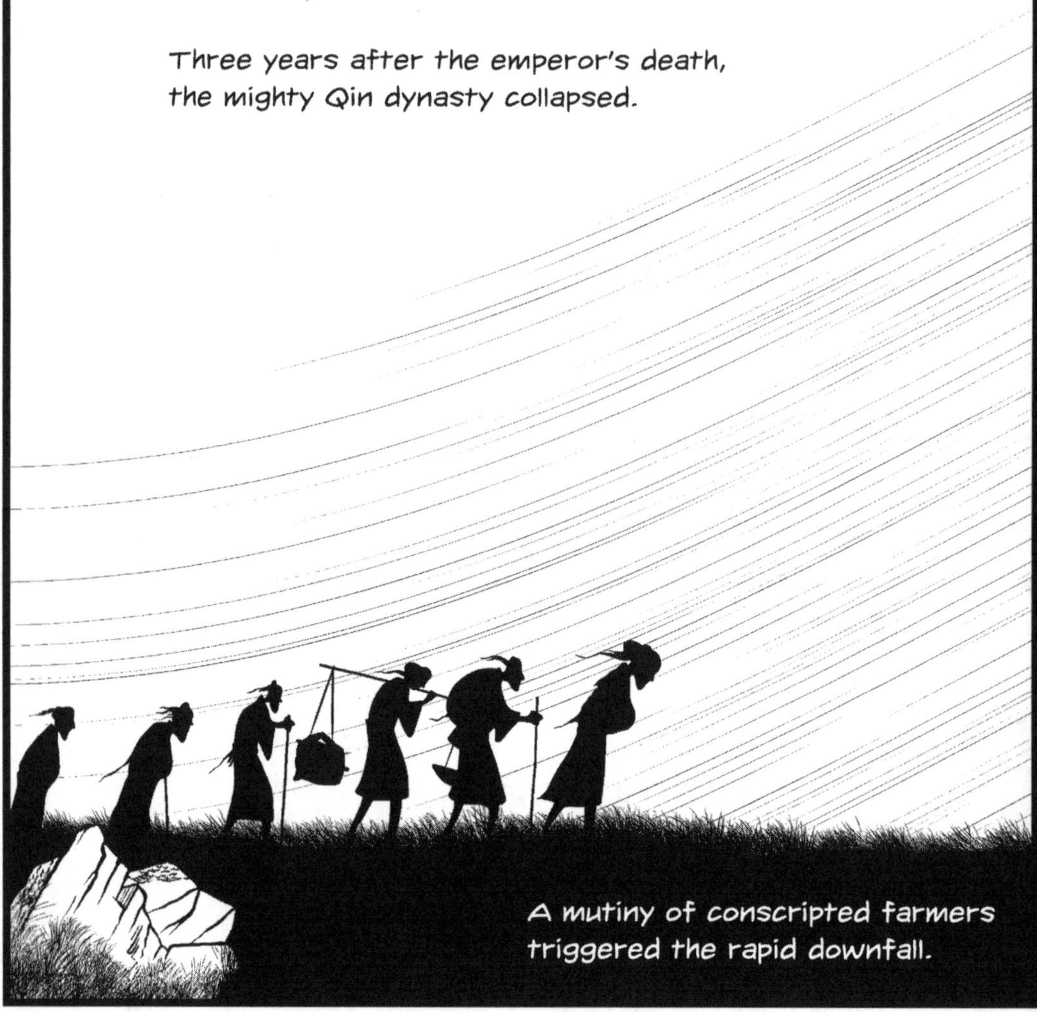
A mutiny of conscripted farmers triggered the rapid downfall.

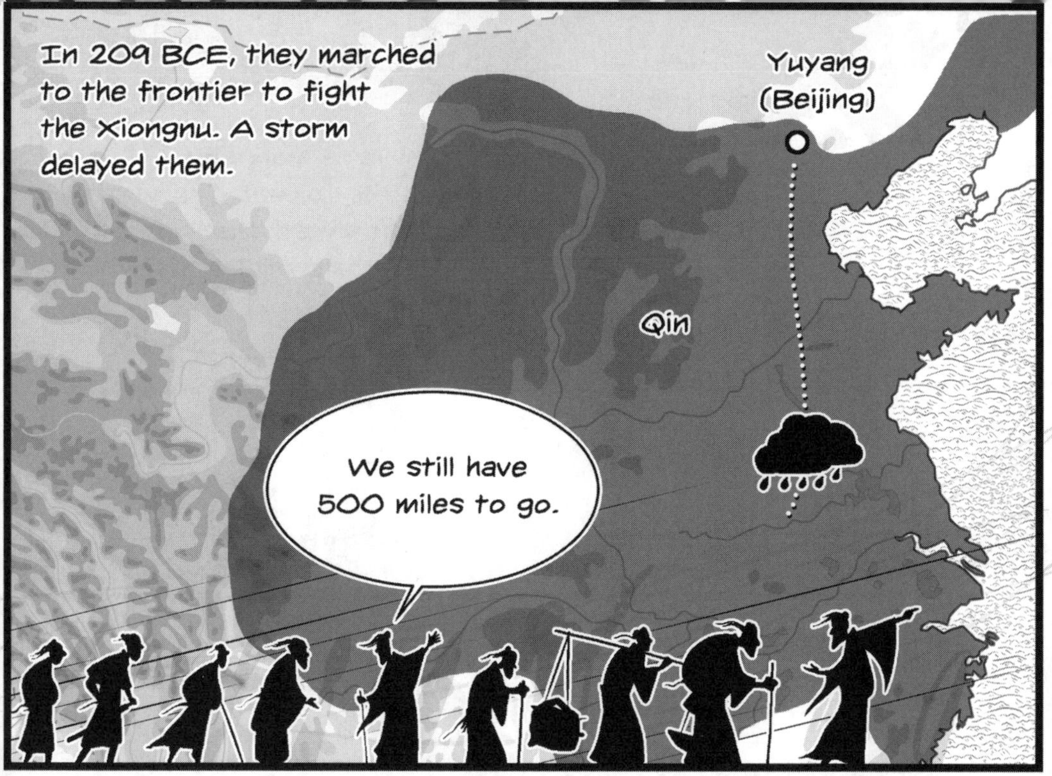
In 209 BCE, they marched to the frontier to fight the Xiongnu. A storm delayed them.
Yuyang (Beijing)
Qin
We still have 500 miles to go.

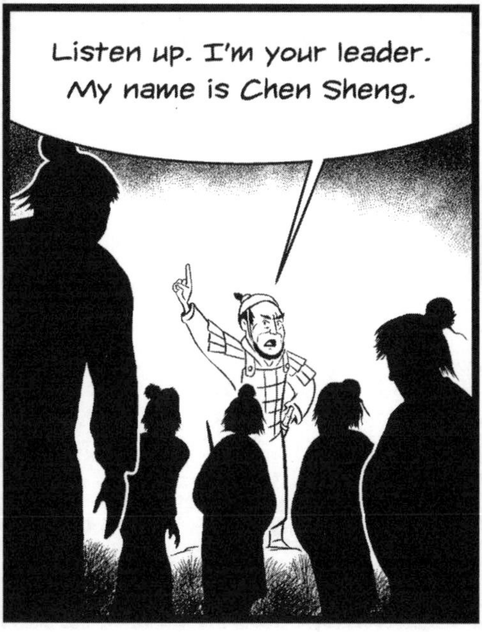
Listen up. I'm your leader. My name is Chen Sheng.

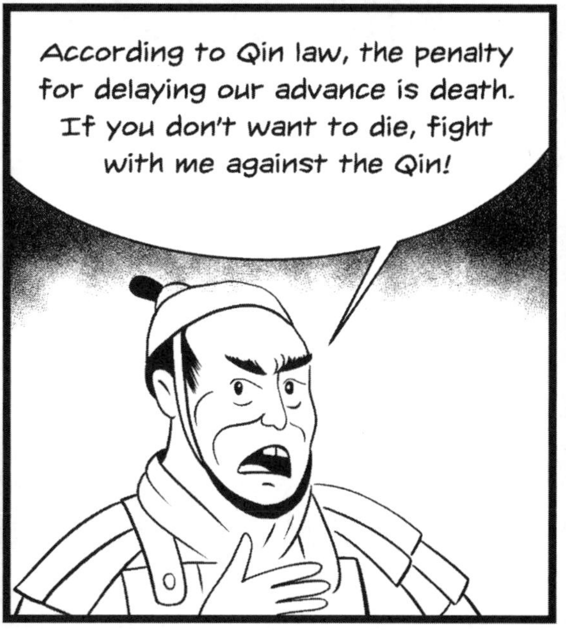
According to Qin law, the penalty for delaying our advance is death. If you don't want to die, fight with me against the Qin!

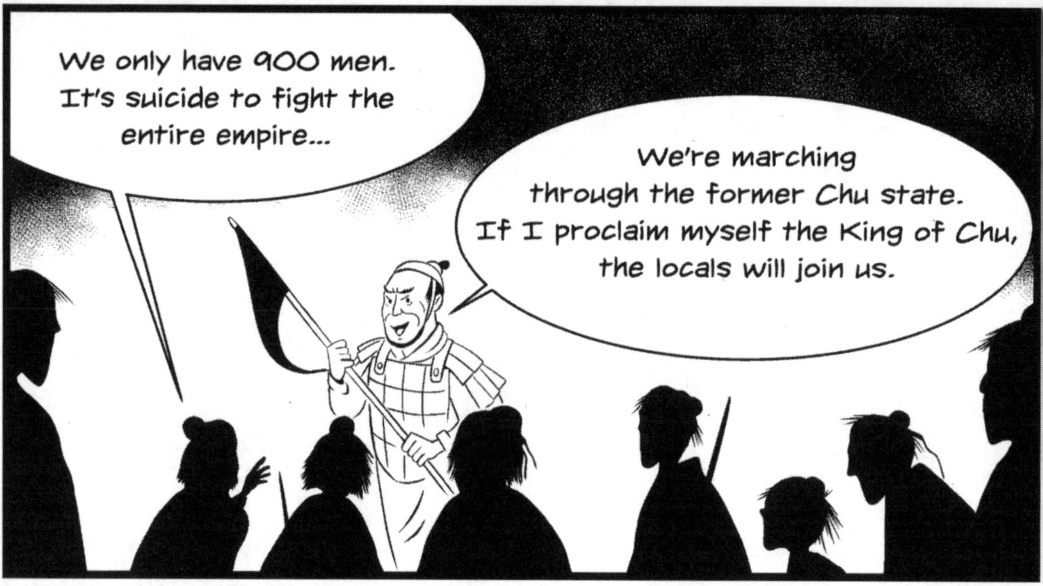
We only have 900 men. It's suicide to fight the entire empire...
We're marching through the former Chu state. If I proclaim myself the King of Chu, the locals will join us.

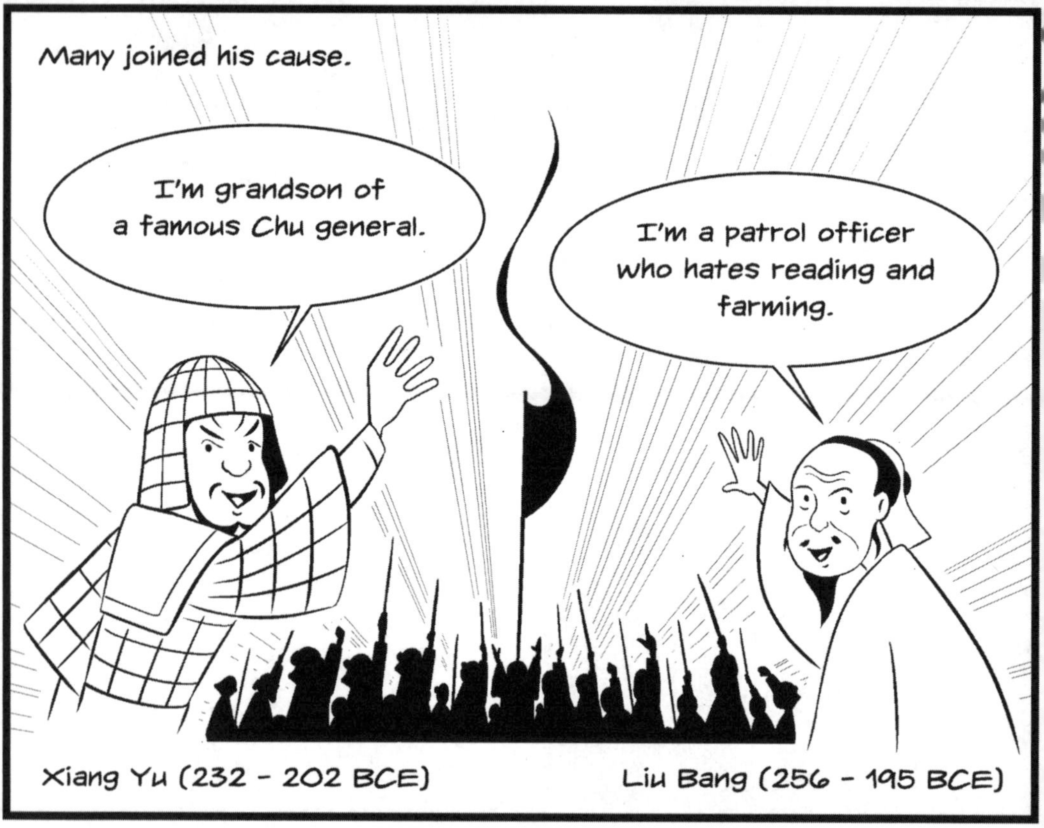
Many joined his cause.
I'm grandson of a famous Chu general.
I'm a patrol officer who hates reading and farming.
Xiang Yu (232 - 202 BCE)
Liu Bang (256 - 195 BCE)

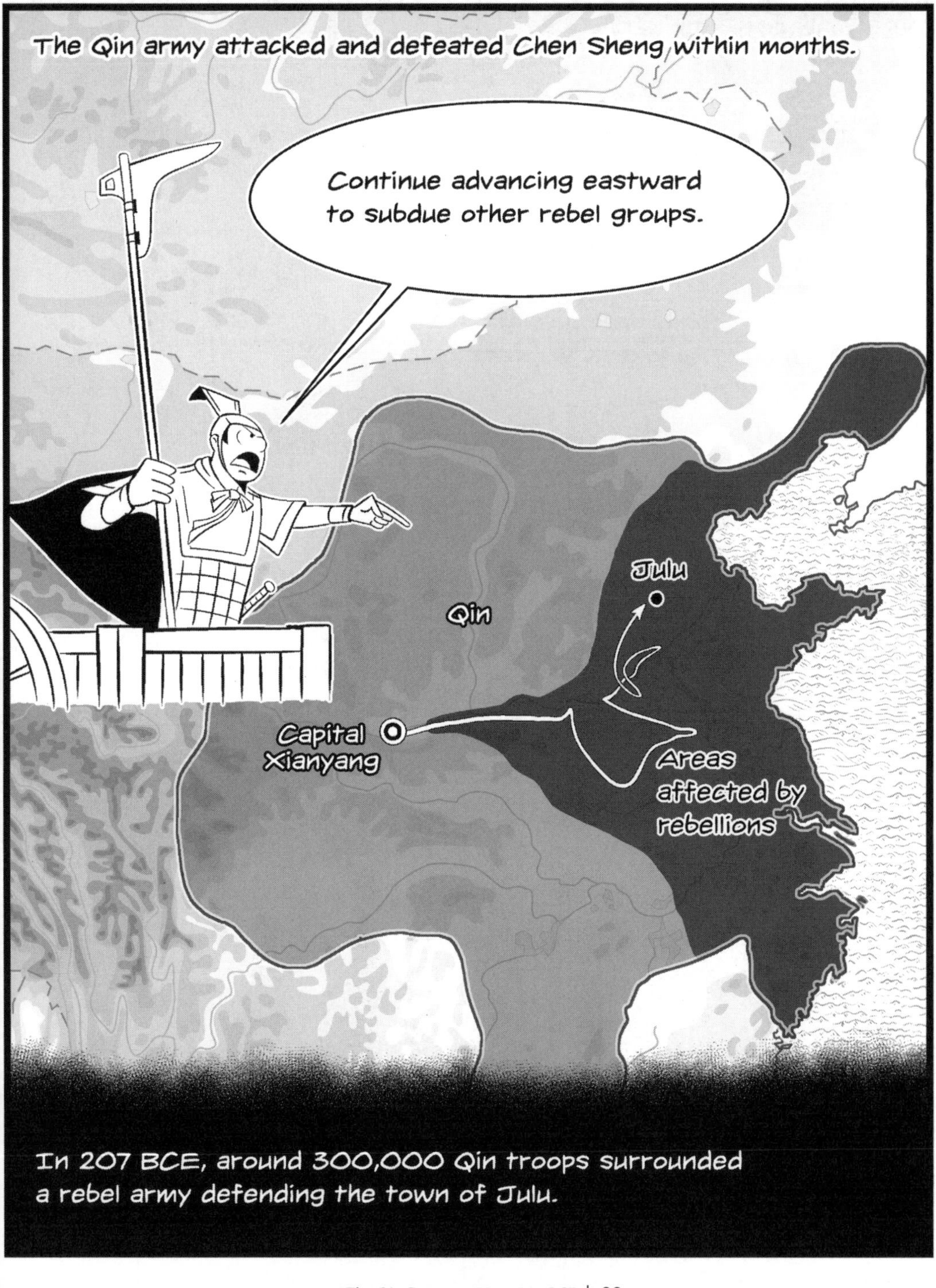

The Qin army attacked and defeated Chen Sheng within months.
Continue advancing eastward to subdue other rebel groups.
Julu
Qin
Capital Xianyang
Areas affected by rebellions
In 207 BCE, around 300,000 Qin troops surrounded a rebel army defending the town of Julu.

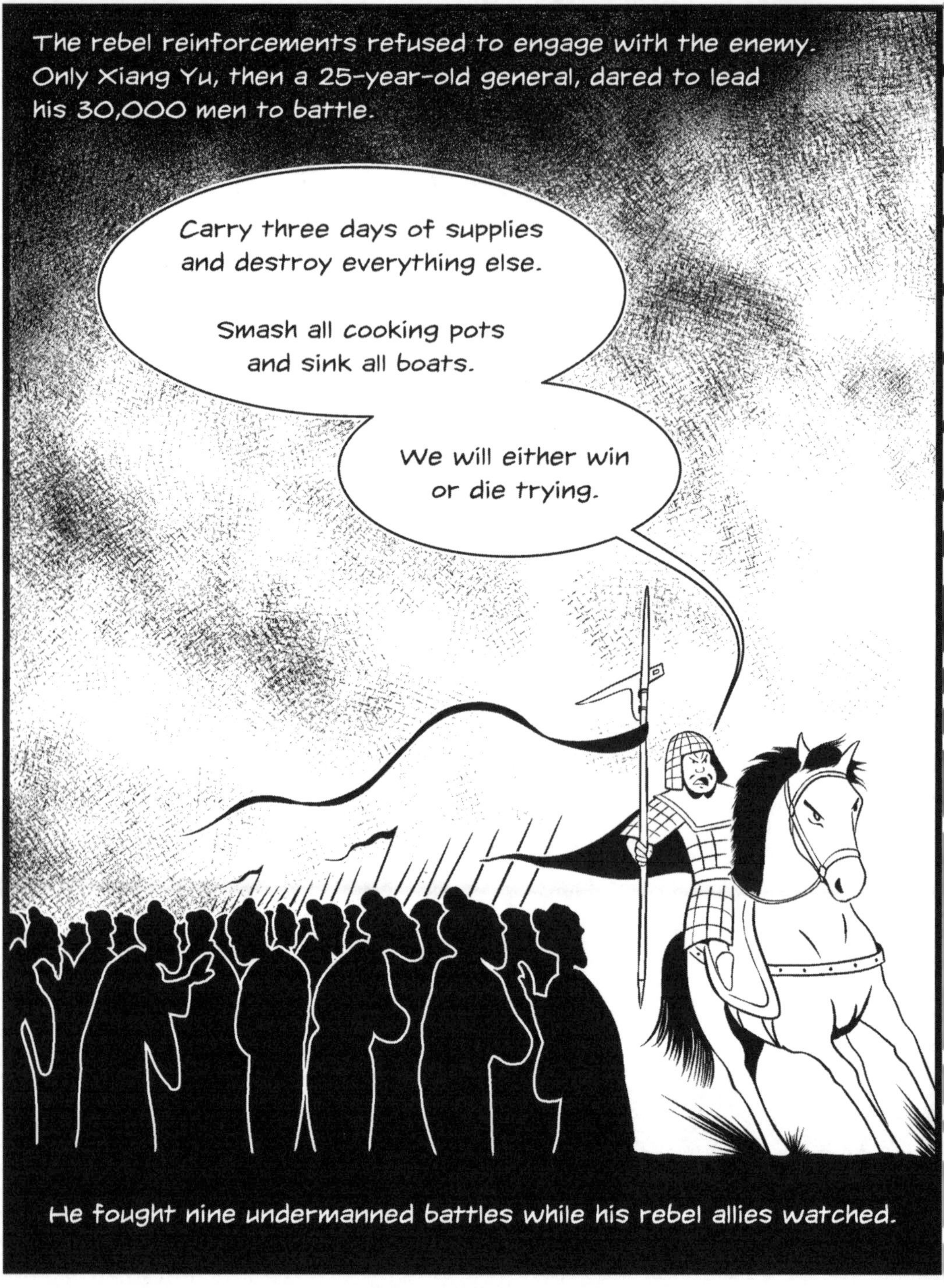
The rebel reinforcements refused to engage with the enemy. Only Xiang Yu, then a 25-year-old general, dared to lead his 30,000 men to battle.
Carry three days of supplies and destroy everything else.
Smash all cooking pots and sink all boats.
We will either win or die trying.
He fought nine undermanned battles while his rebel allies watched.

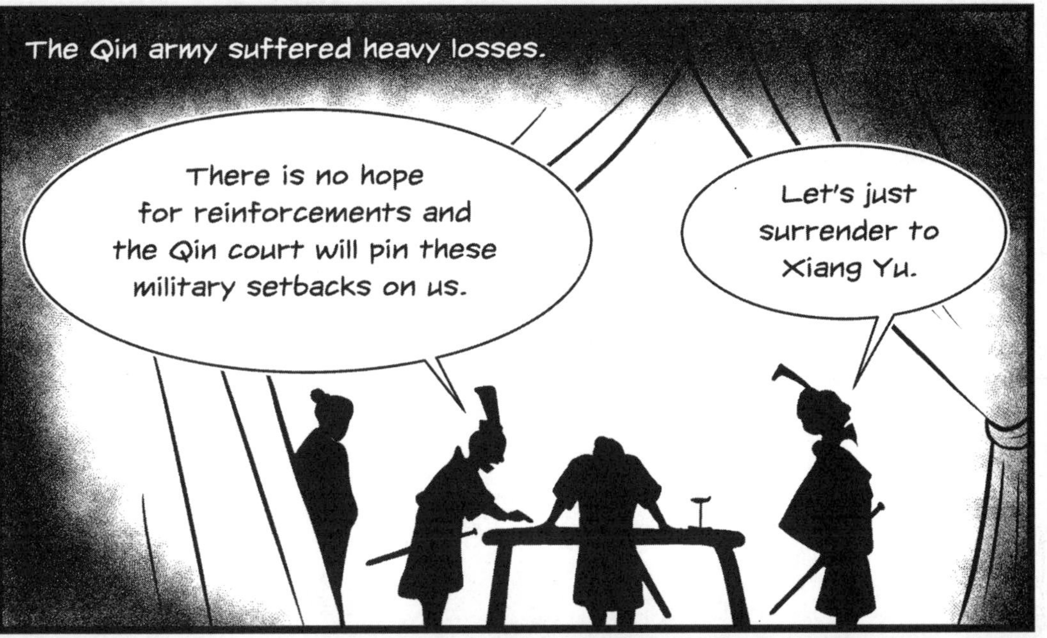
The Qin army suffered heavy losses.
There is no hope for reinforcements and the Qin court will pin these military setbacks on us.
Let's just surrender to Xiang Yu.

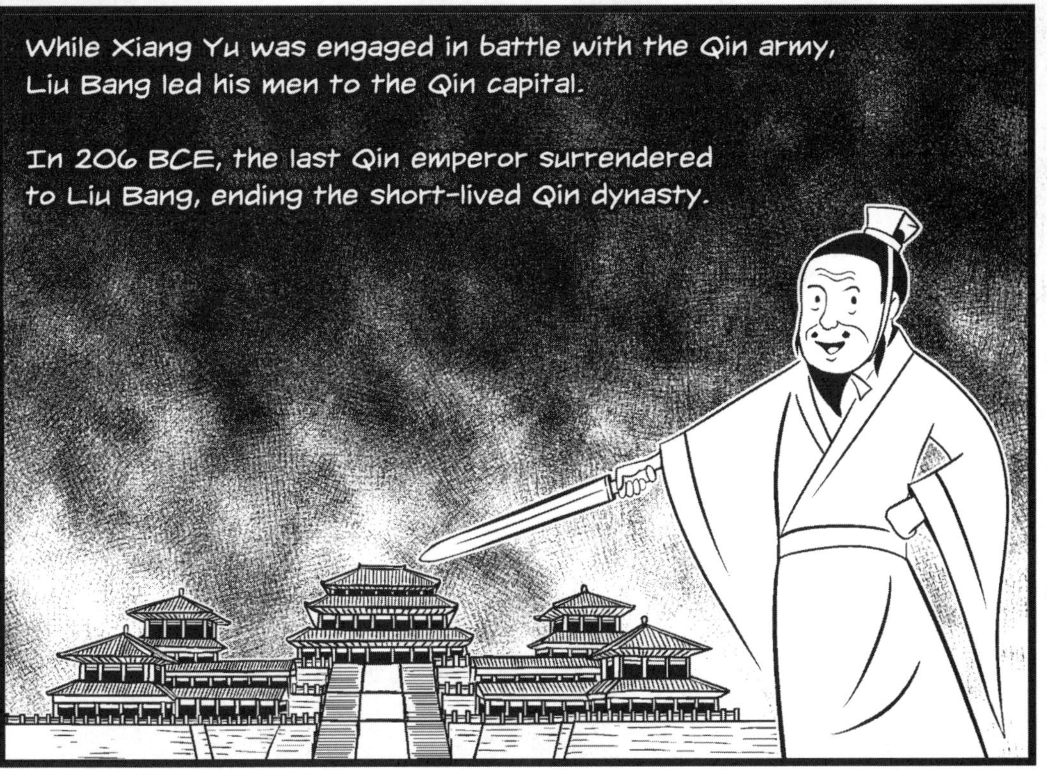
While Xiang Yu was engaged in battle with the Qin army, Liu Bang led his men to the Qin capital.
In 206 BCE, the last Qin emperor surrendered to Liu Bang, ending the short-lived Qin dynasty.

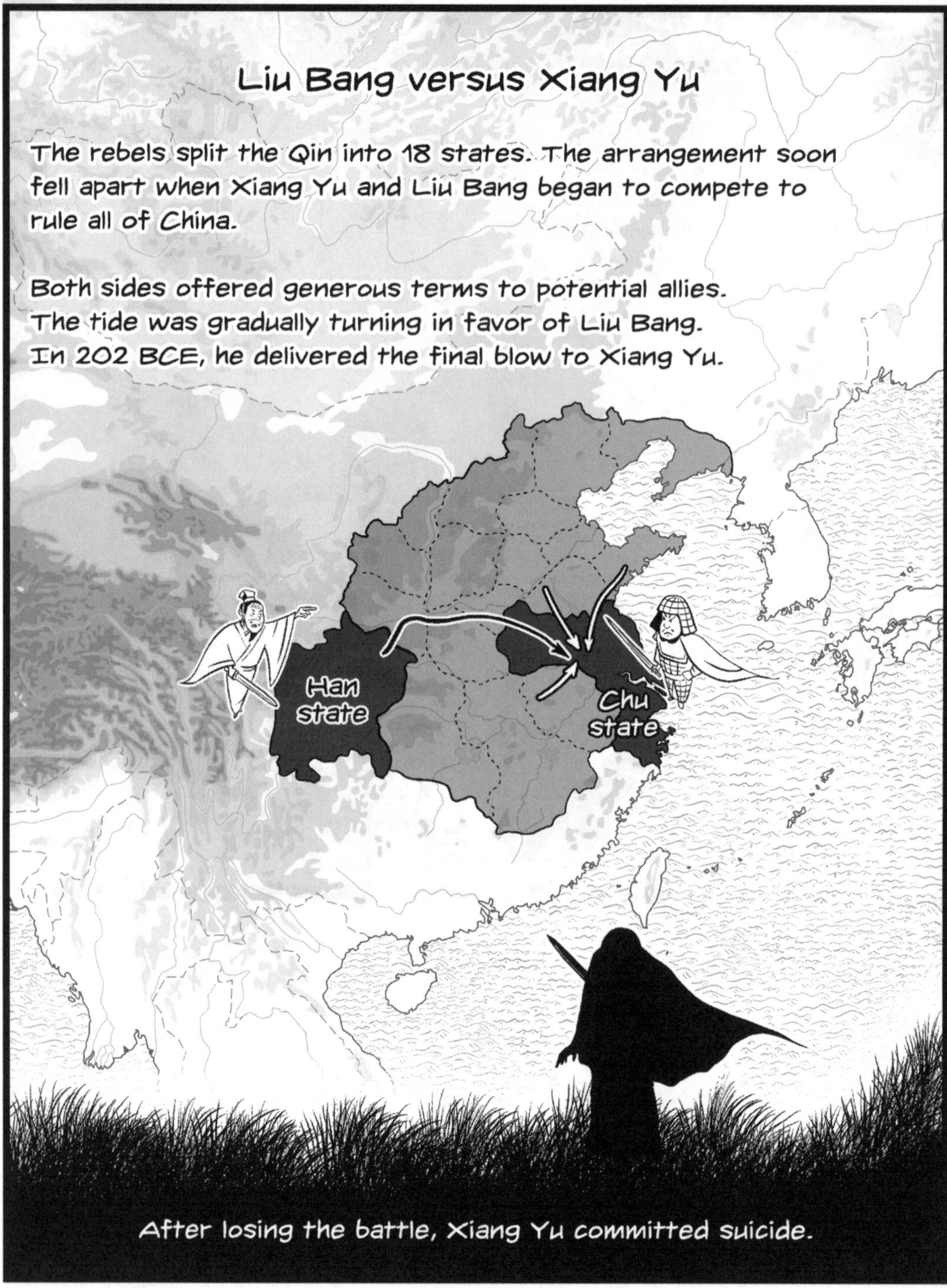
Liu Bang versus Xiang Yu
The rebels split the Qin into 18 states. The arrangement soon fell apart when Xiang Yu and Liu Bang began to compete to rule all of China.
Both sides offered generous terms to potential allies. The tide was gradually turning in favor of Liu Bang. In 202 BCE, he delivered the final blow to Xiang Yu.
Han state
Chu state
After losing the battle, Xiang Yu committed suicide.

In the same year, Liu Bang proclaimed himself emperor of the Han Dynasty.

THE HAN DYNASTY

202 BCE* – 220 CE

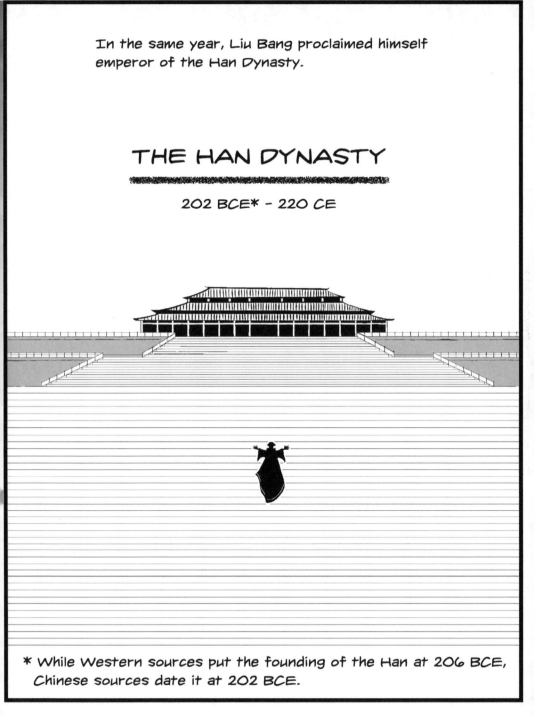

* While Western sources put the founding of the Han at 206 BCE, Chinese sources date it at 202 BCE.

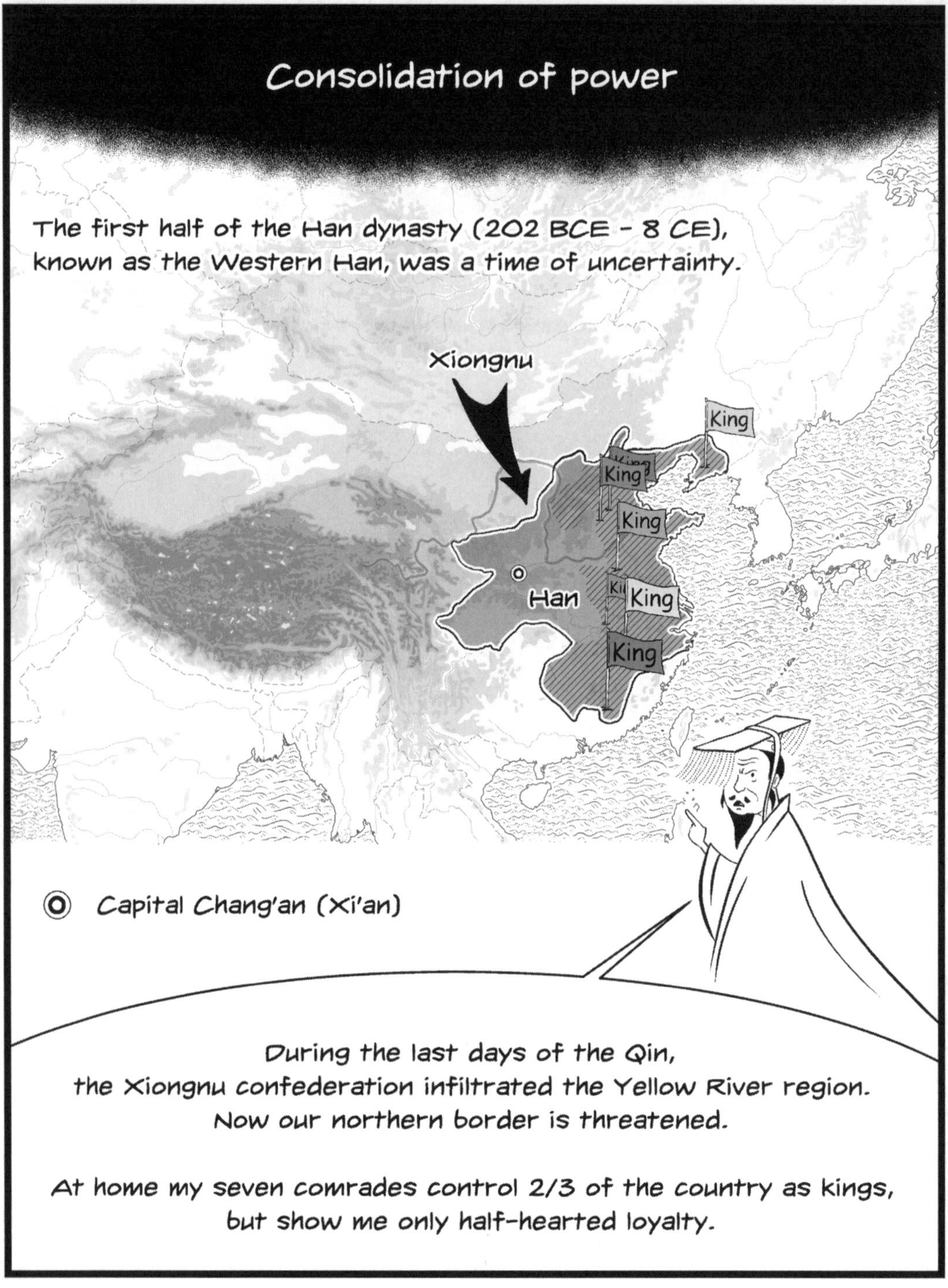
Consolidation of power
The first half of the Han dynasty (202 BCE – 8 CE), known as the Western Han, was a time of uncertainty.
Xiongnu
King
King
King
King
King
Han
Capital Chang'an (Xi'an)
During the last days of the Qin, the Xiongnu confederation infiltrated the Yellow River region. Now our northern border is threatened.
At home my seven comrades control 2/3 of the country as kings, but show me only half-hearted loyalty.

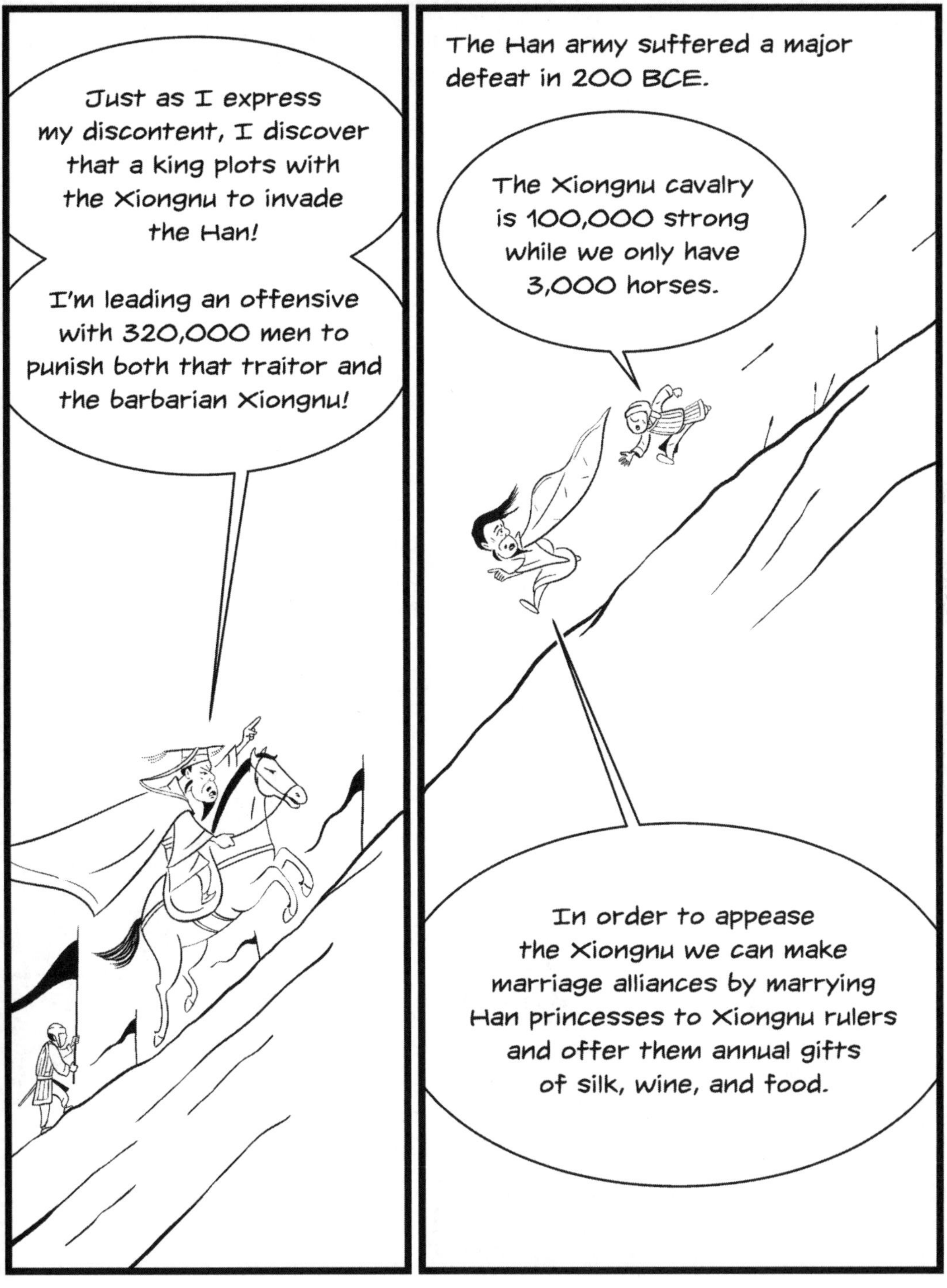
Just as I express my discontent, I discover that a king plots with the Xiongnu to invade the Han!
I'm leading an offensive with 320,000 men to punish both that traitor and the barbarian Xiongnu!
The Han army suffered a major defeat in 200 BCE.
The Xiongnu cavalry is 100,000 strong while we only have 3,000 horses.
In order to appease the Xiongnu we can make marriage alliances by marrying Han princesses to Xiongnu rulers and offer them annual gifts of silk, wine, and food.

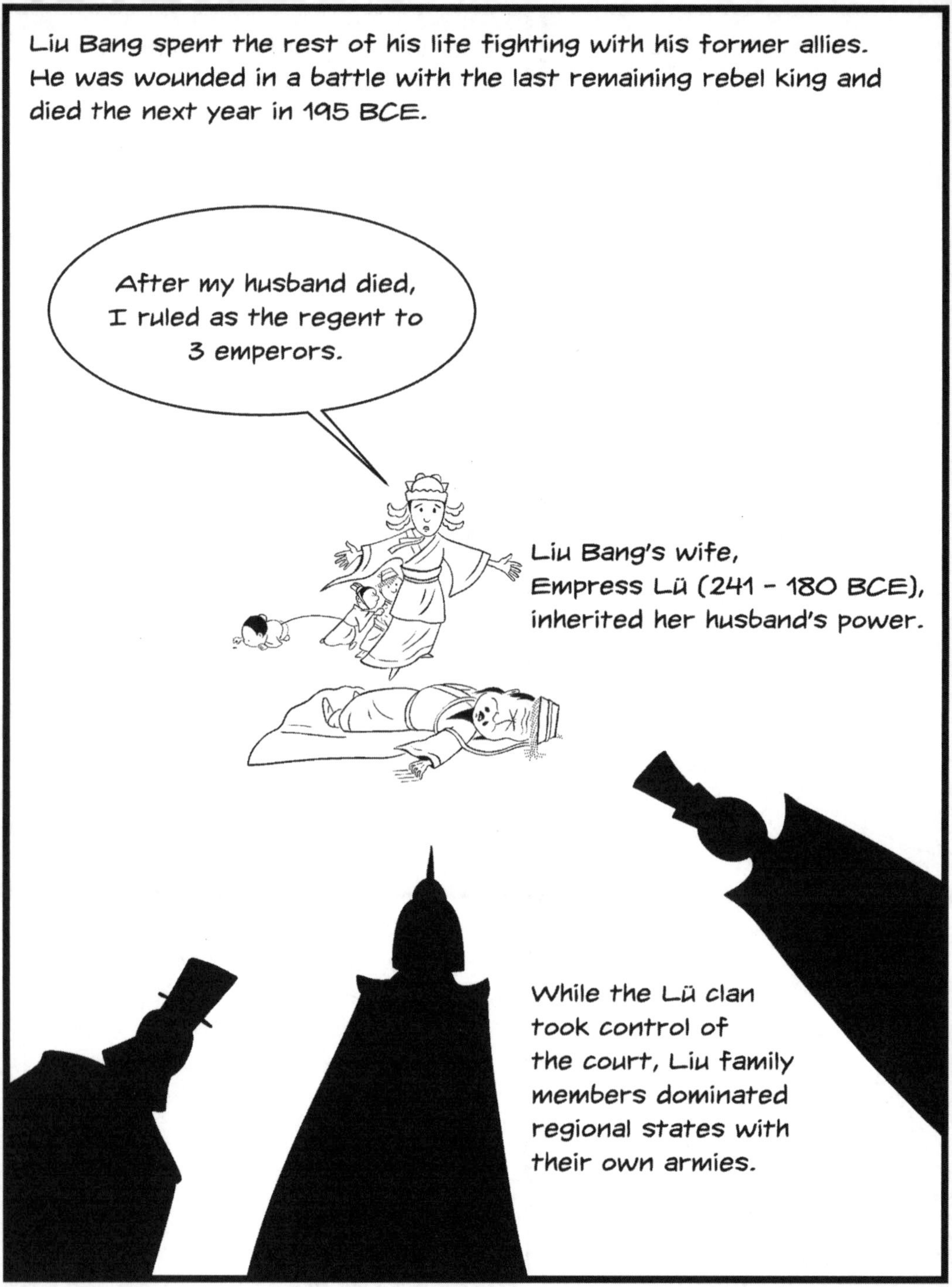
Liu Bang spent the rest of his life fighting with his former allies. He was wounded in a battle with the last remaining rebel king and died the next year in 195 BCE.
After my husband died, I ruled as the regent to 3 emperors.
Liu Bang's wife, Empress Lü (241 - 180 BCE), inherited her husband's power.
While the Lü clan took control of the court, Liu family members dominated regional states with their own armies.

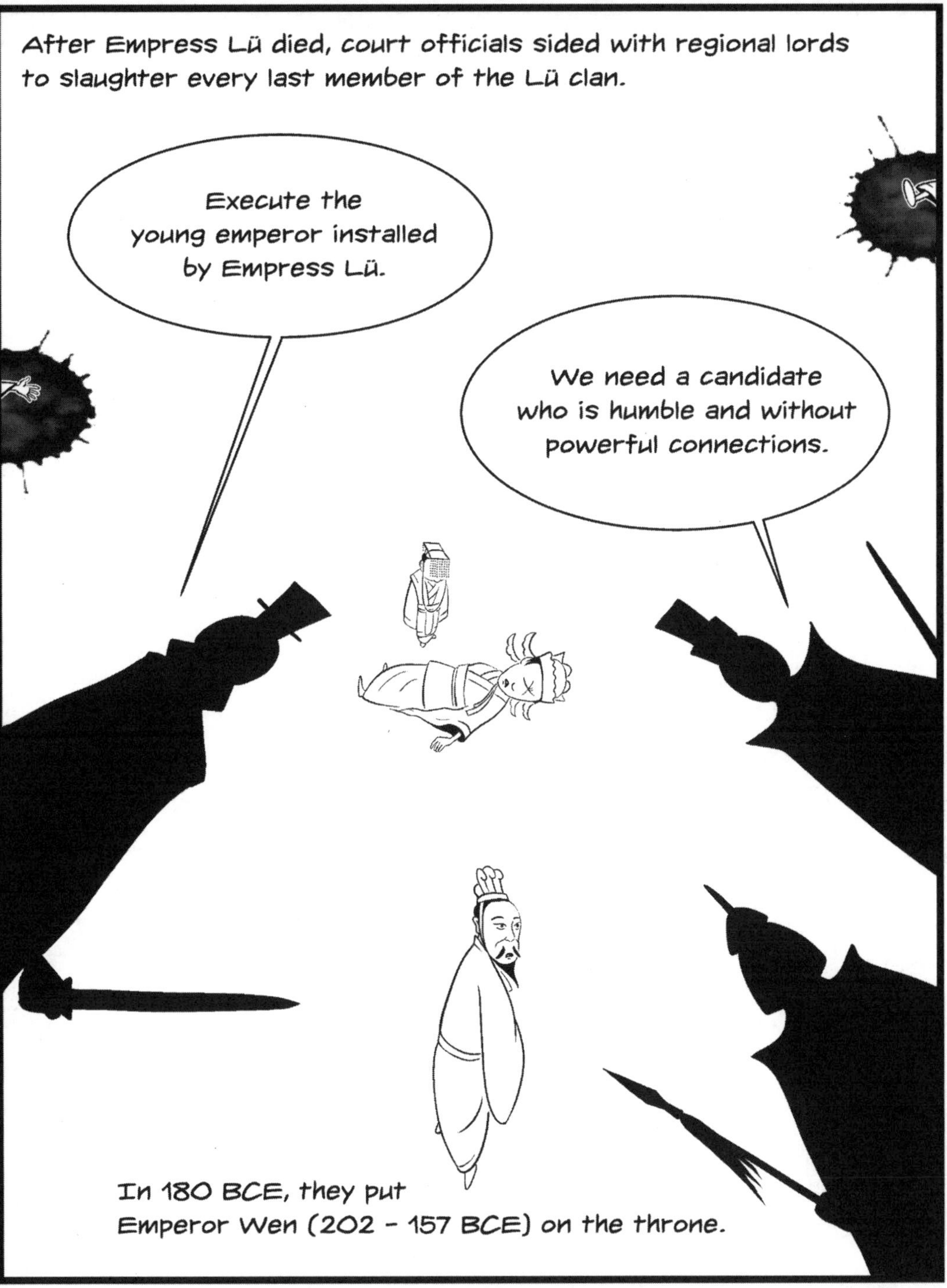
After Empress Lü died, court officials sided with regional lords to slaughter every last member of the Lü clan.
Execute the young emperor installed by Empress Lü.
We need a candidate who is humble and without powerful connections.
In 180 BCE, they put Emperor Wen (202 - 157 BCE) on the throne.

Economic recovery

Despite the palace intrigue, an economic recovery was underway.

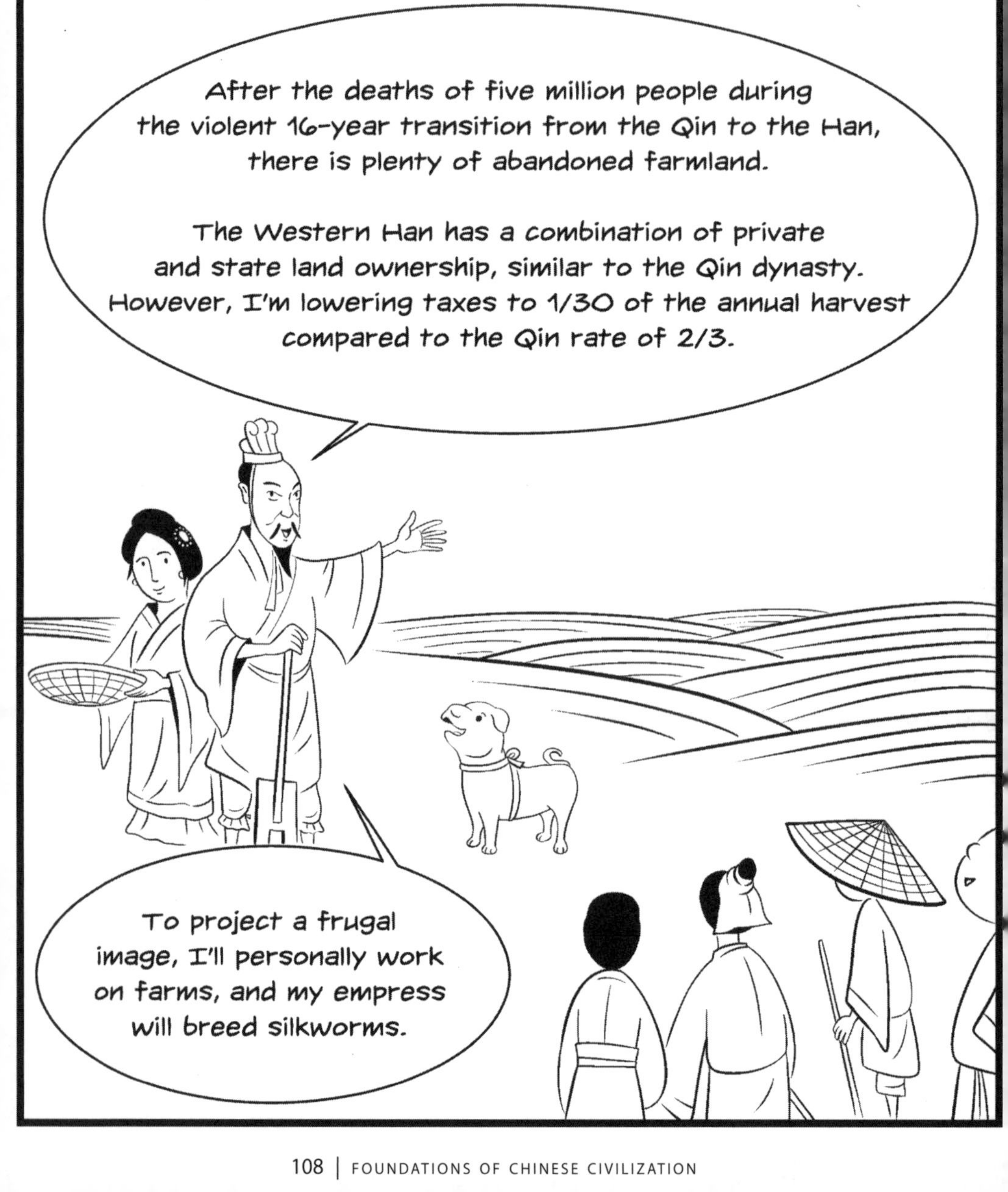
After the deaths of five million people during the violent 16-year transition from the Qin to the Han, there is plenty of abandoned farmland.
The Western Han has a combination of private and state land ownership, similar to the Qin dynasty. However, I'm lowering taxes to 1/30 of the annual harvest compared to the Qin rate of 2/3.
To project a frugal image, I'll personally work on farms, and my empress will breed silkworms.

Imperial expansion under Emperor Wu

After decades of recovery, Emperor Wu was prepared to centralize his rule and make the Western Han into an imperial power.

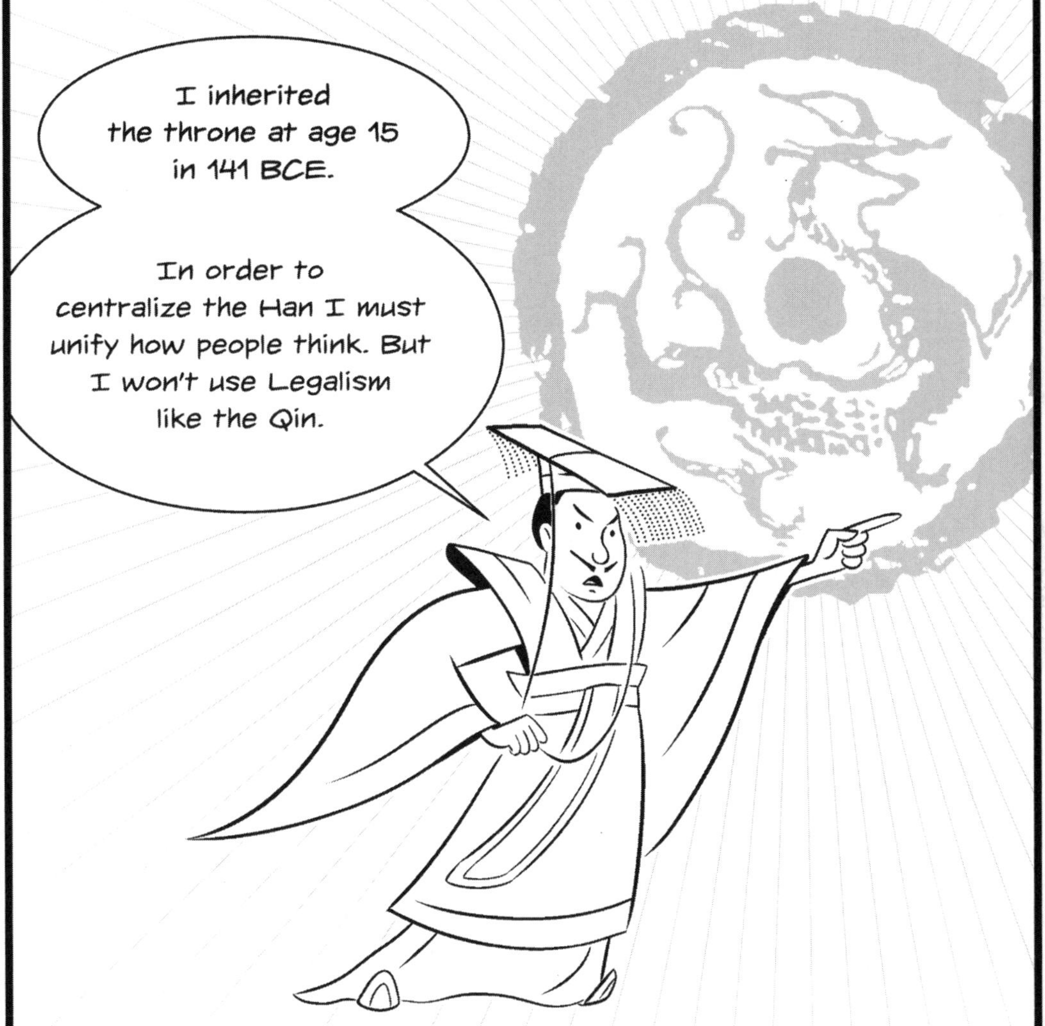
I inherited the throne at age 15 in 141 BCE.
In order to centralize the Han I must unify how people think. But I won't use Legalism like the Qin.

Emperor Wu of Han (156 - 87 BCE)

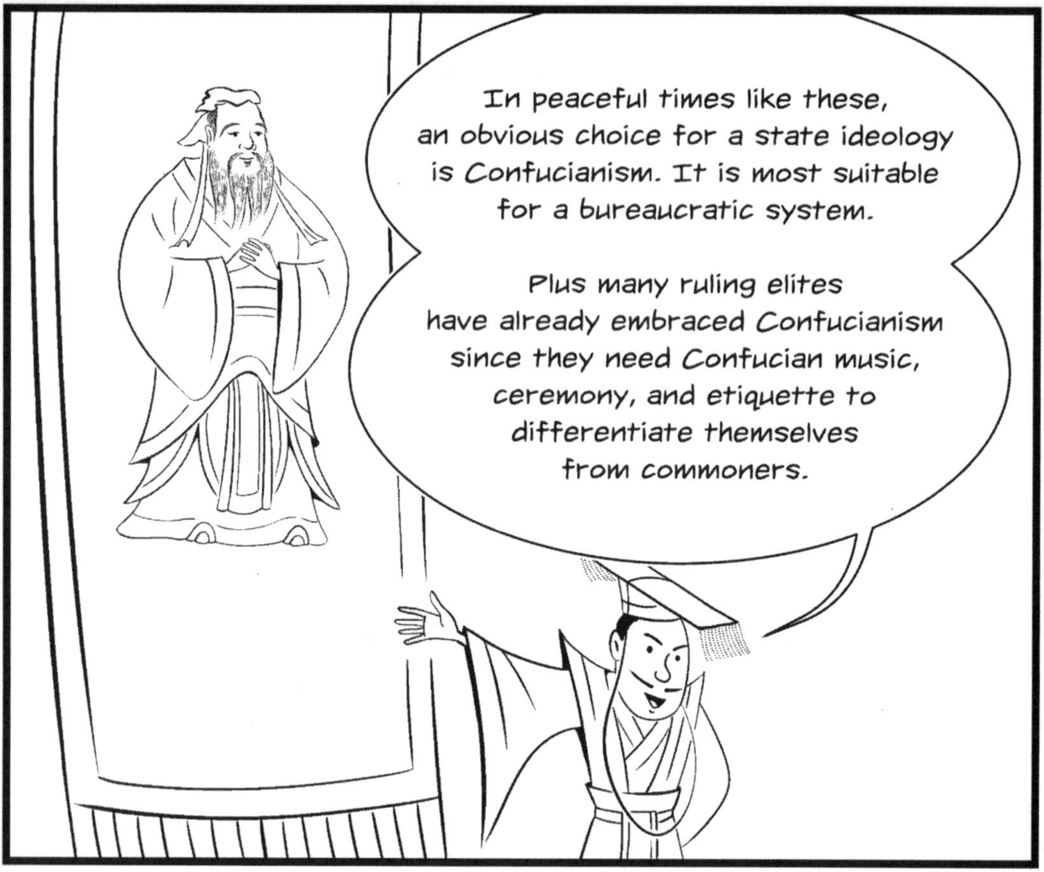
In peaceful times like these, an obvious choice for a state ideology is Confucianism. It is most suitable for a bureaucratic system.
Plus many ruling elites have already embraced Confucianism since they need Confucian music, ceremony, and etiquette to differentiate themselves from commoners.

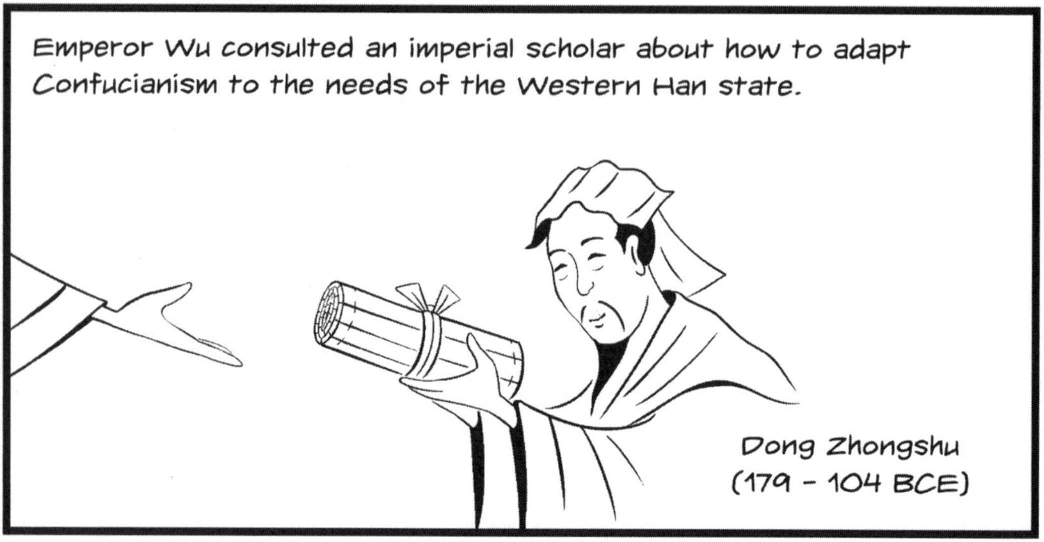
Emperor Wu consulted an imperial scholar about how to adapt Confucianism to the needs of the Western Han state.
Dong Zhongshu (179 - 104 BCE)

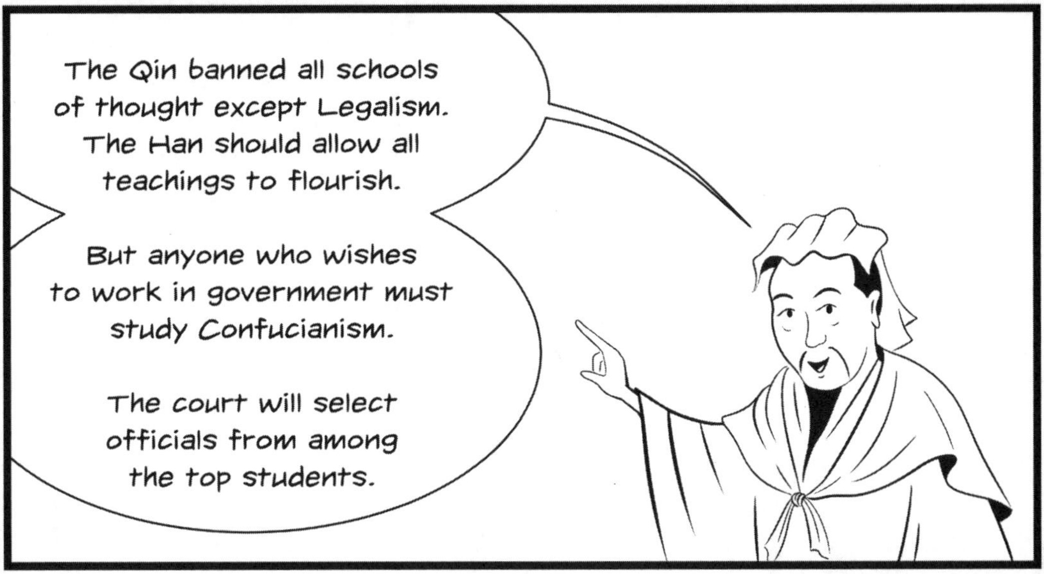
The Qin banned all schools of thought except Legalism. The Han should allow all teachings to flourish.
But anyone who wishes to work in government must study Confucianism.
The court will select officials from among the top students.

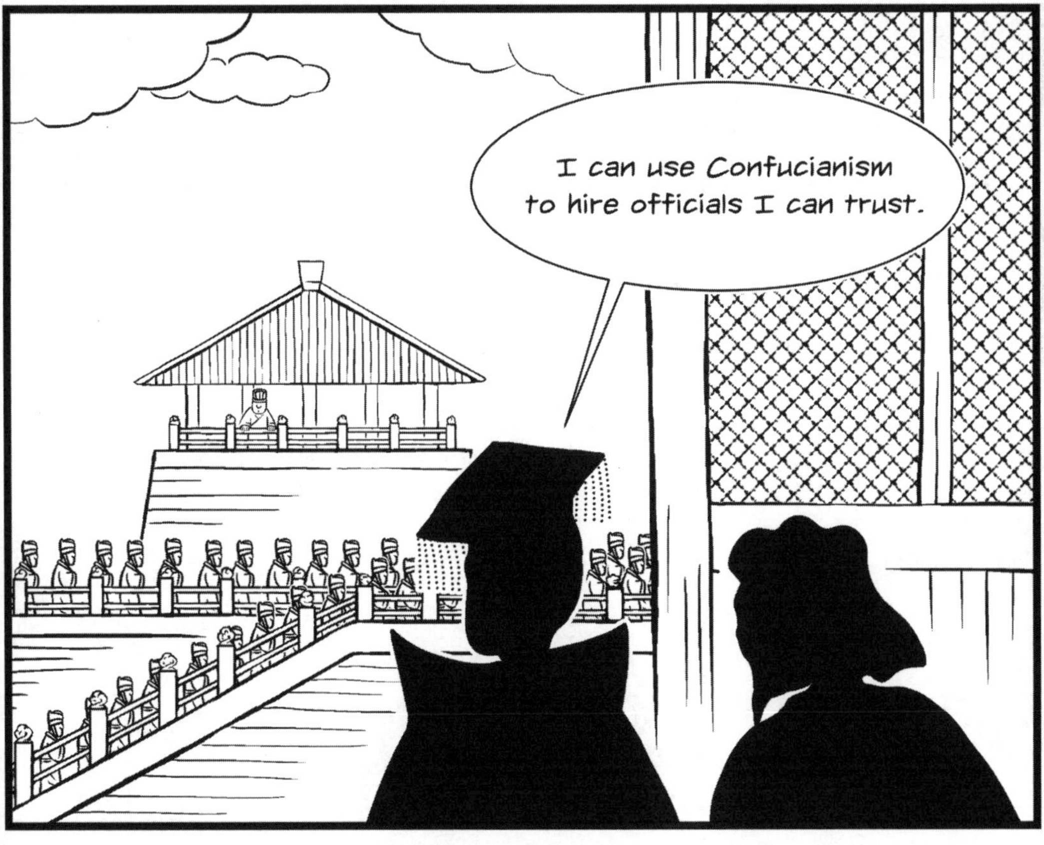
I can use Confucianism to hire officials I can trust.

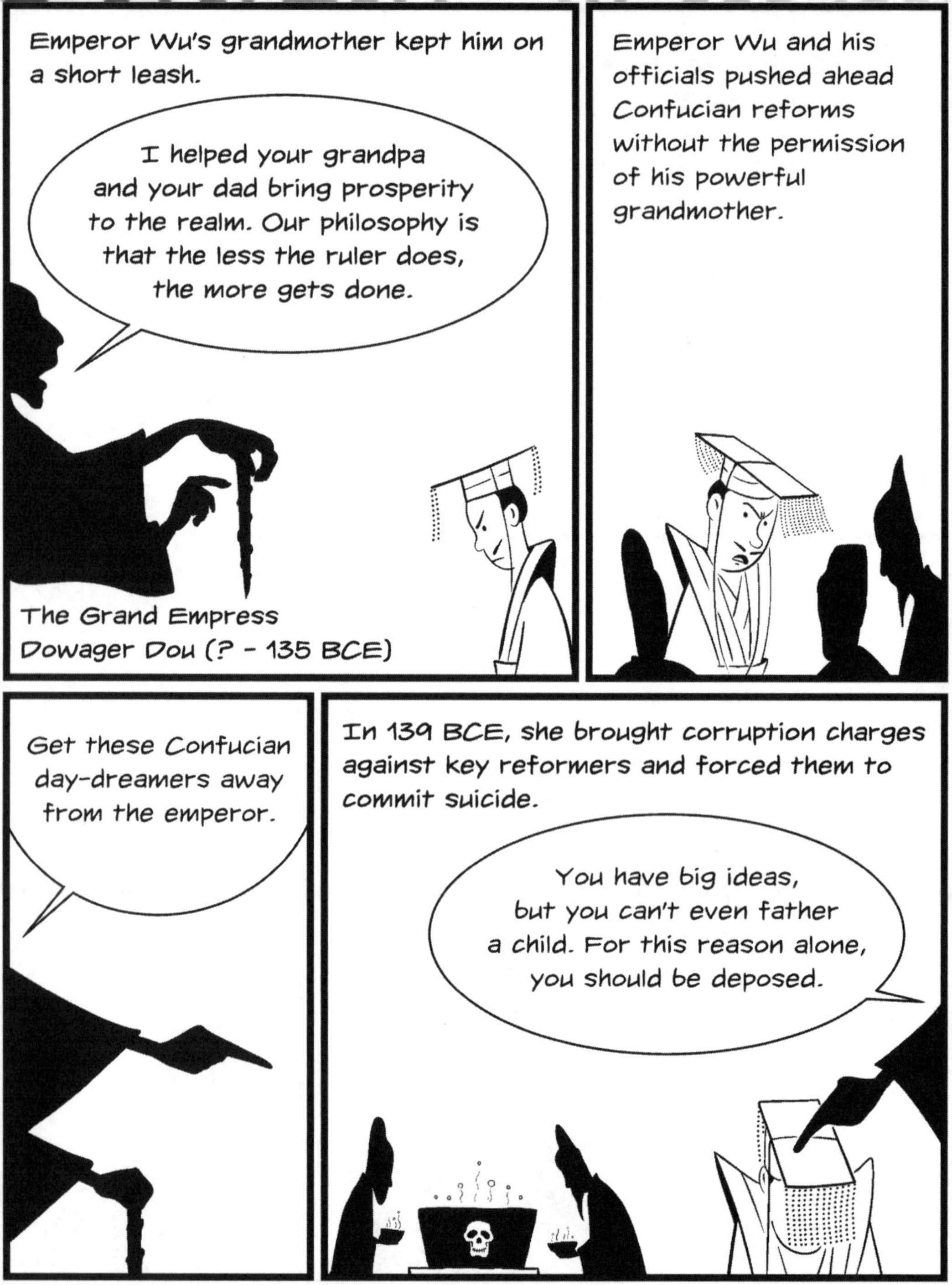
Emperor Wu's grandmother kept him on a short leash.
I helped your grandpa and your dad bring prosperity to the realm. Our philosophy is that the less the ruler does, the more gets done.
The Grand Empress Dowager Dou (? - 135 BCE)
Emperor Wu and his officials pushed ahead Confucian reforms without the permission of his powerful grandmother.
Get these Confucian day-dreamers away from the emperor.
In 139 BCE, she brought corruption charges against key reformers and forced them to commit suicide.
You have big ideas, but you can't even father a child. For this reason alone, you should be deposed.

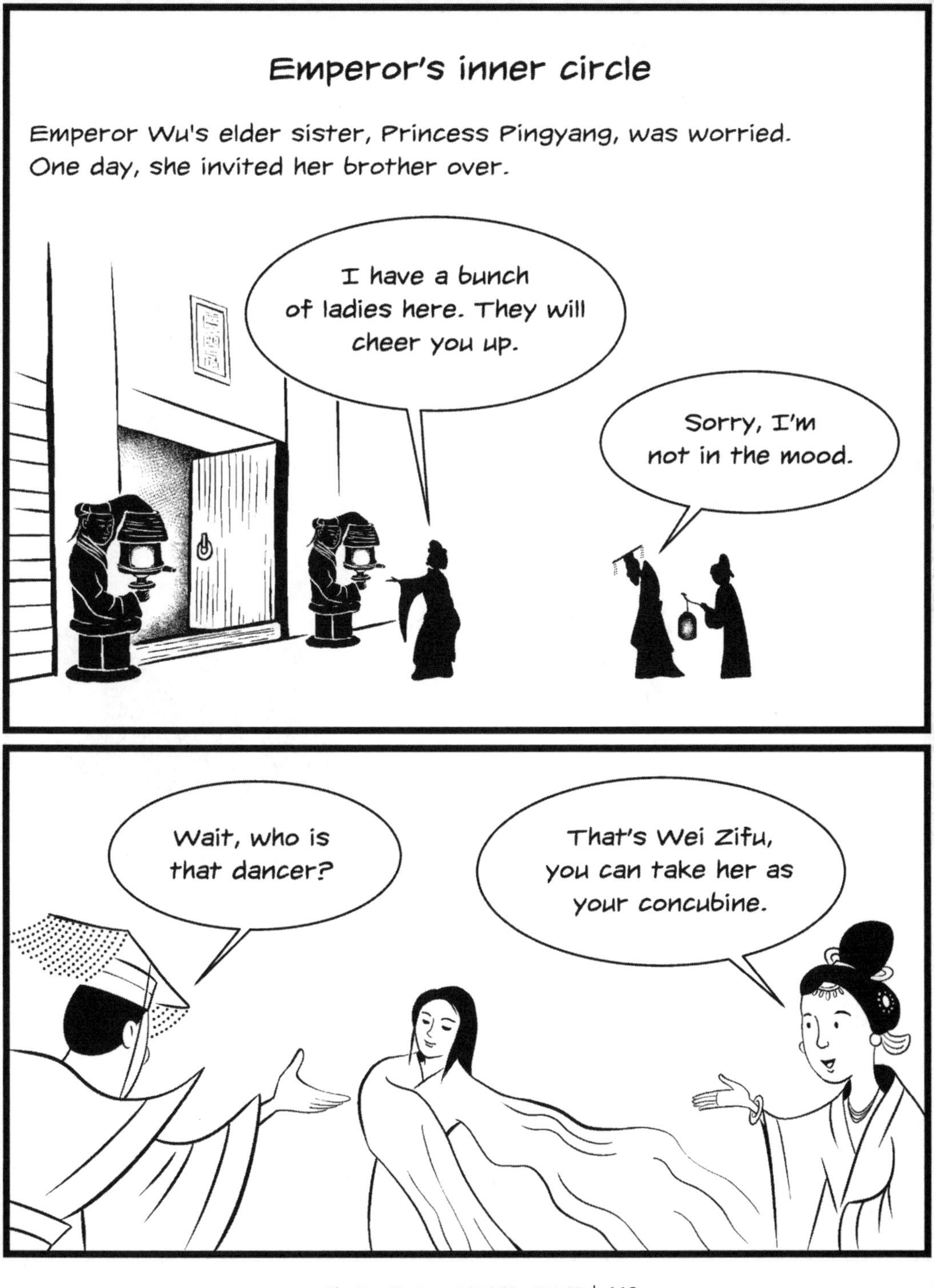
Emperor's inner circle
Emperor Wu's elder sister, Princess Pingyang, was worried. One day, she invited her brother over.
I have a bunch of ladies here. They will cheer you up.
Sorry, I'm not in the mood.
Wait, who is that dancer?
That's Wei Zifu, you can take her as your concubine.

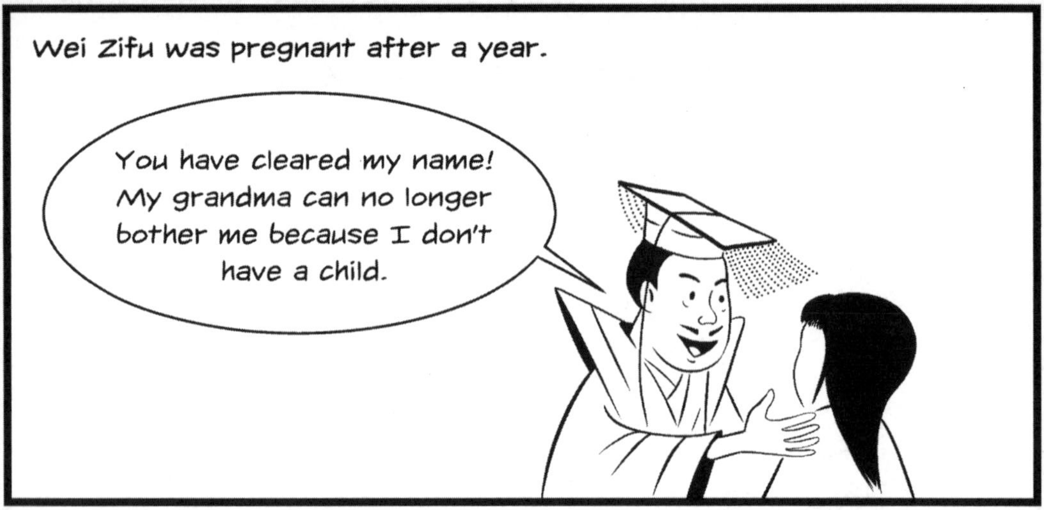
Wei Zifu was pregnant after a year.
You have cleared my name! My grandma can no longer bother me because I don't have a child.

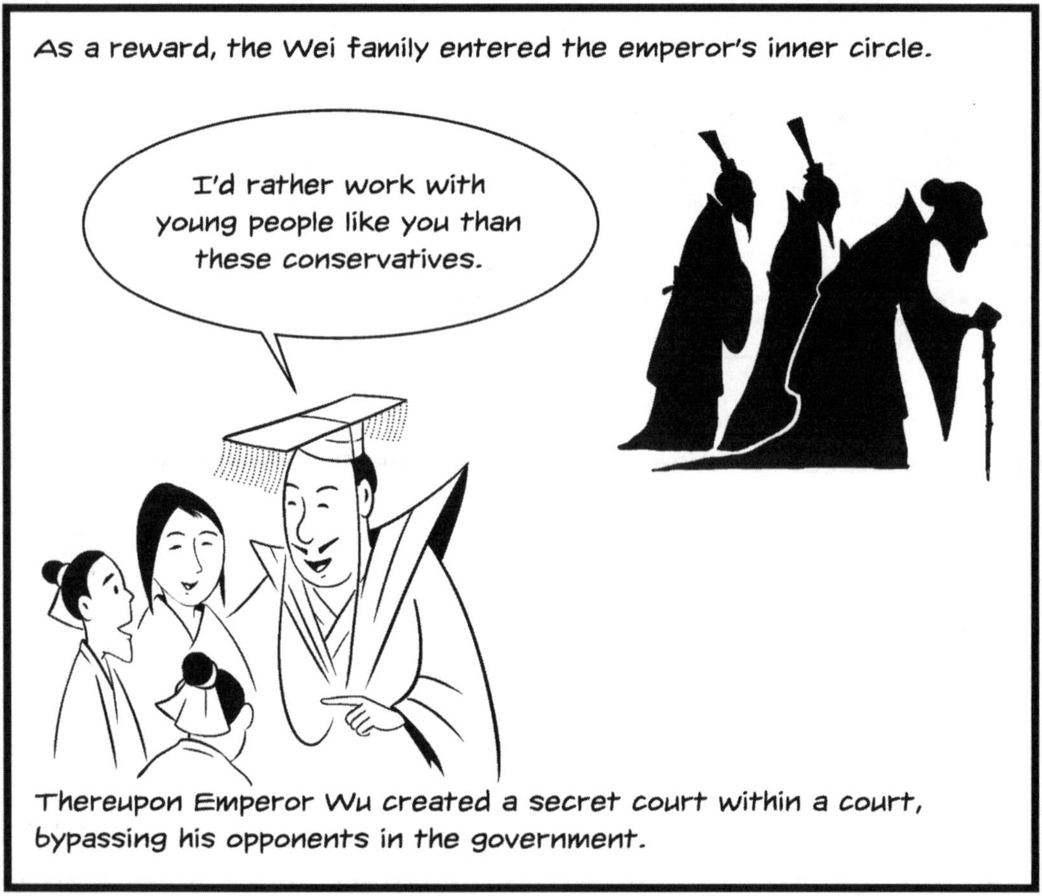
As a reward, the Wei family entered the emperor's inner circle.
I'd rather work with young people like you than these conservatives.
Thereupon Emperor Wu created a secret court within a court, bypassing his opponents in the government.

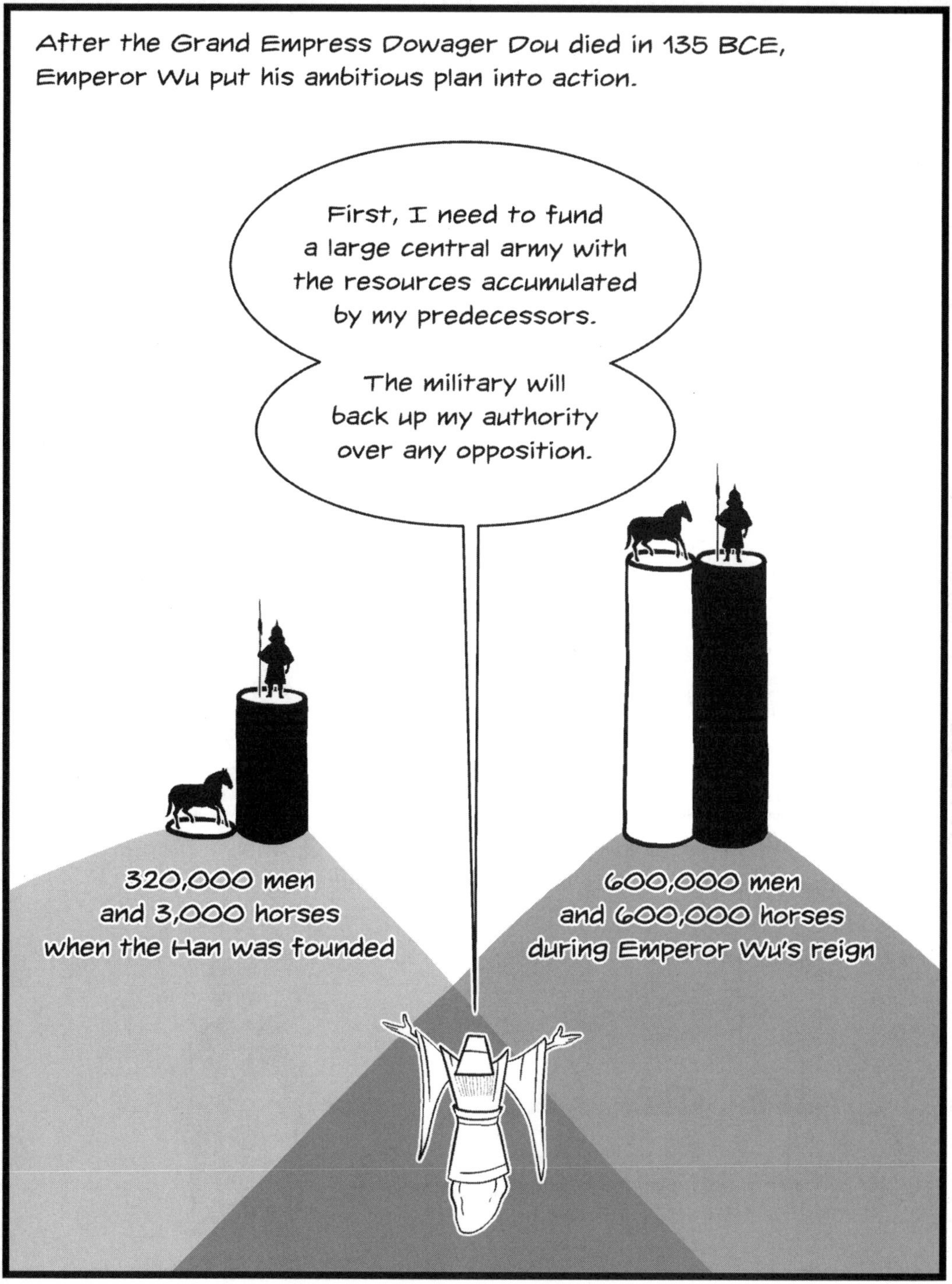
After the Grand Empress Dowager Dou died in 135 BCE, Emperor Wu put his ambitious plan into action.
First, I need to fund a large central army with the resources accumulated by my predecessors.
The military will back up my authority over any opposition.
320,000 men and 3,000 horses when the Han was founded
600,000 men and 600,000 horses during Emperor Wu's reign

Equal inheritance law

Then the emperor issued an equal-inheritance law in 128 BCE.

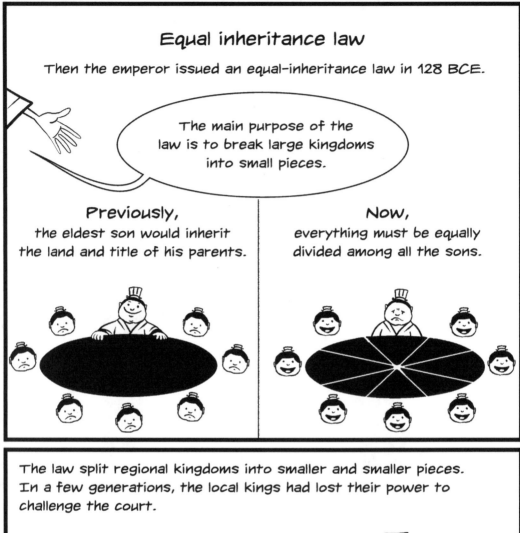

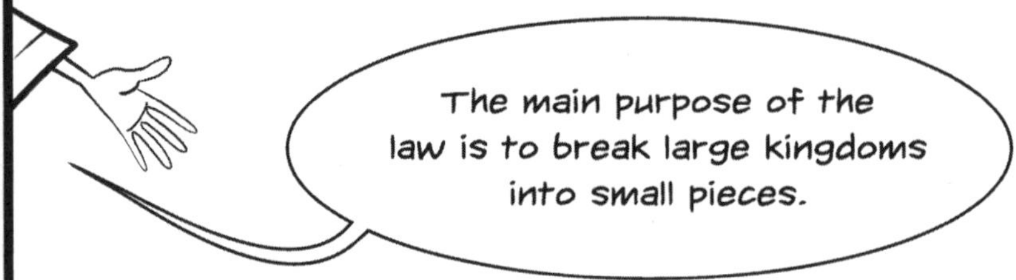
The main purpose of the law is to break large kingdoms into small pieces.

Previously,
the eldest son would inherit the land and title of his parents.

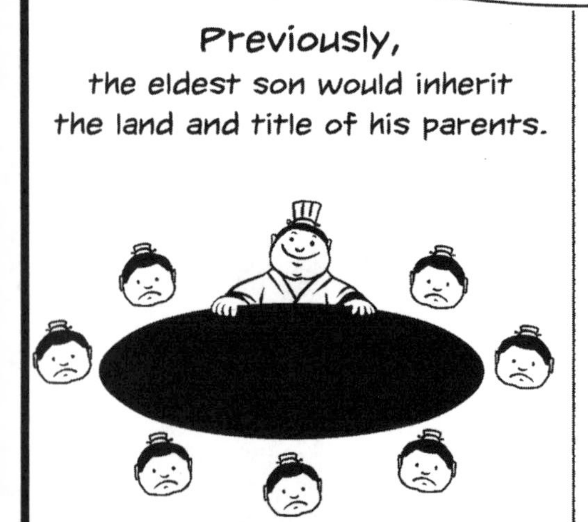

Now,
everything must be equally divided among all the sons.

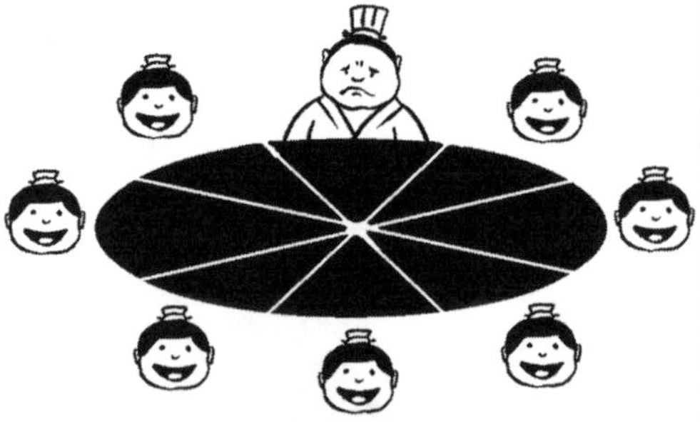

The law split regional kingdoms into smaller and smaller pieces. In a few generations, the local kings had lost their power to challenge the court.

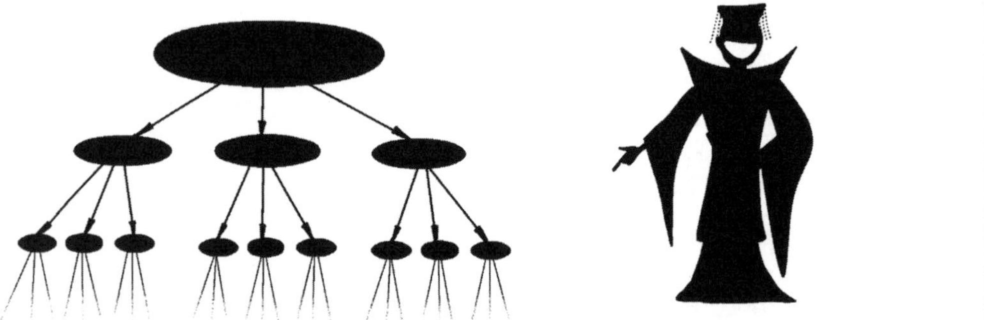

Offensive against the north

Once Emperor Wu consolidated power at home, he turned his attention to the borders, especially in the north.

Emperor Wu's army fought 11 major wars with the Xiongnu during his 54-year reign.

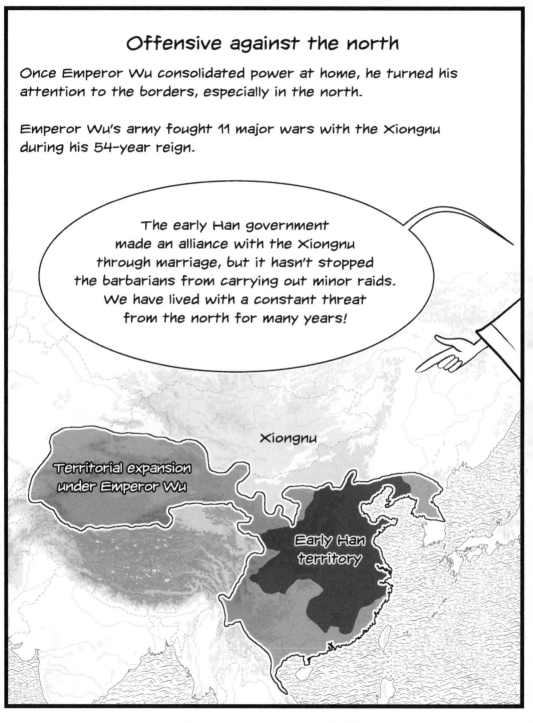

The early Han government made an alliance with the Xiongnu through marriage, but it hasn't stopped the barbarians from carrying out minor raids. We have lived with a constant threat from the north for many years!

Xiongnu

Territorial expansion under Emperor Wu

Early Han territory

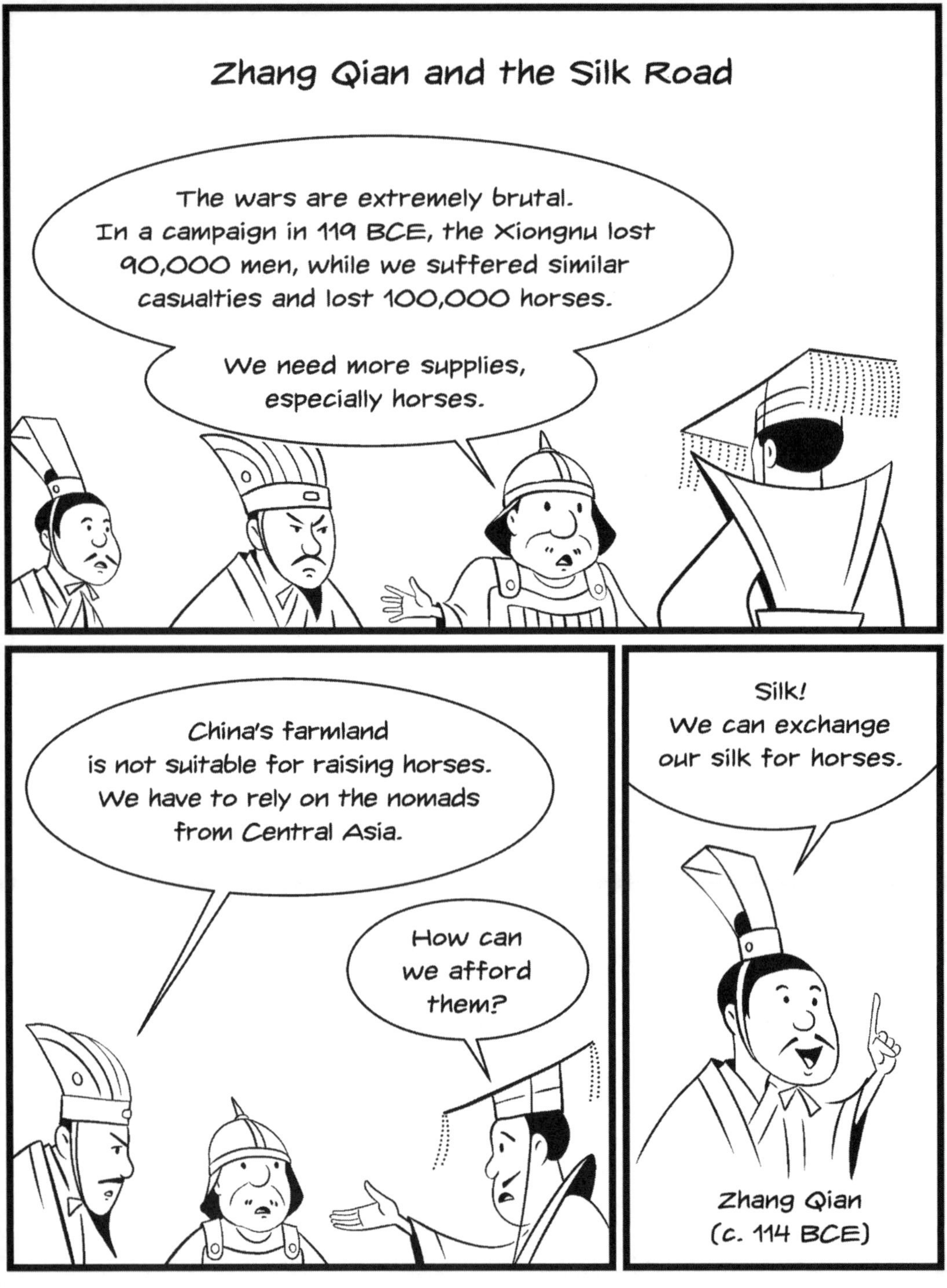
Zhang Qian and the Silk Road
The wars are extremely brutal. In a campaign in 119 BCE, the Xiongnu lost 90,000 men, while we suffered similar casualties and lost 100,000 horses.
We need more supplies, especially horses.
China's farmland is not suitable for raising horses. We have to rely on the nomads from Central Asia.
How can we afford them?
Silk! We can exchange our silk for horses.
Zhang Qian (c. 114 BCE)

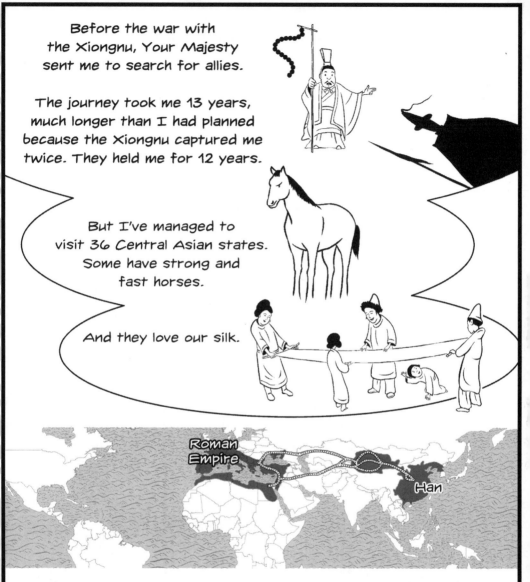

Before the war with the Xiongnu, Your Majesty sent me to search for allies.

The journey took me 13 years, much longer than I had planned because the Xiongnu captured me twice. They held me for 12 years.

But I've managed to visit 36 Central Asian states. Some have strong and fast horses.

And they love our silk.

Roman Empire

Han

At Zhang Qian's suggestion, the Western Han set up diplomatic outposts in Central Asia to facilitate the trade of silk for horses.

Some of the silk traveled 4,000 miles and passed through many middlemen until it reached the Roman Empire. This network of trade routes was later known as the Silk Road.

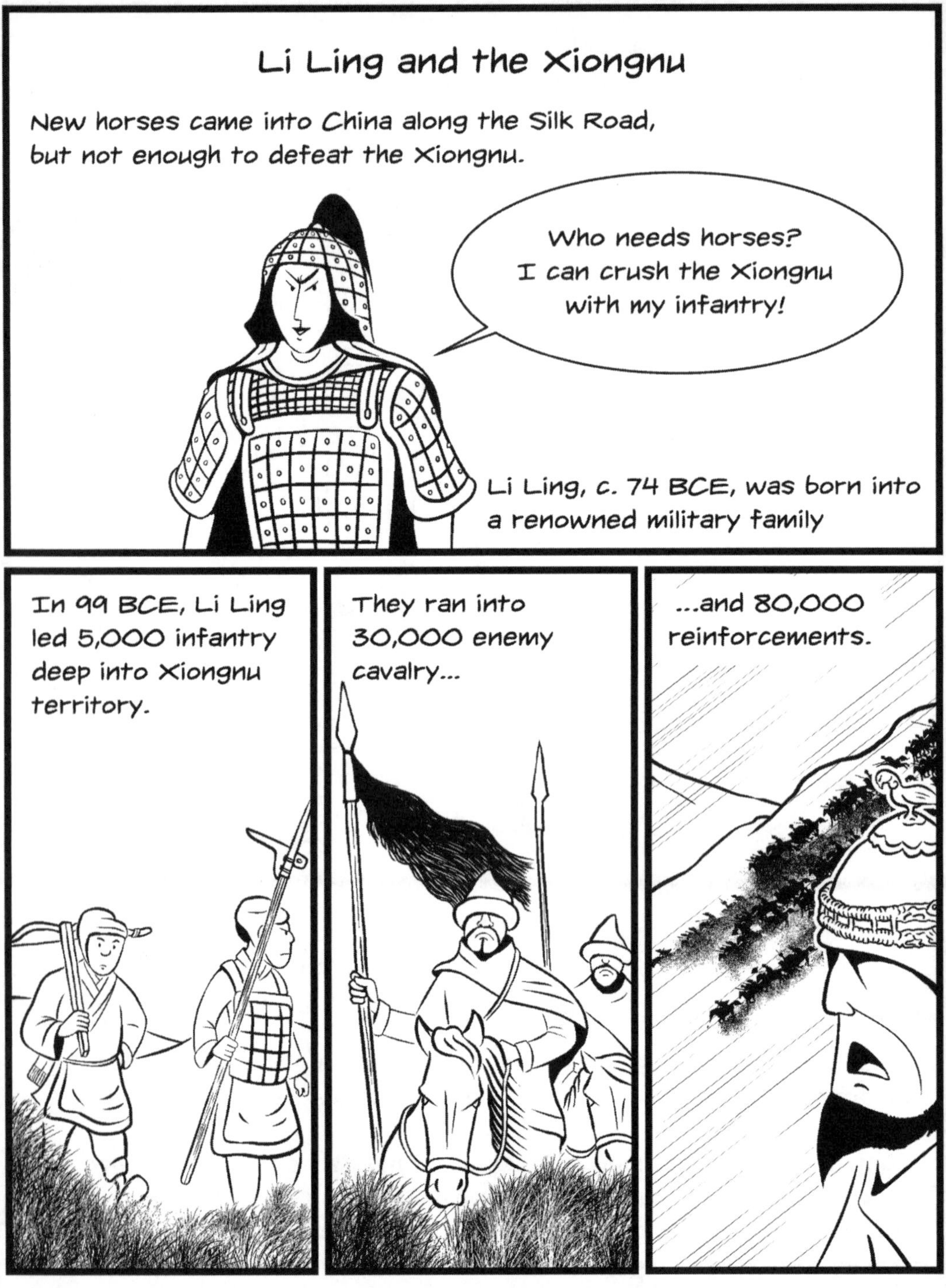
Li Ling and the Xiongnu
New horses came into China along the Silk Road, but not enough to defeat the Xiongnu.
Who needs horses? I can crush the Xiongnu with my infantry!
Li Ling, c. 74 BCE, was born into a renowned military family
In 99 BCE, Li Ling led 5,000 infantry deep into Xiongnu territory.
They ran into 30,000 enemy cavalry...
...and 80,000 reinforcements.

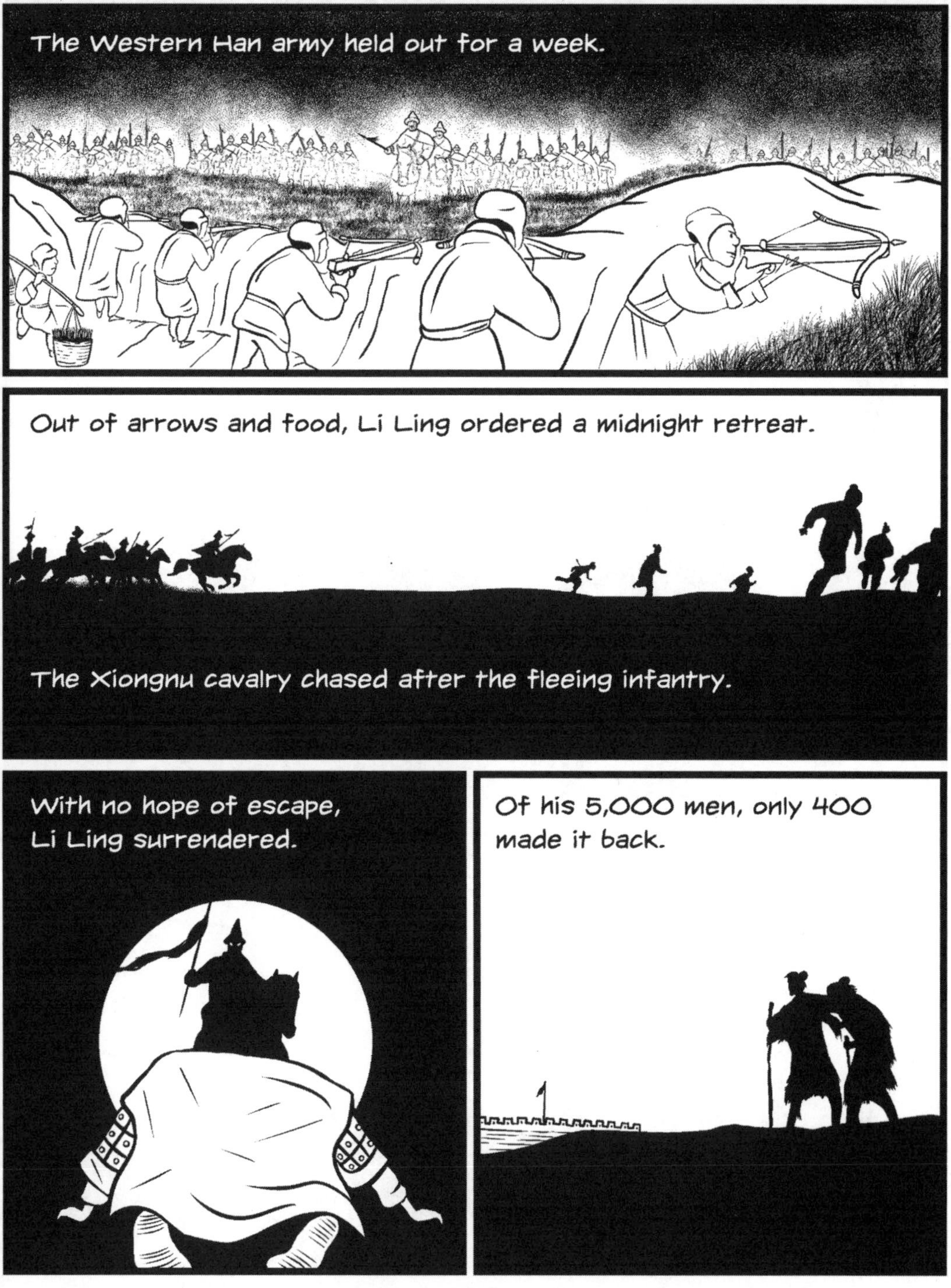
The Western Han army held out for a week.
Out of arrows and food, Li Ling ordered a midnight retreat.
The Xiongnu cavalry chased after the fleeing infantry.
With no hope of escape,
Li Ling surrendered.
Of his 5,000 men, only 400
made it back.

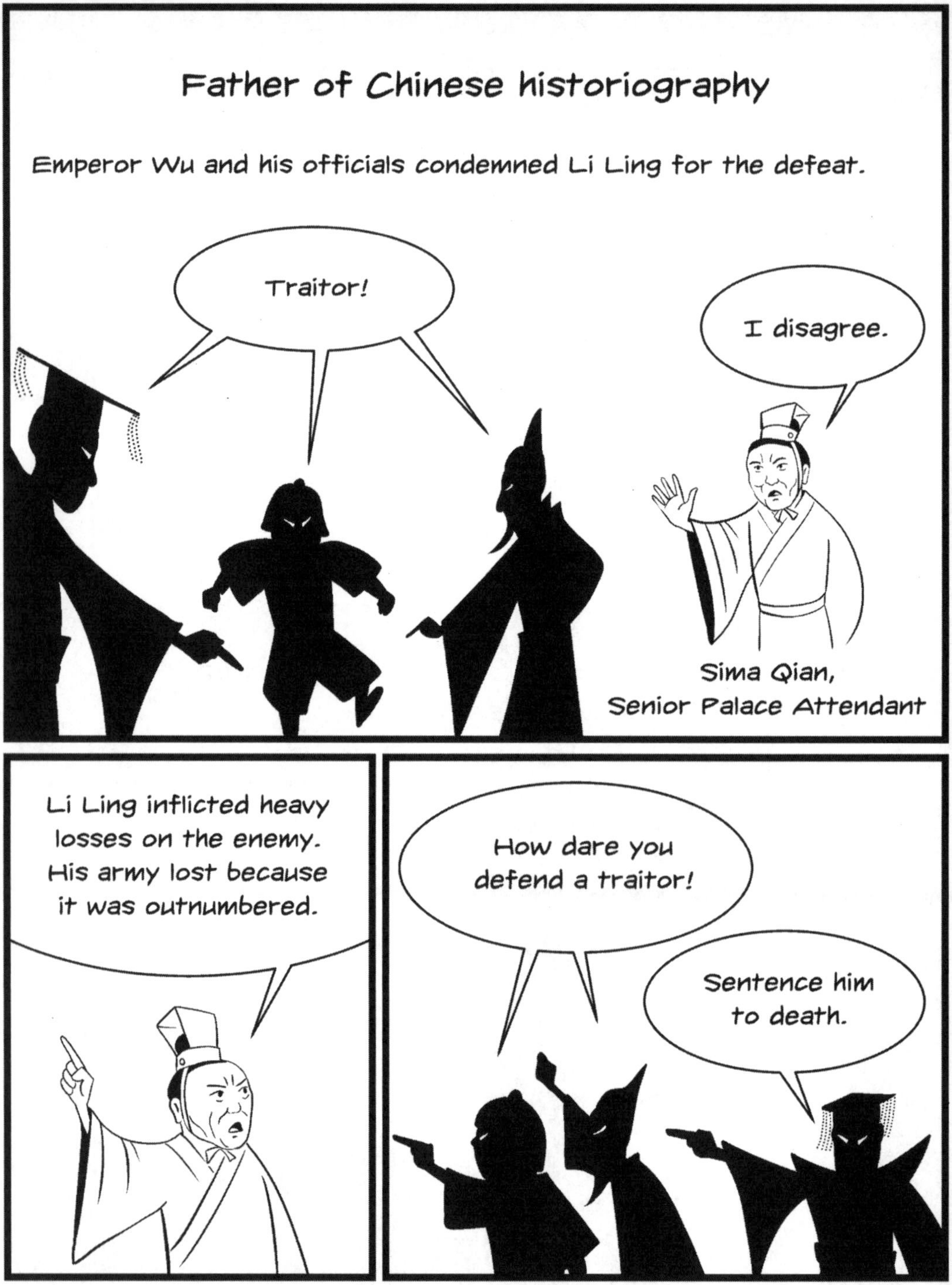
Father of Chinese historiography
Emperor Wu and his officials condemned Li Ling for the defeat.
Traitor!
I disagree.
Sima Qian,
Senior Palace Attendant
Li Ling inflicted heavy losses on the enemy. His army lost because it was outnumbered.
How dare you defend a traitor!
Sentence him to death.

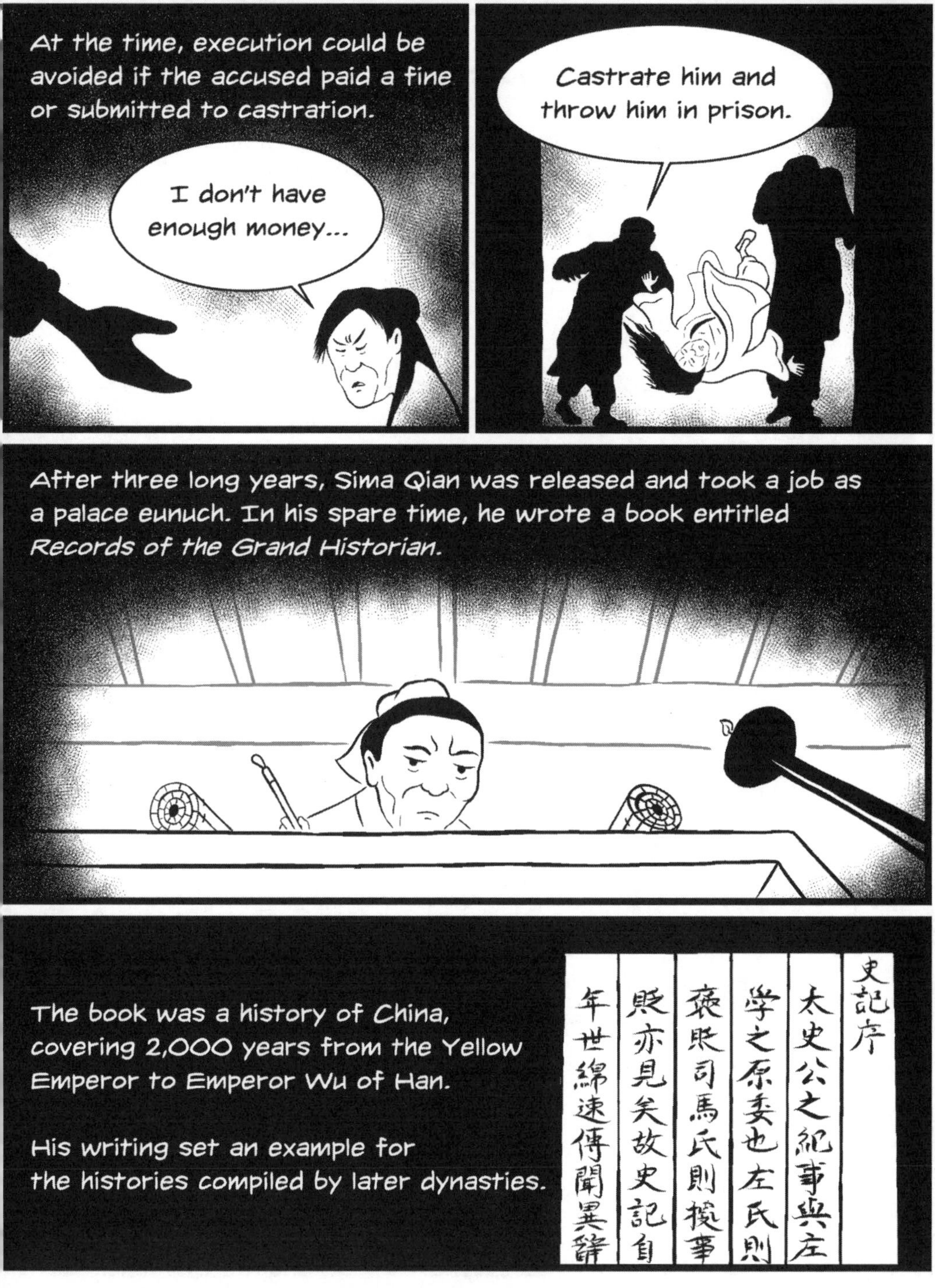
At the time, execution could be avoided if the accused paid a fine or submitted to castration.
I don't have enough money...
Castrate him and throw him in prison.
After three long years, Sima Qian was released and took a job as a palace eunuch. In his spare time, he wrote a book entitled *Records of the Grand Historian.*
The book was a history of China, covering 2,000 years from the Yellow Emperor to Emperor Wu of Han.
His writing set an example for the histories compiled by later dynasties.
史記序
太史公之紀事與左
學之原委也左氏則
褒貶司馬氏則撰事
貶亦見矣故史記自
年世綿速傳聞異辭

An exhausted country

In his *Records of the Grand Historian*, Sima Qian detailed the costs associated with Emperor Wu's campaigns.

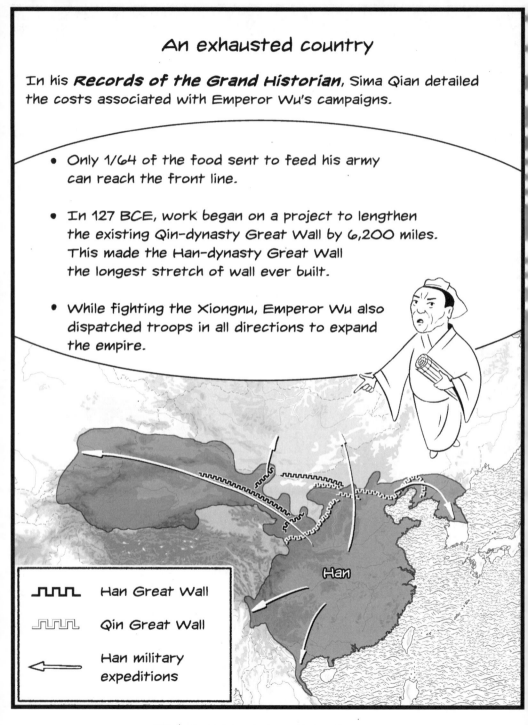

- Only 1/64 of the food sent to feed his army can reach the front line.

- In 127 BCE, work began on a project to lengthen the existing Qin-dynasty Great Wall by 6,200 miles. This made the Han-dynasty Great Wall the longest stretch of wall ever built.

- While fighting the Xiongnu, Emperor Wu also dispatched troops in all directions to expand the empire.

Han

ПППЛ Han Great Wall

ЛППЛ Qin Great Wall

← Han military expeditions

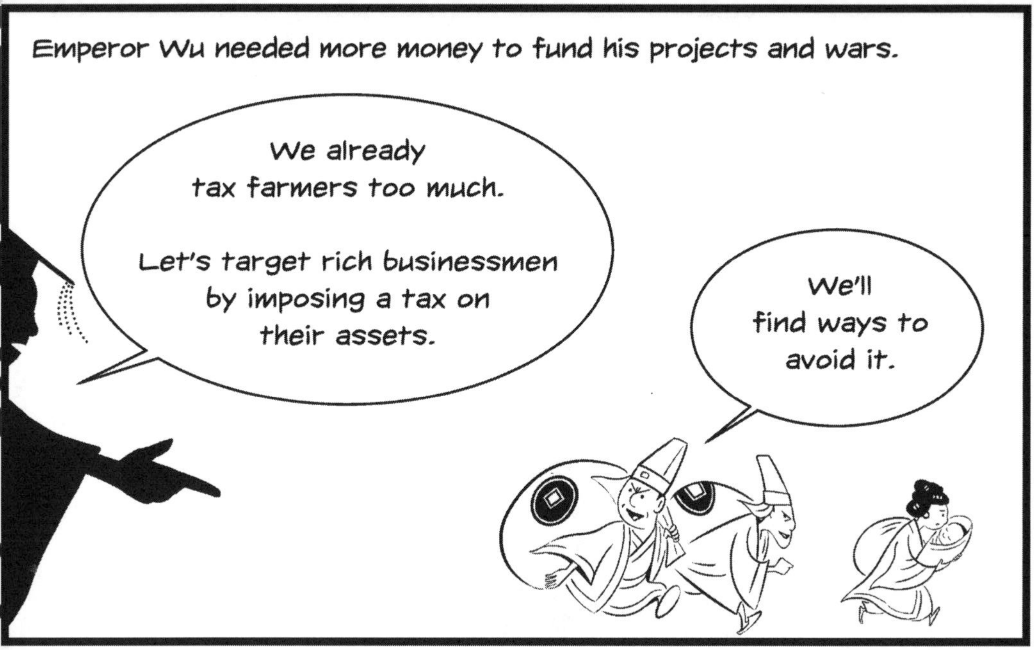
Emperor Wu needed more money to fund his projects and wars.
We already tax farmers too much.
Let's target rich businessmen by imposing a tax on their assets.
We'll find ways to avoid it.

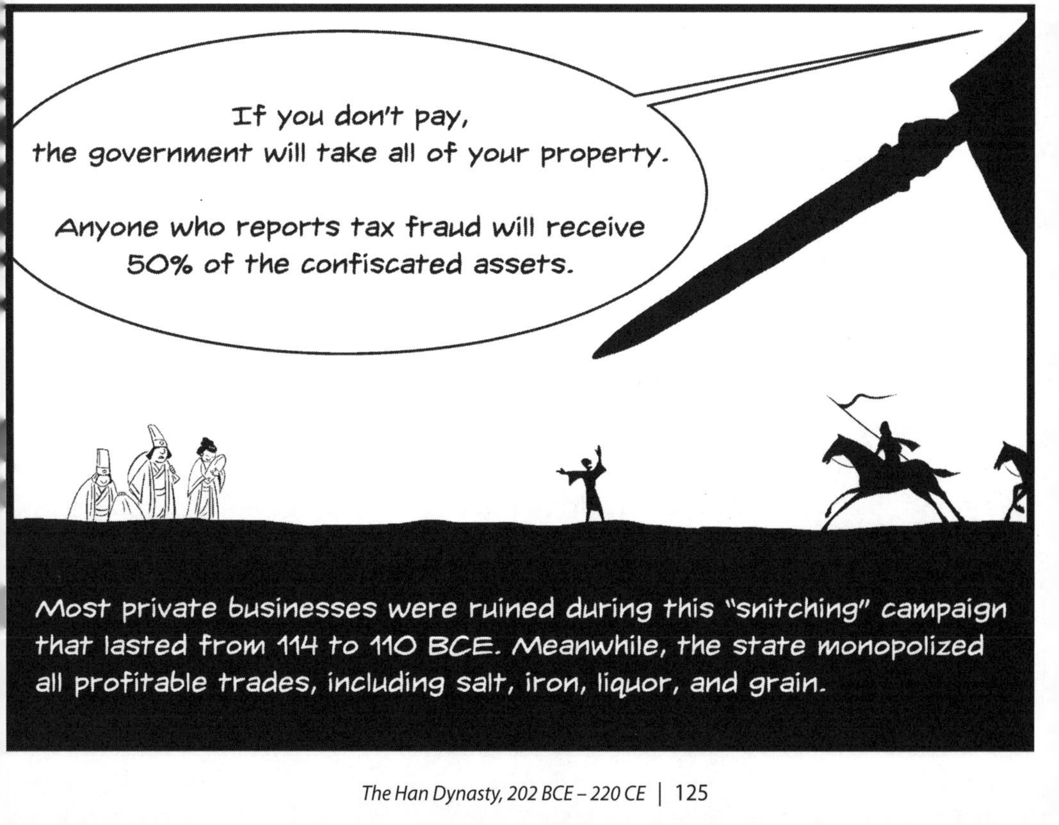
If you don't pay, the government will take all of your property.
Anyone who reports tax fraud will receive 50% of the confiscated assets.
Most private businesses were ruined during this "snitching" campaign that lasted from 114 to 110 BCE. Meanwhile, the state monopolized all profitable trades, including salt, iron, liquor, and grain.

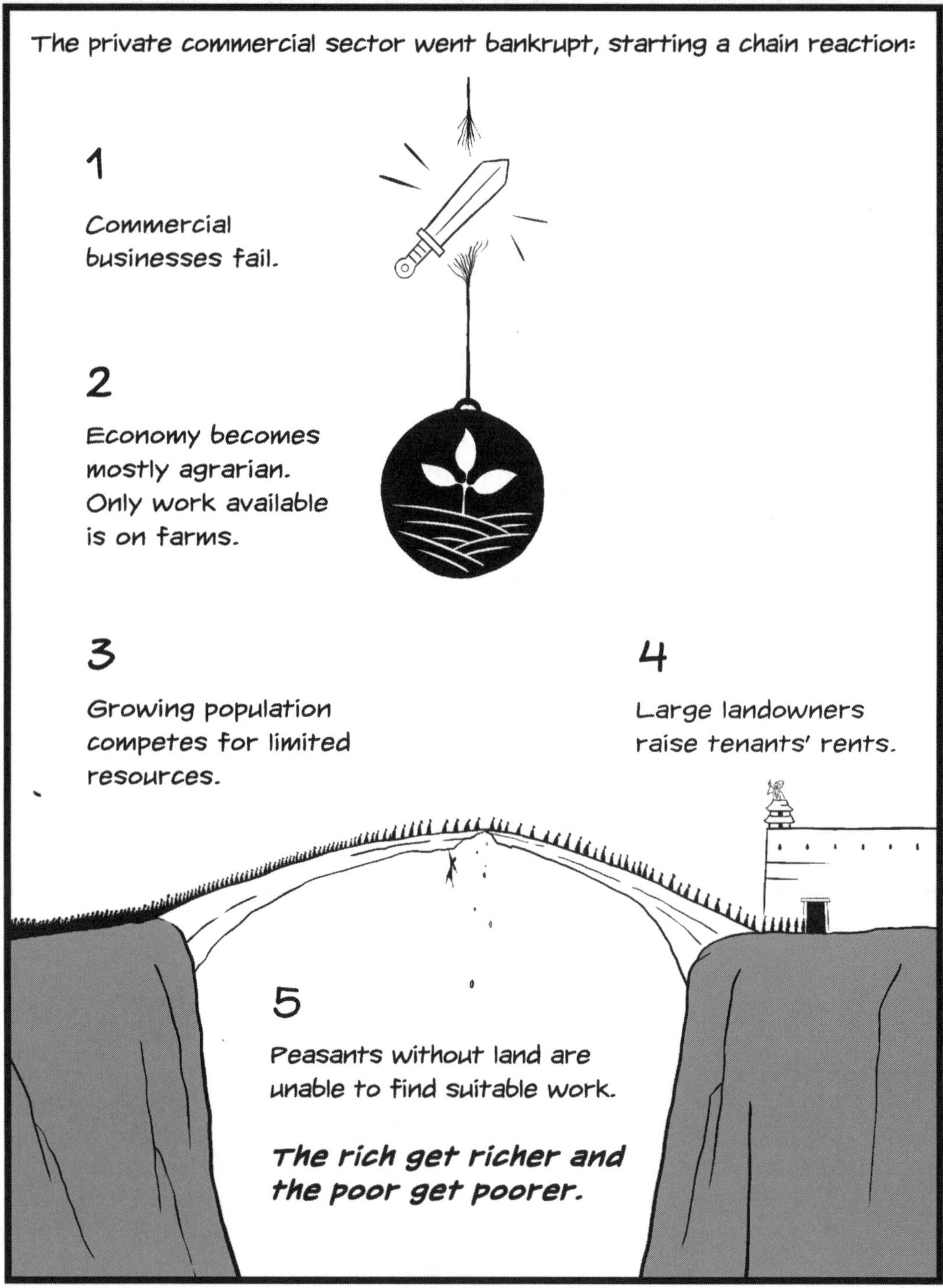
The private commercial sector went bankrupt, starting a chain reaction:
1
Commercial businesses fail.
2
Economy becomes mostly agrarian. Only work available is on farms.
3
Growing population competes for limited resources.
4
Large landowners raise tenants' rents.
5
Peasants without land are unable to find suitable work.
The rich get richer and the poor get poorer.

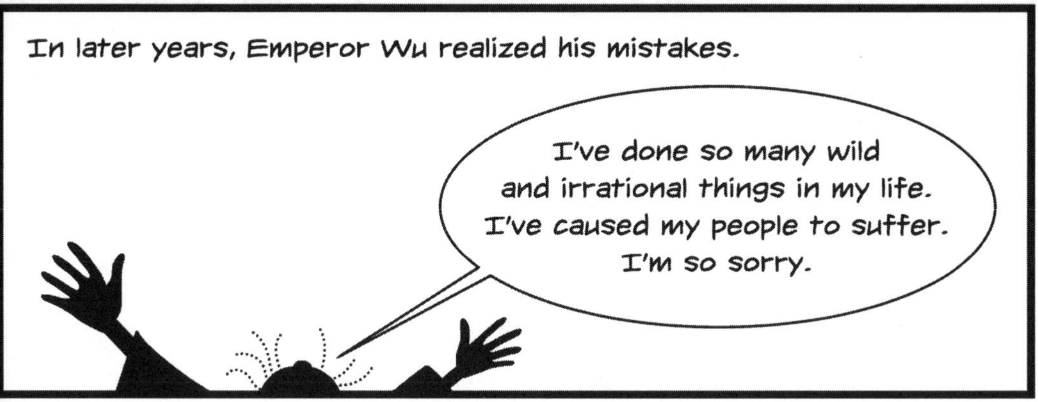
In later years, Emperor Wu realized his mistakes.
I've done so many wild and irrational things in my life. I've caused my people to suffer. I'm so sorry.

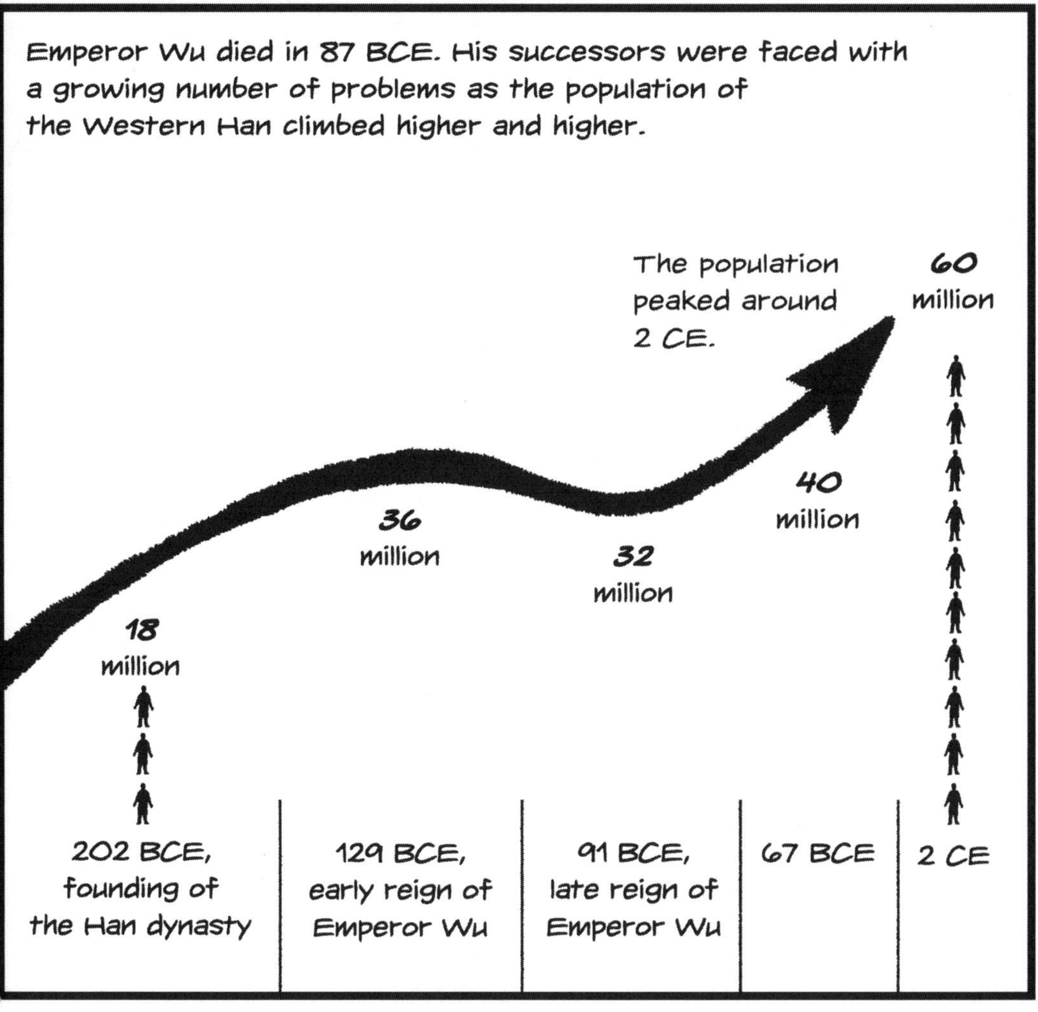
Emperor Wu died in 87 BCE. His successors were faced with a growing number of problems as the population of the Western Han climbed higher and higher.
The population peaked around 2 CE.
18 million
36 million
32 million
40 million
60 million
202 BCE, founding of the Han dynasty
129 BCE, early reign of Emperor Wu
91 BCE, late reign of Emperor Wu
67 BCE
2 CE

Life of a farmer

A pattern quickly emerged in the life of the typical Chinese farmer during this time.

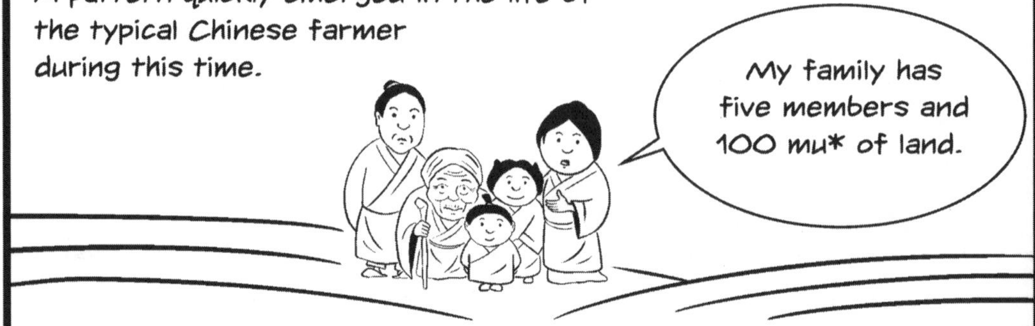
My family has five members and 100 mu* of land.

Food income	Food expense	Food balance (Dan**)
Each mu can produce 1.5 dan of grain, so our annual harvest is 150 dan.		150
	The current land tax is 1/15 of my annual harvest or 10 dan.	140
	I require 90 dan of grain to feed my family each year.	50

* 1 mu = 0.165 acres

** Dan: a traditional Chinese unit of volume equal to around 26 gallons

Cash income	*Cash expenses*	*Cash balance* (Coins)
I sell my grain surplus of 50 dan on the market at 30 coins per dan.		1,500
	I use 300 coins for community rituals and events.	1,200
	I use 300 coins annually to buy clothes for each family member. That's a total of 1,500 coins.	-300

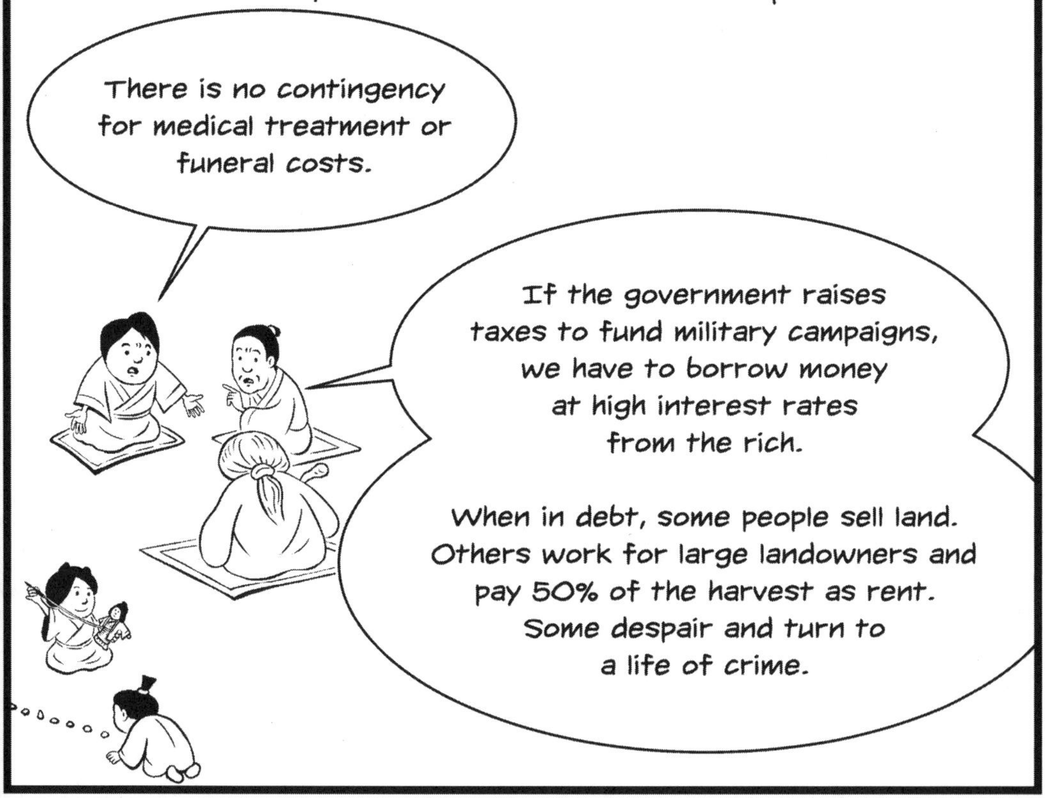

There is no contingency for medical treatment or funeral costs.
If the government raises taxes to fund military campaigns, we have to borrow money at high interest rates from the rich.
When in debt, some people sell land. Others work for large landowners and pay 50% of the harvest as rent. Some despair and turn to a life of crime.

Xin dynasty and Confucian reforms

While poor farmers couldn't afford taxes, large landowners always found ways to pay less.

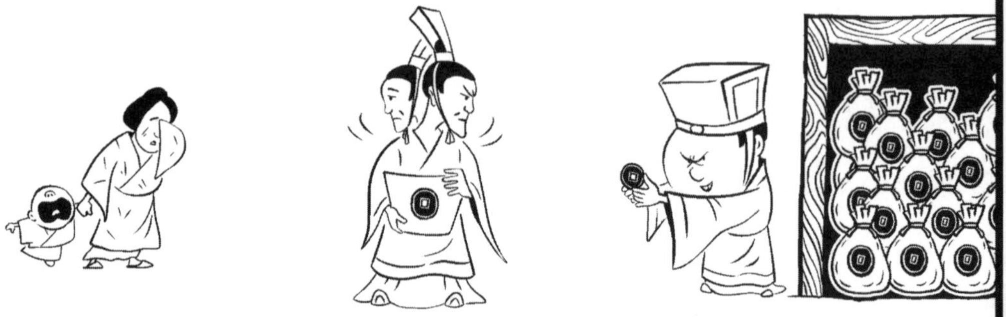

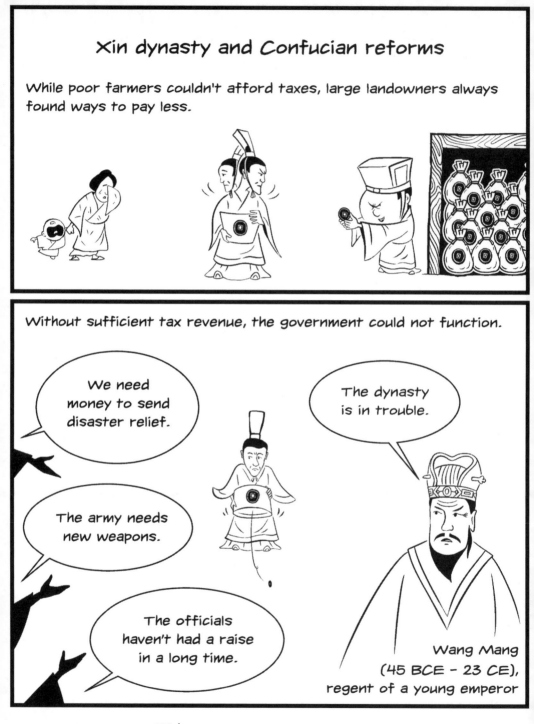

Without sufficient tax revenue, the government could not function.

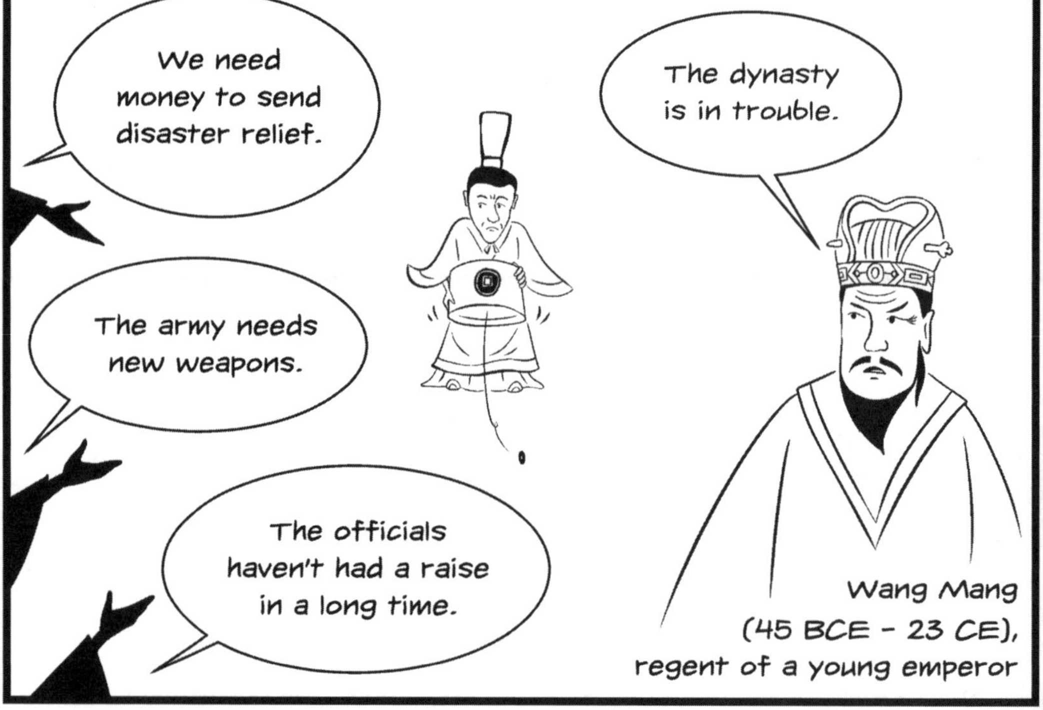
We need money to send disaster relief.
The army needs new weapons.
The officials haven't had a raise in a long time.
The dynasty is in trouble.
Wang Mang (45 BCE – 23 CE), regent of a young emperor

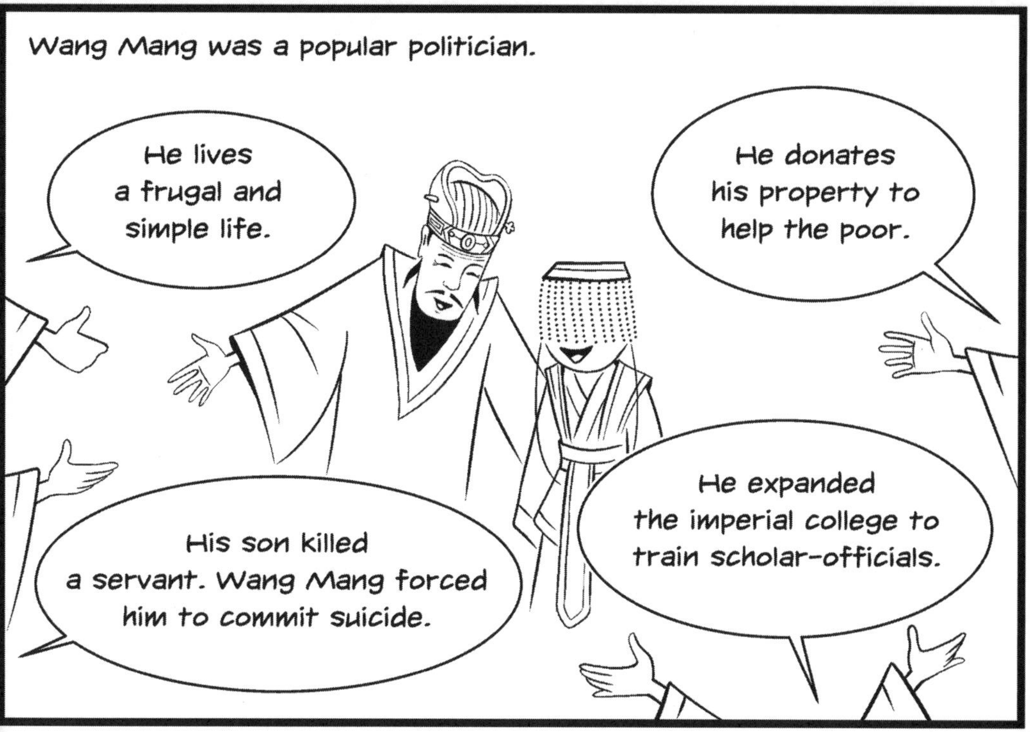
Wang Mang was a popular politician.
He lives a frugal and simple life.
He donates his property to help the poor.
His son killed a servant. Wang Mang forced him to commit suicide.
He expanded the imperial college to train scholar-officials.

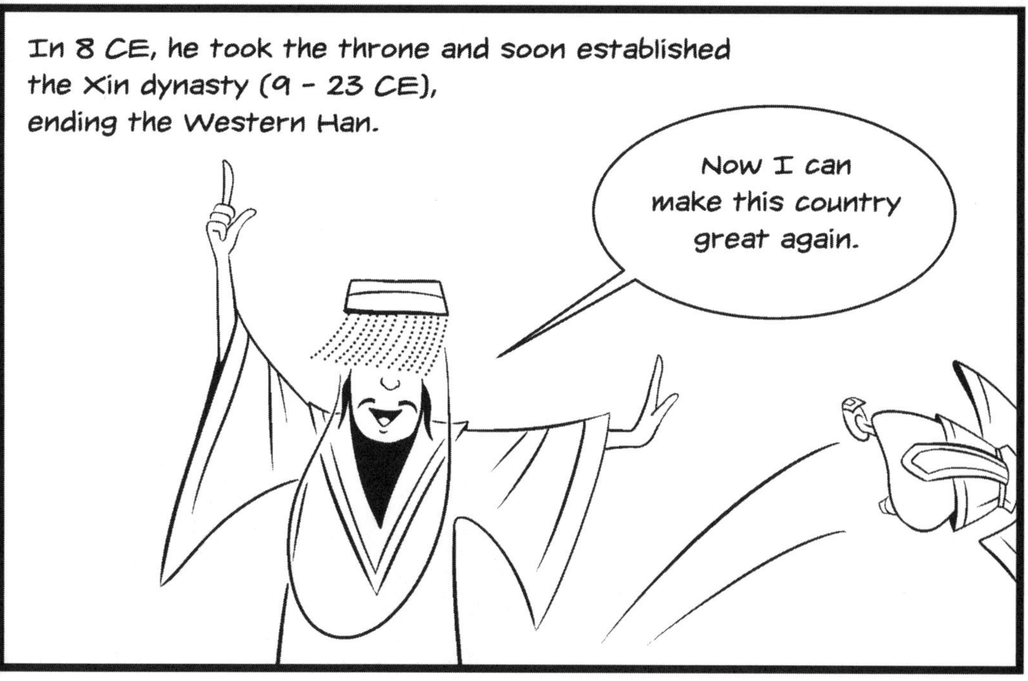
In 8 CE, he took the throne and soon established the Xin dynasty (9 - 23 CE), ending the Western Han.
Now I can make this country great again.

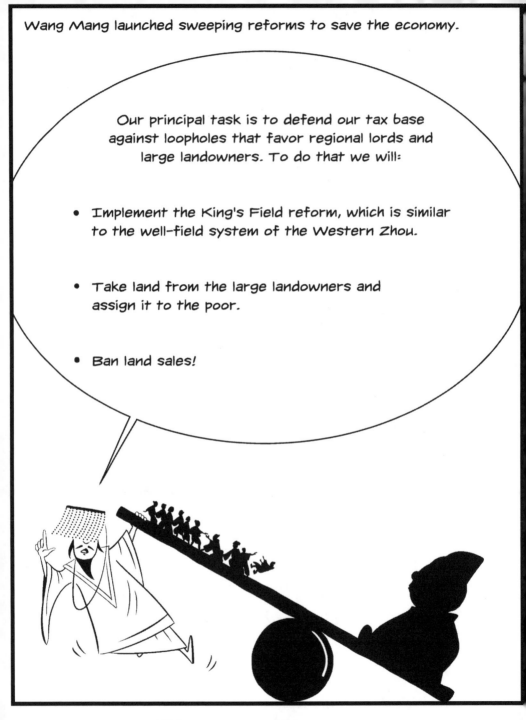

Wang Mang launched sweeping reforms to save the economy.

Our principal task is to defend our tax base against loopholes that favor regional lords and large landowners. To do that we will:

- Implement the King's Field reform, which is similar to the well-field system of the Western Zhou.

- Take land from the large landowners and assign it to the poor.

- Ban land sales!

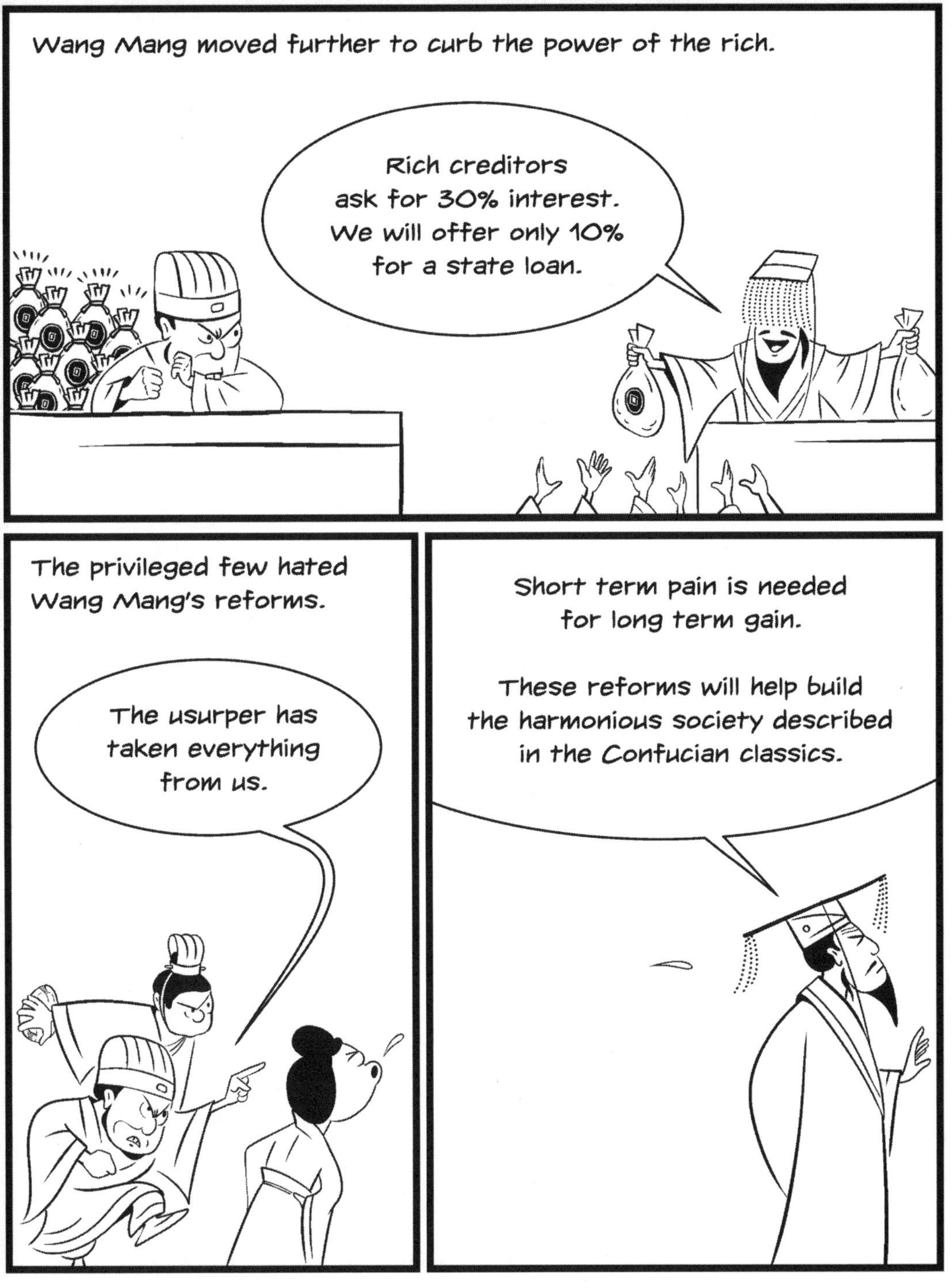
Wang Mang moved further to curb the power of the rich.
Rich creditors ask for 30% interest. We will offer only 10% for a state loan.
The privileged few hated Wang Mang's reforms.
The usurper has taken everything from us.
Short term pain is needed for long term gain.
These reforms will help build the harmonious society described in the Confucian classics.

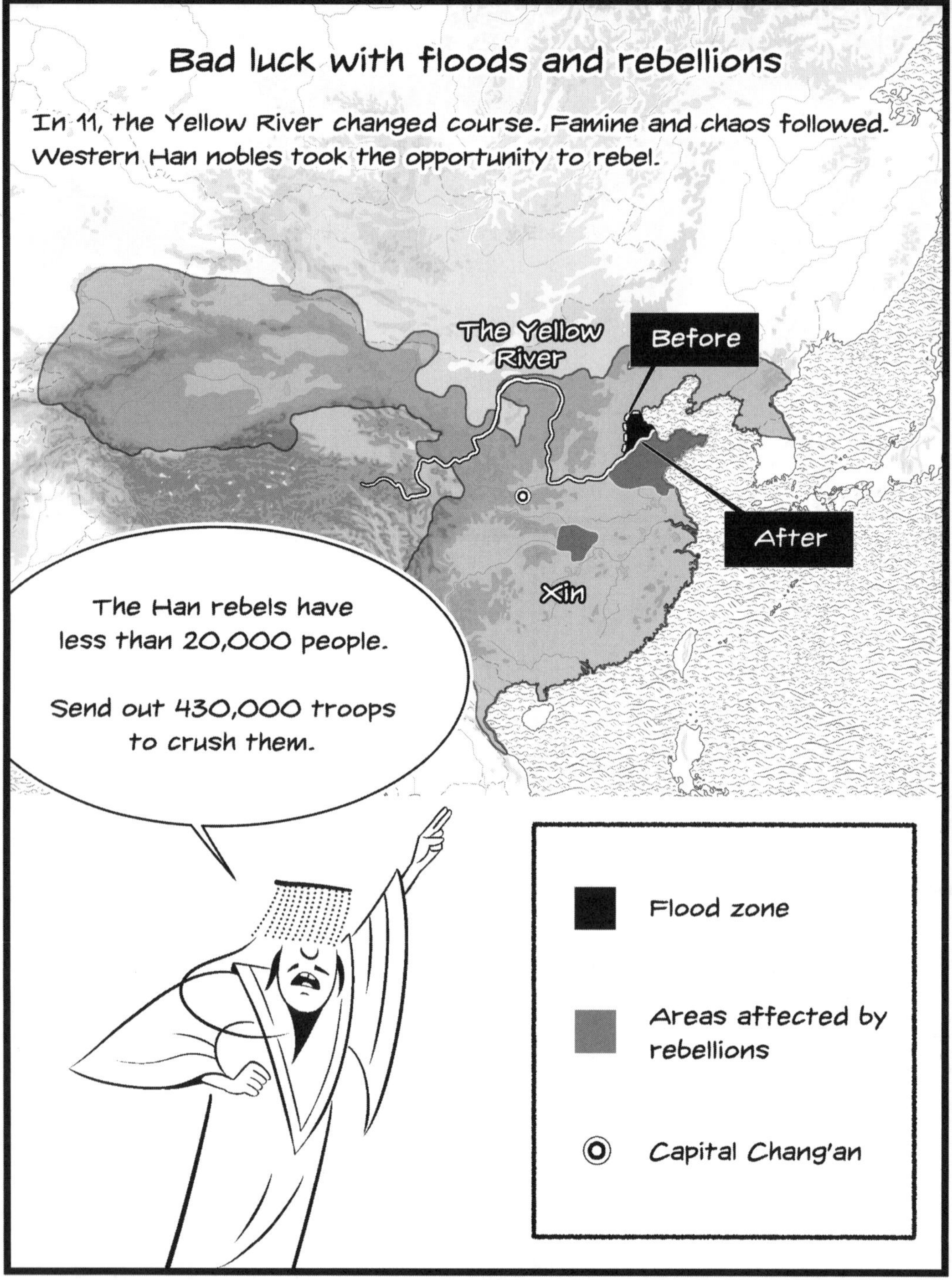
Bad luck with floods and rebellions
In 11, the Yellow River changed course. Famine and chaos followed. Western Han nobles took the opportunity to rebel.
The Yellow River
Before
After
Xin
The Han rebels have less than 20,000 people.
Send out 430,000 troops to crush them.
Flood zone
Areas affected by rebellions
Capital Chang'an

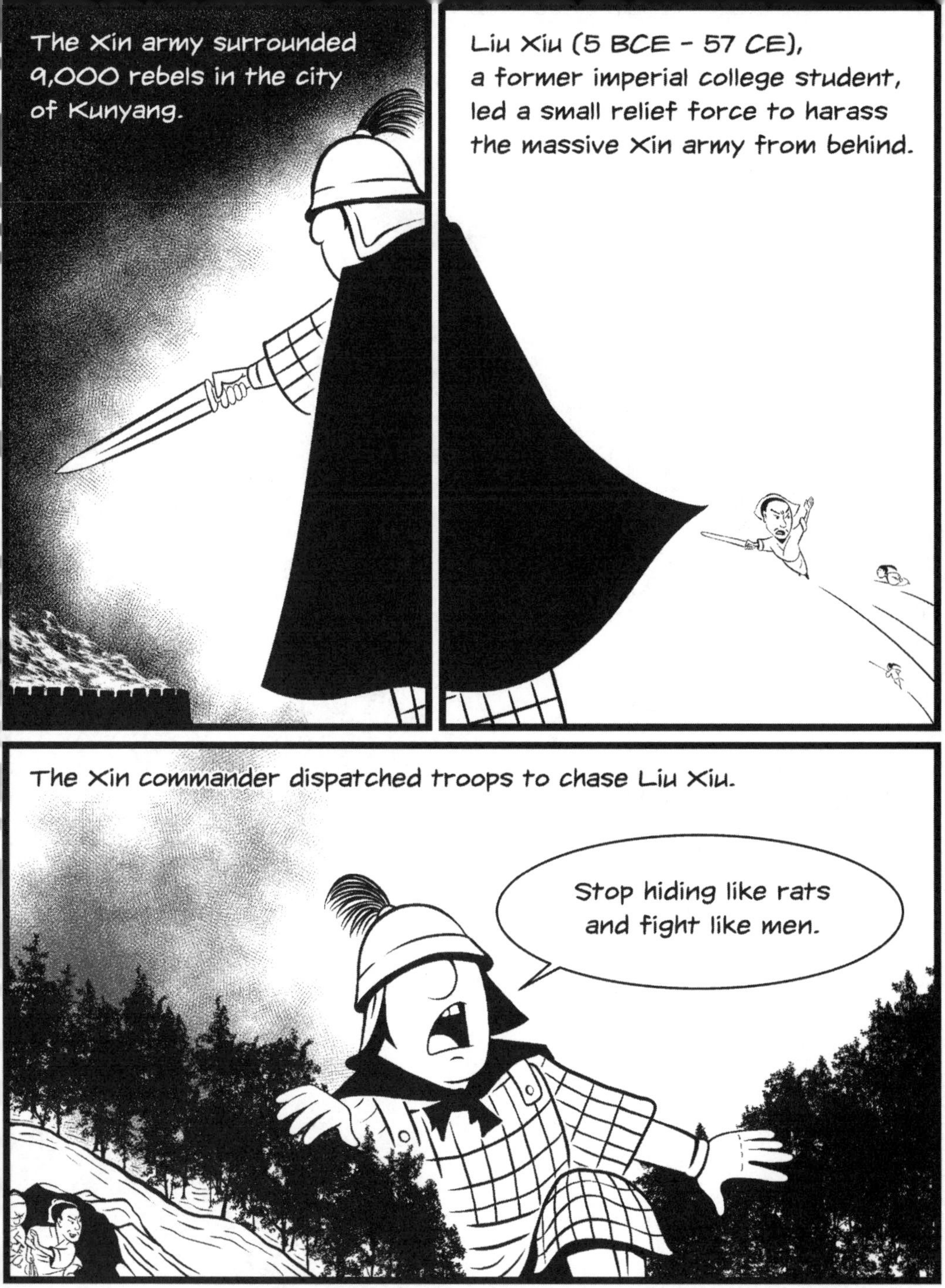
The Xin army surrounded 9,000 rebels in the city of Kunyang.
Liu Xiu (5 BCE - 57 CE), a former imperial college student, led a small relief force to harass the massive Xin army from behind.
The Xin commander dispatched troops to chase Liu Xiu.
Stop hiding like rats and fight like men.

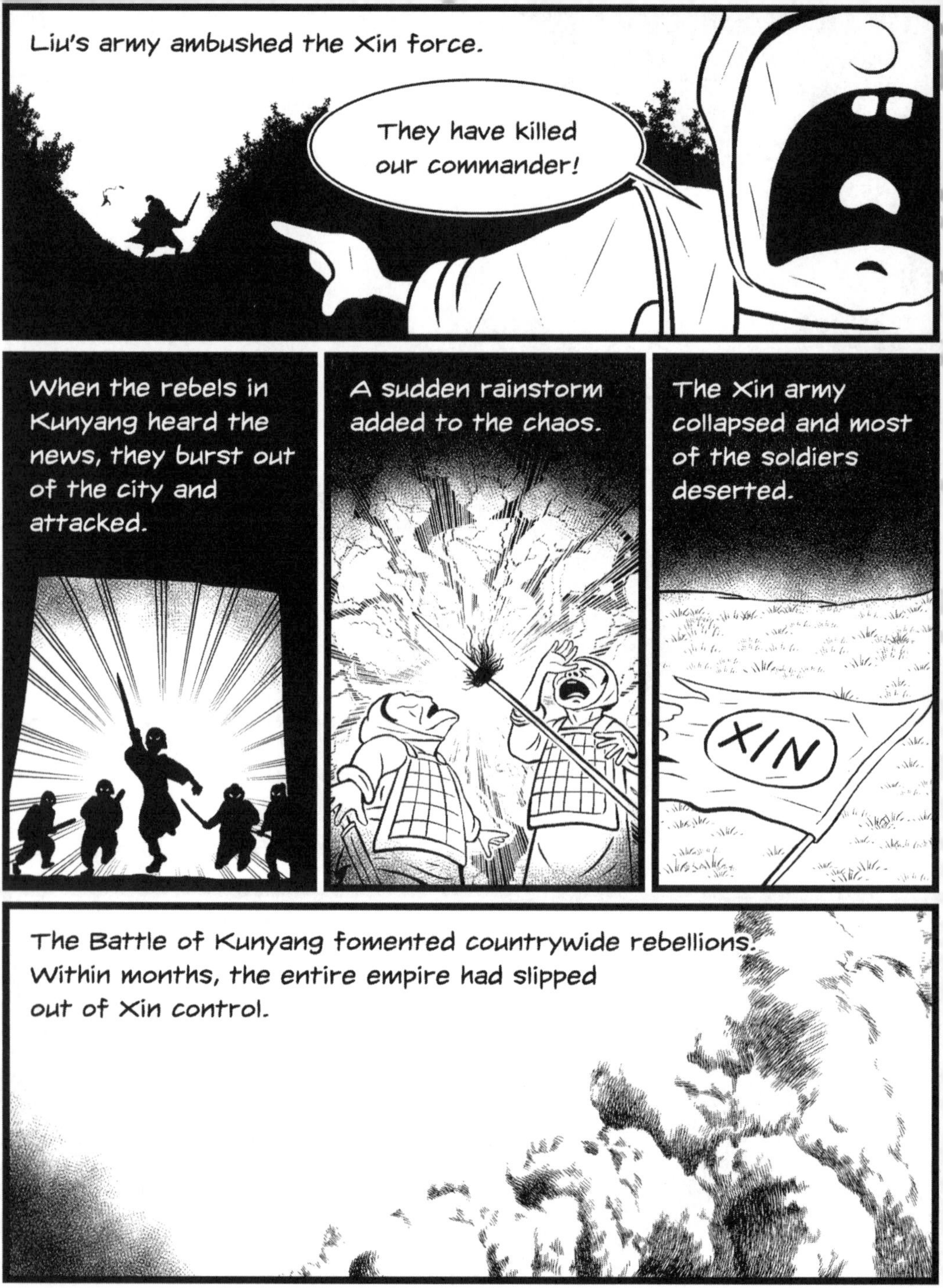
Liu's army ambushed the Xin force.
They have killed our commander!
When the rebels in Kunyang heard the news, they burst out of the city and attacked.
A sudden rainstorm added to the chaos.
The Xin army collapsed and most of the soldiers deserted.
XIN
The Battle of Kunyang fomented countrywide rebellions. Within months, the entire empire had slipped out of Xin control.

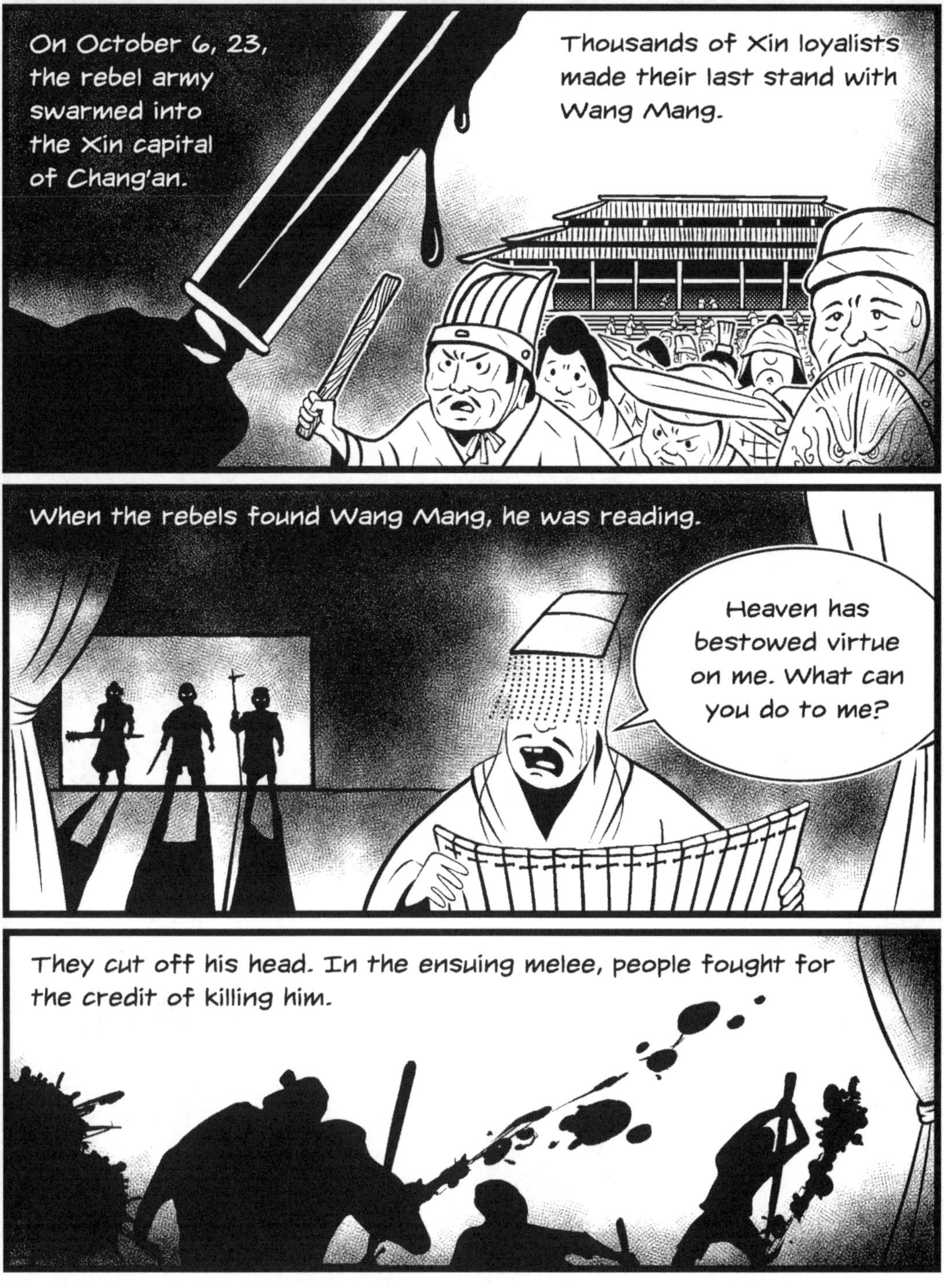
On October 6, 23, the rebel army swarmed into the Xin capital of Chang'an.
Thousands of Xin loyalists made their last stand with Wang Mang.
When the rebels found Wang Mang, he was reading.
Heaven has bestowed virtue on me. What can you do to me?
They cut off his head. In the ensuing melee, people fought for the credit of killing him.

Han restoration

Within two years of Wang Mang's death, several rebel groups had named their own emperors. Millions died in the 14-year war to determine the true Son of Heaven.

In 37, Liu Xiu vanquished these rebels. He re-established the Han, beginning the Eastern Han dynasty (25 - 220) period.

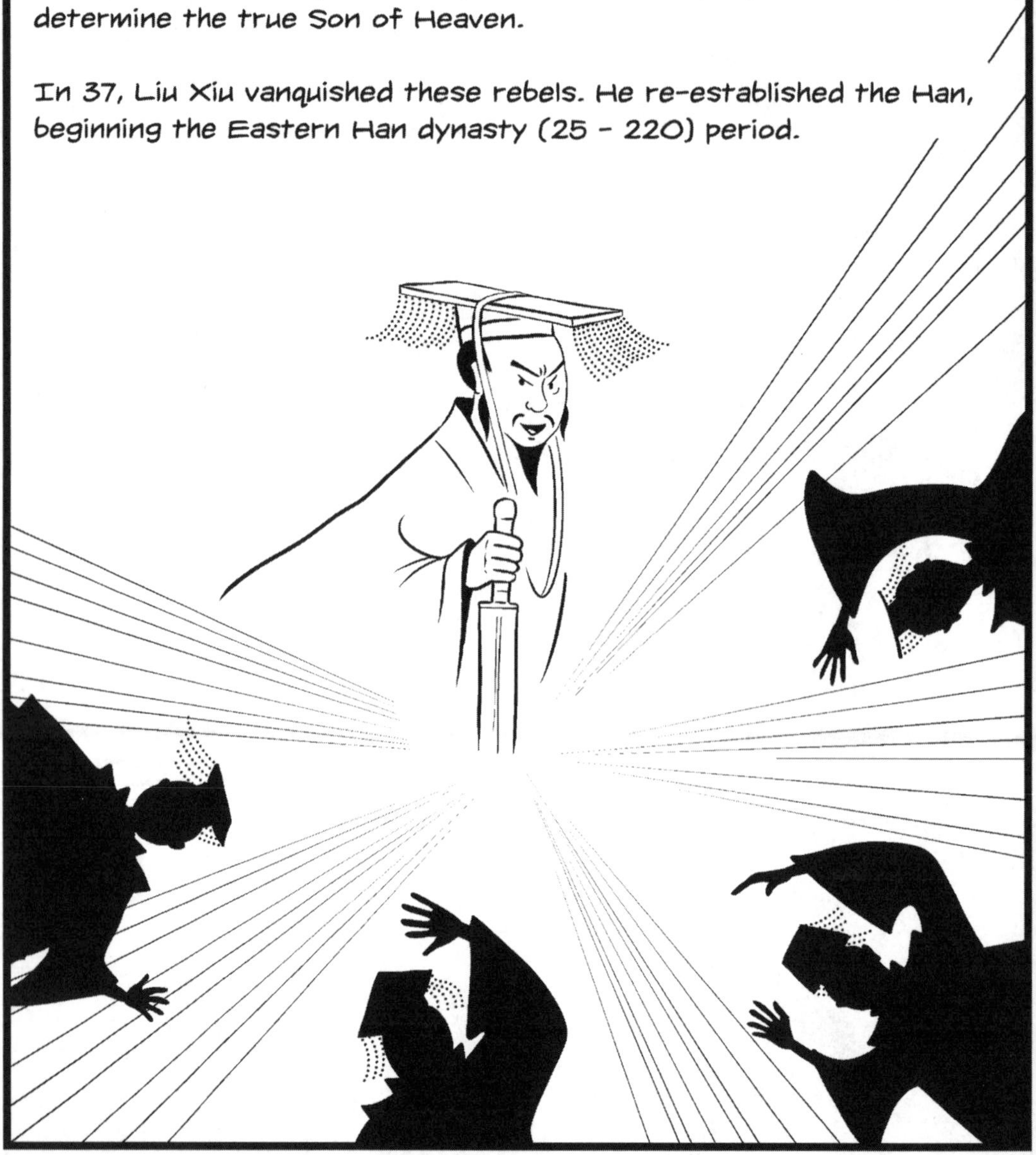

Reasserting control

While Chinese factions fought for the throne, the Xiongnu rose up and once more took control of the profitable Silk Road. The Eastern Han then spent decades rallying other nomad forces to defend its far-flung borders.

In 91, the Eastern Han crushed the Xiongnu in a battle 1,500 miles away from the Chinese border. It was the westernmost distance a Chinese imperial army had ever traveled.

The remaining Xiongnu fled west. Some historians believe they settled in Hungary, assimilating into the local population.

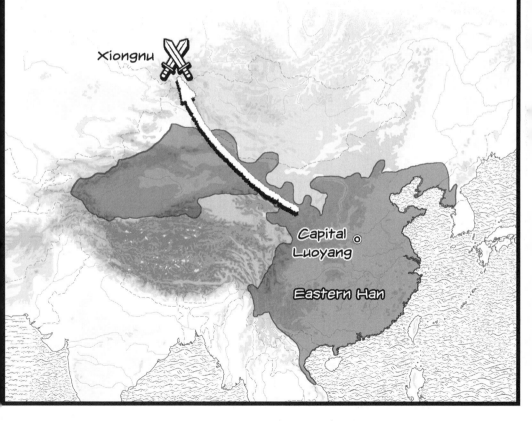

Xiongnu

Capital ◦
Luoyang

Eastern Han

Educating officials

In addition to securing the border, early Eastern Han rulers also devoted themselves to restoring imperial institutions.

The court ordered the construction of a new college in the capital, the largest ever built in Chinese imperial history.

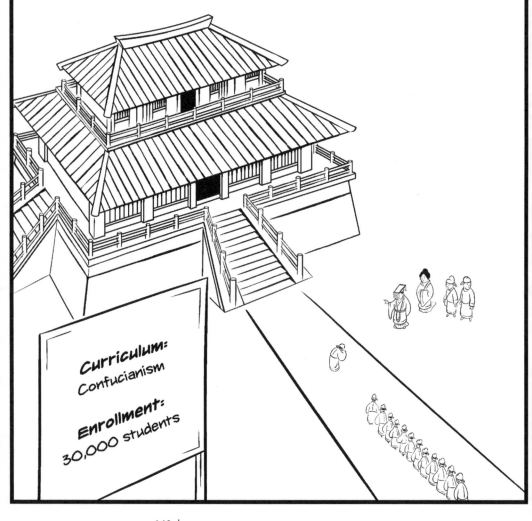

Curriculum:
Confucianism

Enrollment:
30,000 students

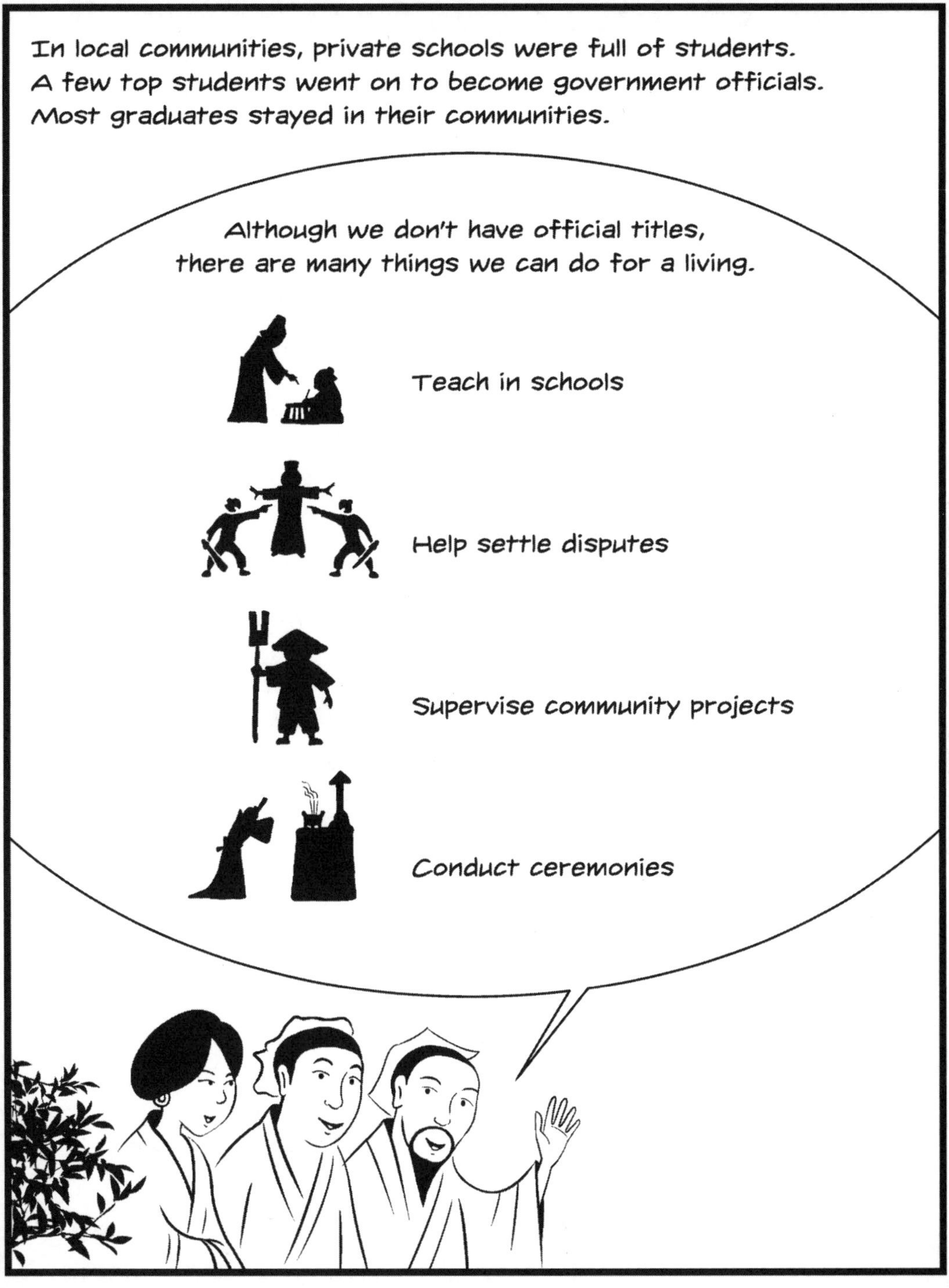
In local communities, private schools were full of students. A few top students went on to become government officials. Most graduates stayed in their communities.
Although we don't have official titles, there are many things we can do for a living.
Teach in schools
Help settle disputes
Supervise community projects
Conduct ceremonies

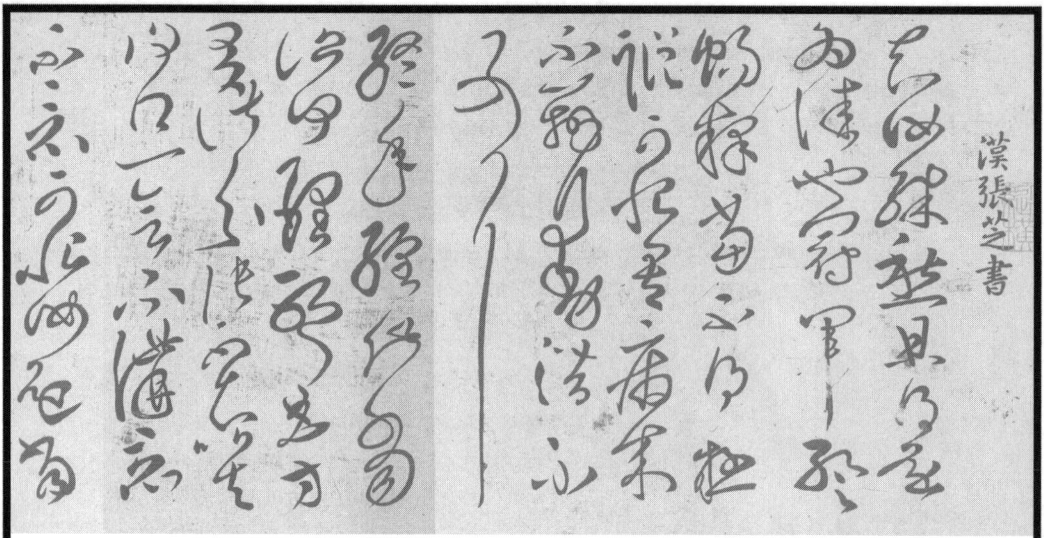
漢張芝書

As access to education expanded, major Chinese art forms thrived.

Literature

Painting

Calligraphy

Seal carving

Antique preservation

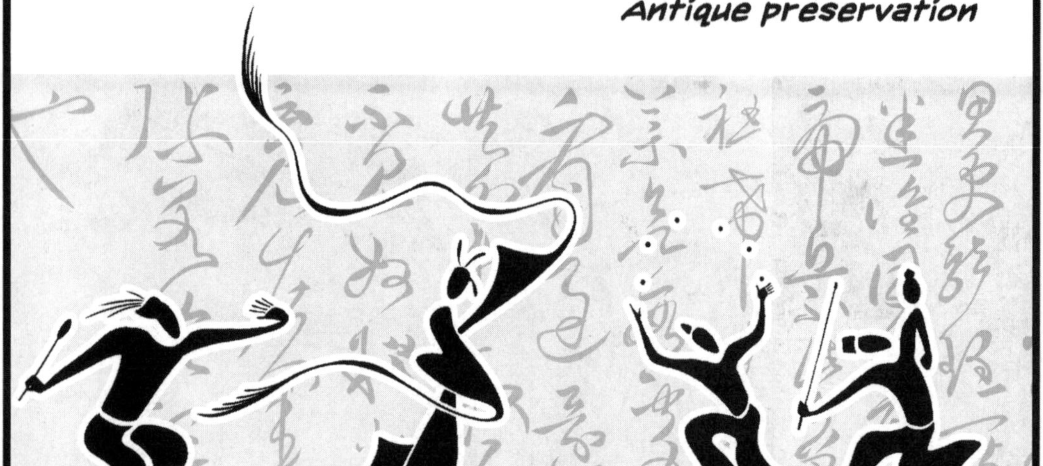

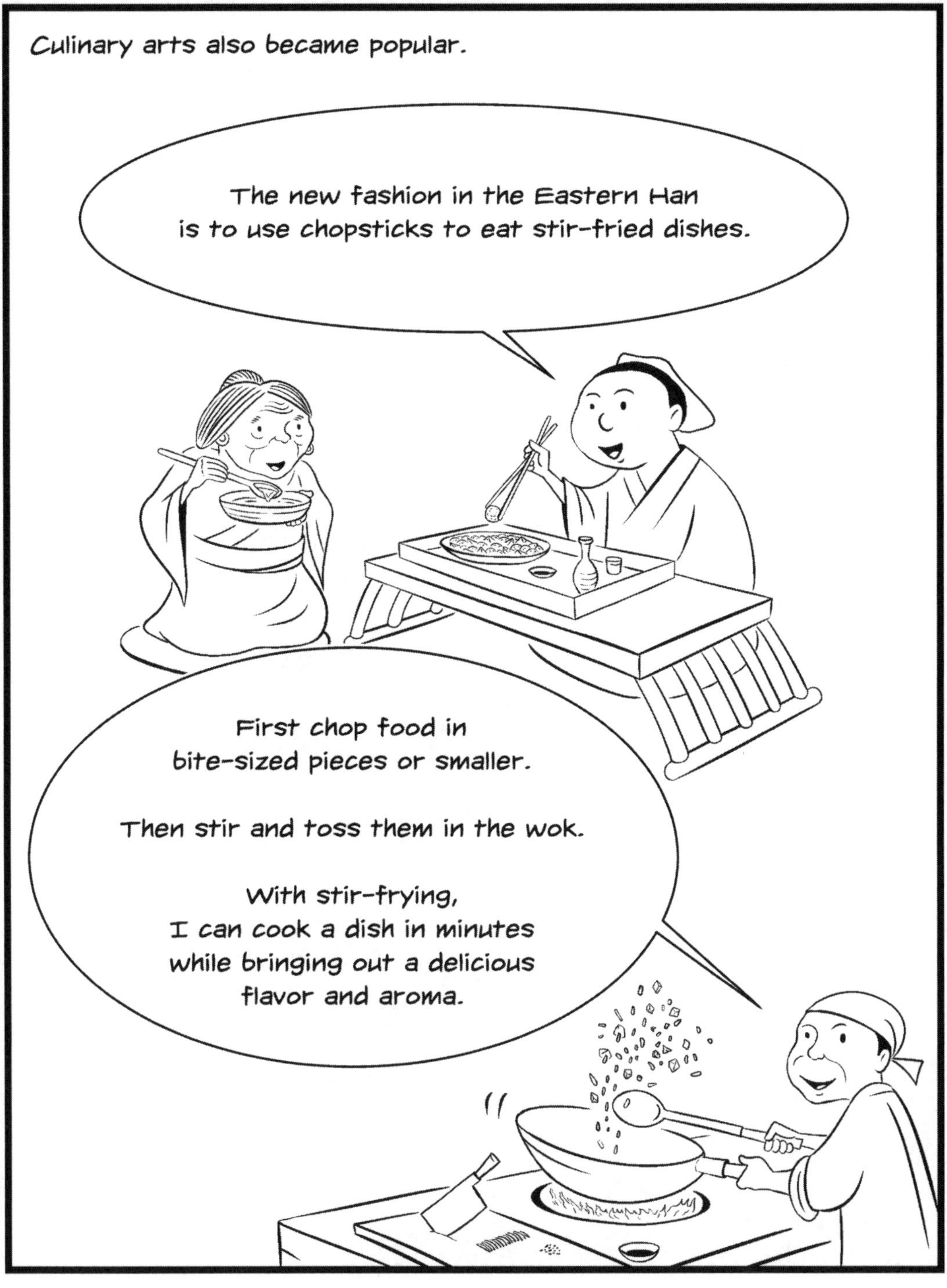
Culinary arts also became popular.
The new fashion in the Eastern Han is to use chopsticks to eat stir-fried dishes.
First chop food in bite-sized pieces or smaller.
Then stir and toss them in the wok.
With stir-frying, I can cook a dish in minutes while bringing out a delicious flavor and aroma.

Trouble at the inner court

While the outer court was filled with diligent scholar-officials, the inner court was in trouble.

Except for the first three emperors, Eastern Han rulers all ascended the throne under the age of 16. A young emperor was often under the control of his mother and her clan.

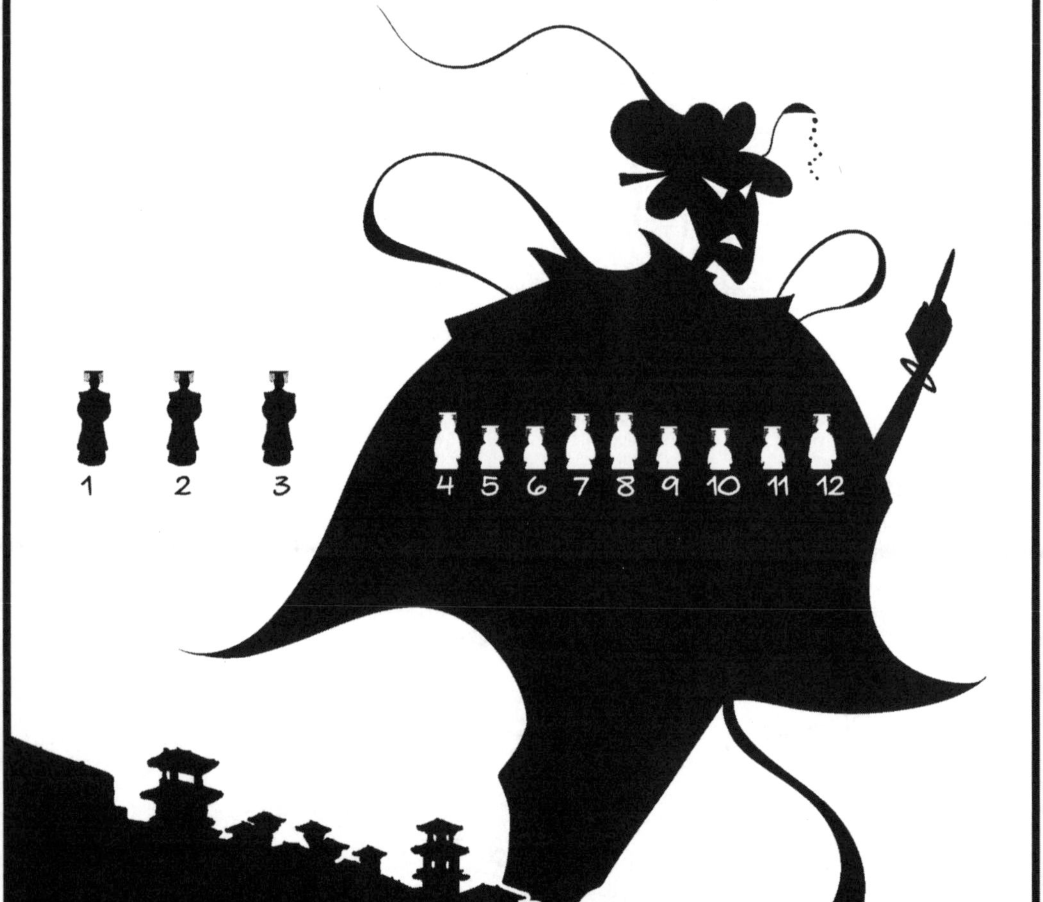
1
2
3
4
5
6
7
8
9
10
11
12

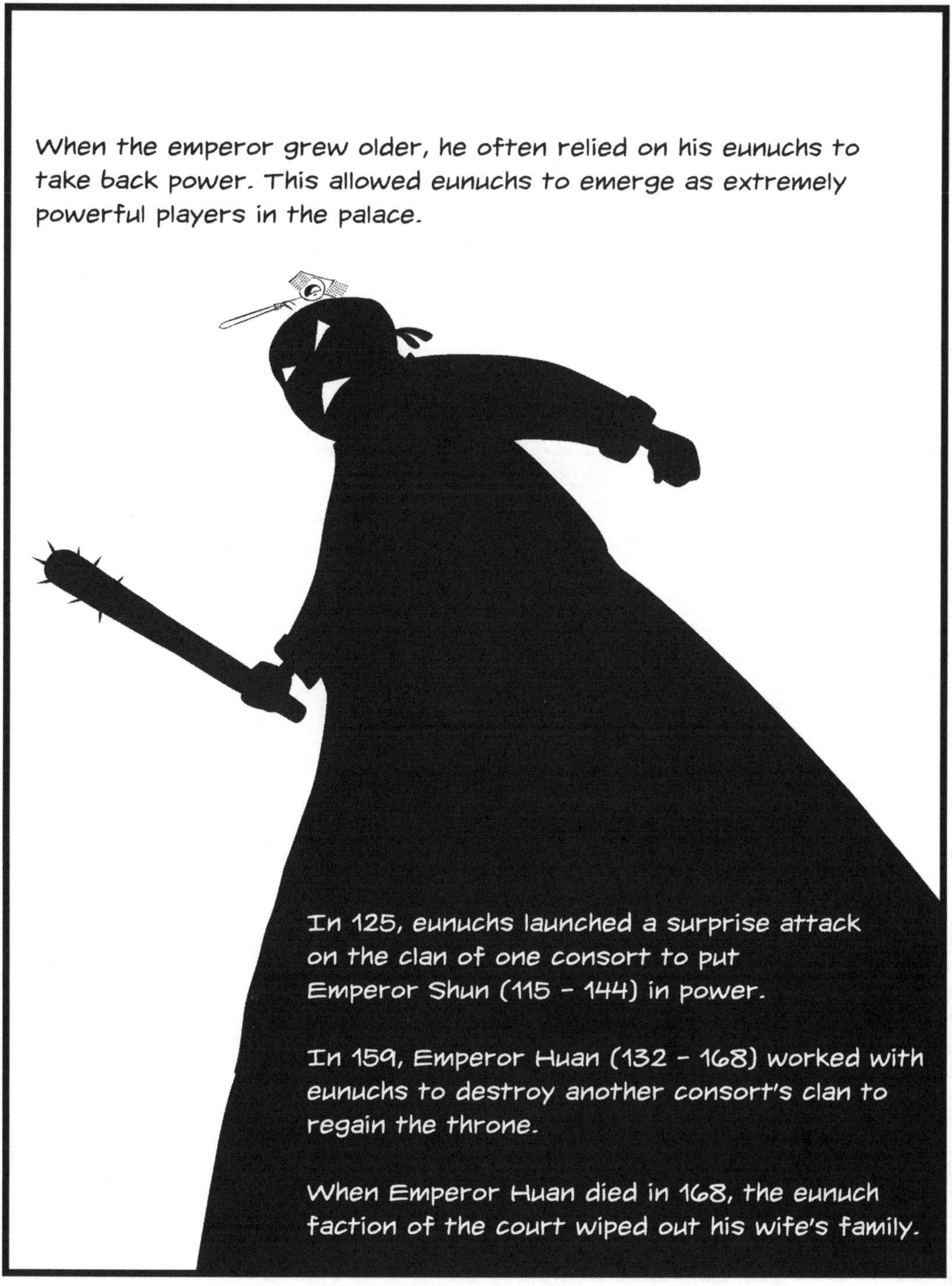
When the emperor grew older, he often relied on his eunuchs to take back power. This allowed eunuchs to emerge as extremely powerful players in the palace.
In 125, eunuchs launched a surprise attack on the clan of one consort to put Emperor Shun (115 - 144) in power.
In 159, Emperor Huan (132 - 168) worked with eunuchs to destroy another consort's clan to regain the throne.
When Emperor Huan died in 168, the eunuch faction of the court wiped out his wife's family.

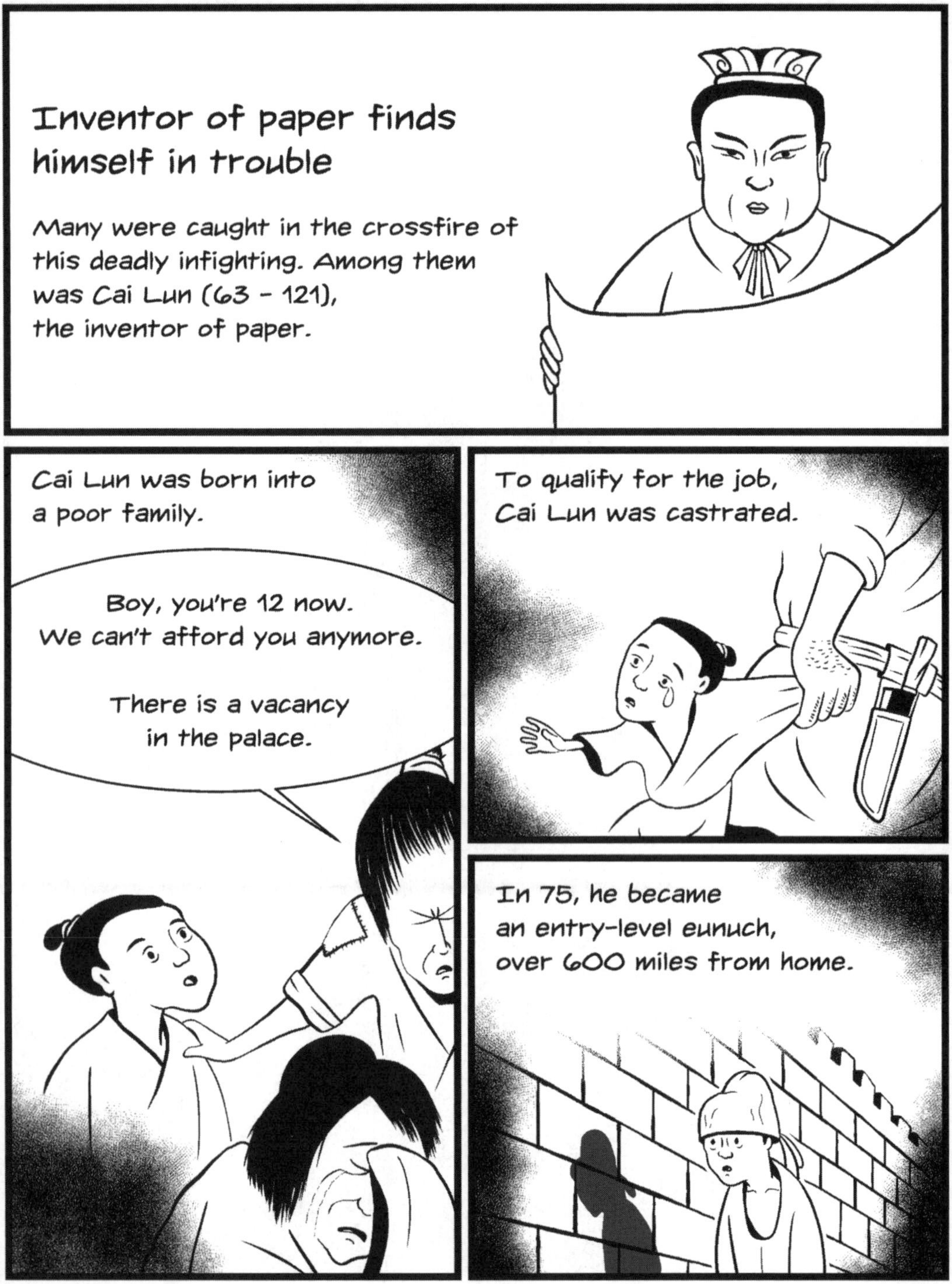
Inventor of paper finds himself in trouble
Many were caught in the crossfire of this deadly infighting. Among them was Cai Lun (63 – 121), the inventor of paper.
Cai Lun was born into a poor family.
Boy, you're 12 now. We can't afford you anymore.
There is a vacancy in the palace.
To qualify for the job, Cai Lun was castrated.
In 75, he became an entry-level eunuch, over 600 miles from home.

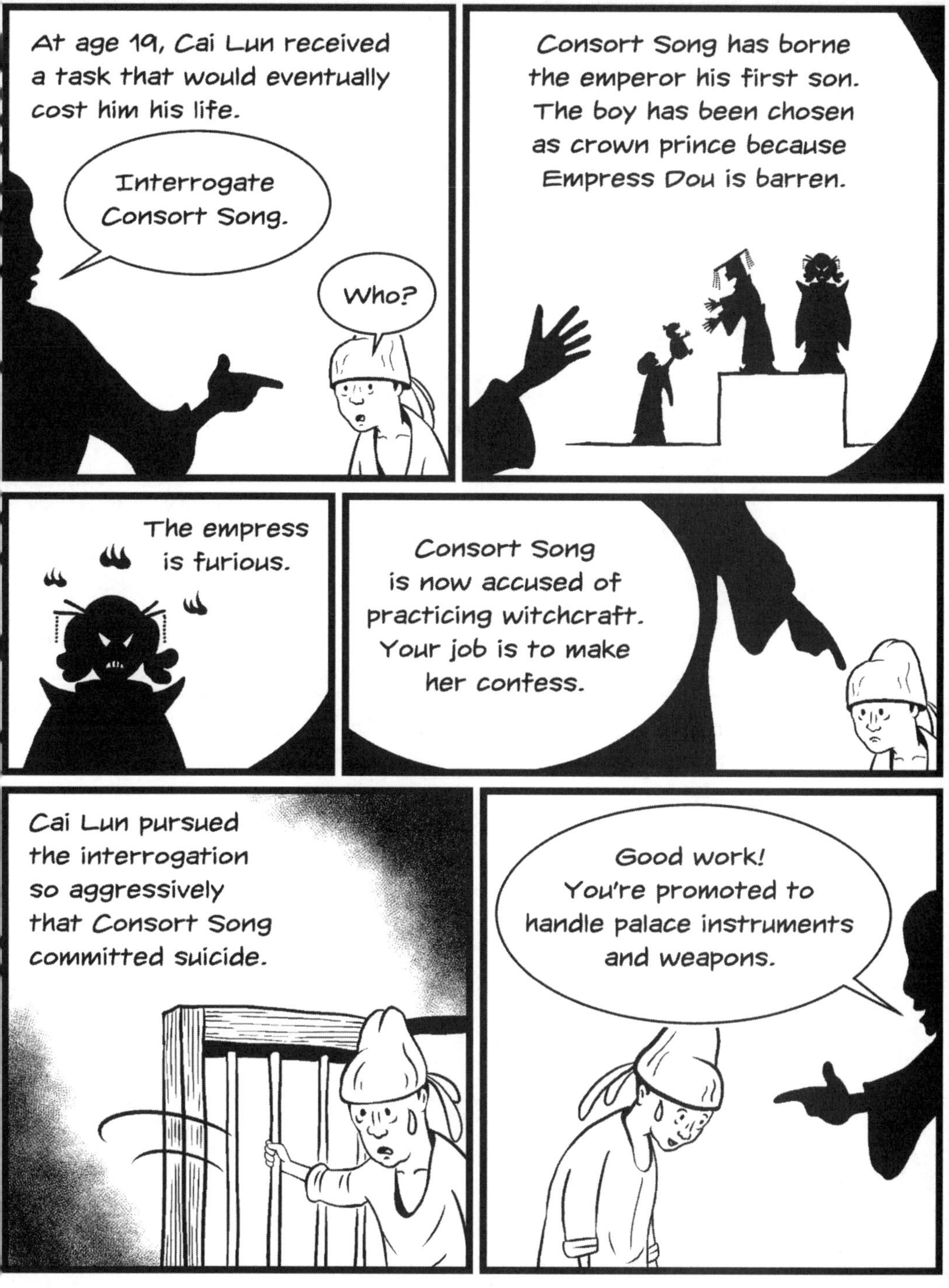
At age 19, Cai Lun received a task that would eventually cost him his life.
Interrogate Consort Song.
Who?
Consort Song has borne the emperor his first son. The boy has been chosen as crown prince because Empress Dou is barren.
The empress is furious.
Consort Song is now accused of practicing witchcraft. Your job is to make her confess.
Cai Lun pursued the interrogation so aggressively that Consort Song committed suicide.
Good work! You're promoted to handle palace instruments and weapons.

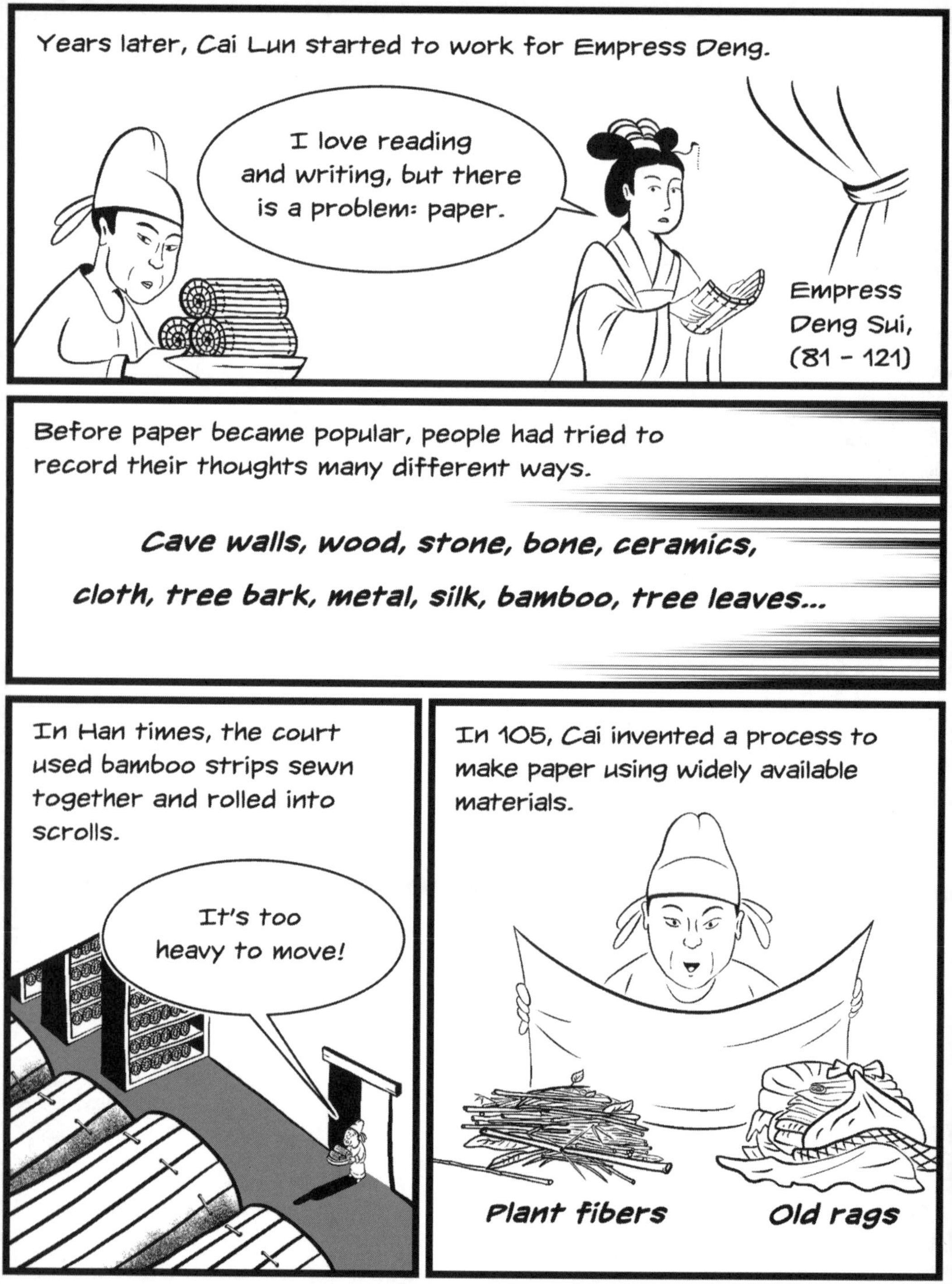
Years later, Cai Lun started to work for Empress Deng.
I love reading and writing, but there is a problem: paper.
Empress Deng Sui, (81 – 121)
Before paper became popular, people had tried to record their thoughts many different ways.
Cave walls, wood, stone, bone, ceramics,
cloth, tree bark, metal, silk, bamboo, tree leaves...
In Han times, the court used bamboo strips sewn together and rolled into scrolls.
It's too heavy to move!
In 105, Cai invented a process to make paper using widely available materials.
Plant fibers
Old rags

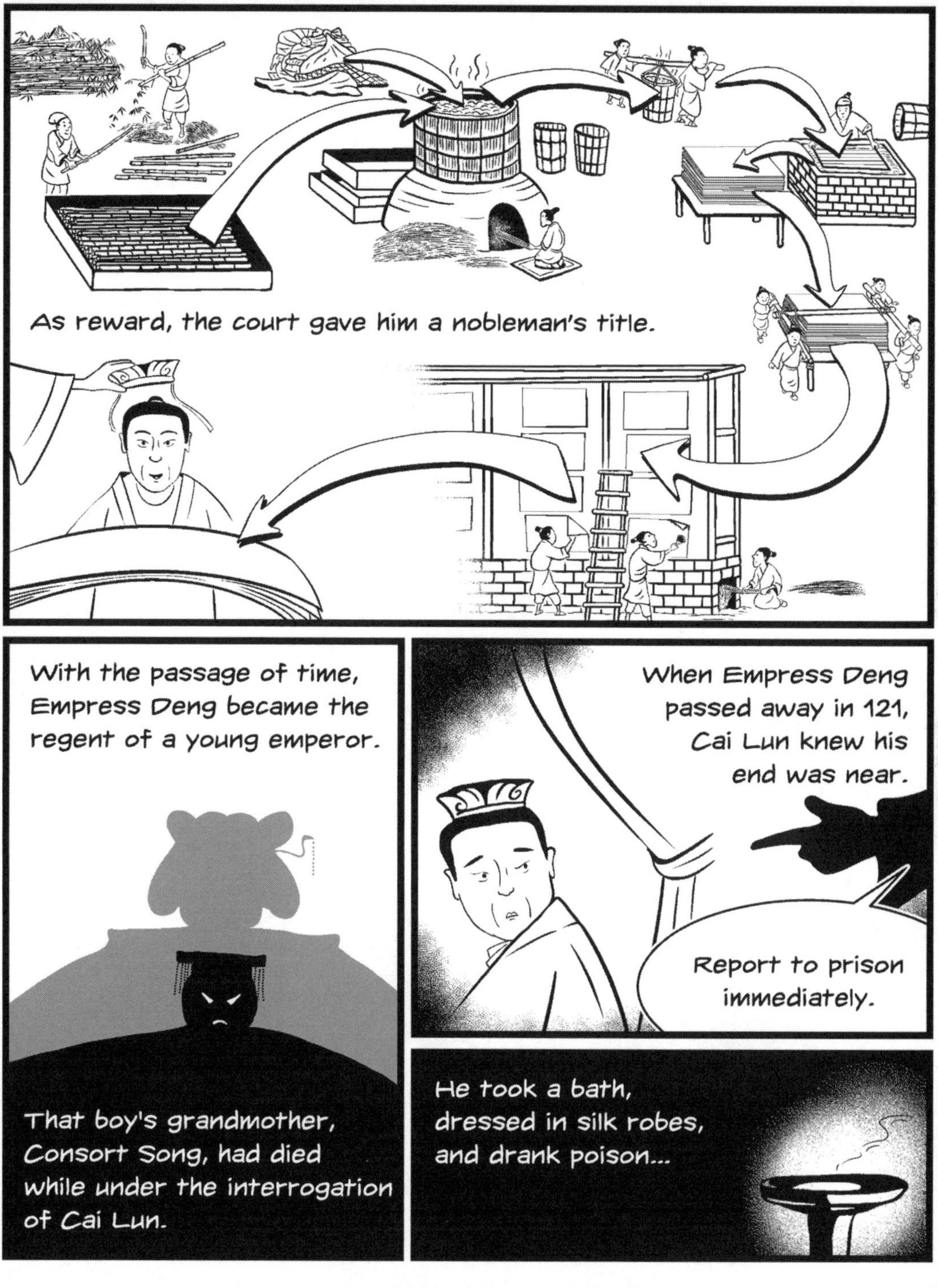
As reward, the court gave him a nobleman's title.
With the passage of time, Empress Deng became the regent of a young emperor.
That boy's grandmother, Consort Song, had died while under the interrogation of Cai Lun.
When Empress Deng passed away in 121, Cai Lun knew his end was near.
Report to prison immediately.
He took a bath, dressed in silk robes, and drank poison...

Beginning of the end

After Cai Lun, palace intrigues became even bloodier. When Emperor Ling (156 - 189) ascended the throne, a showdown between the consort clan and eunuchs spread to the imperial university. In 169, tens of thousands of students took to the streets.

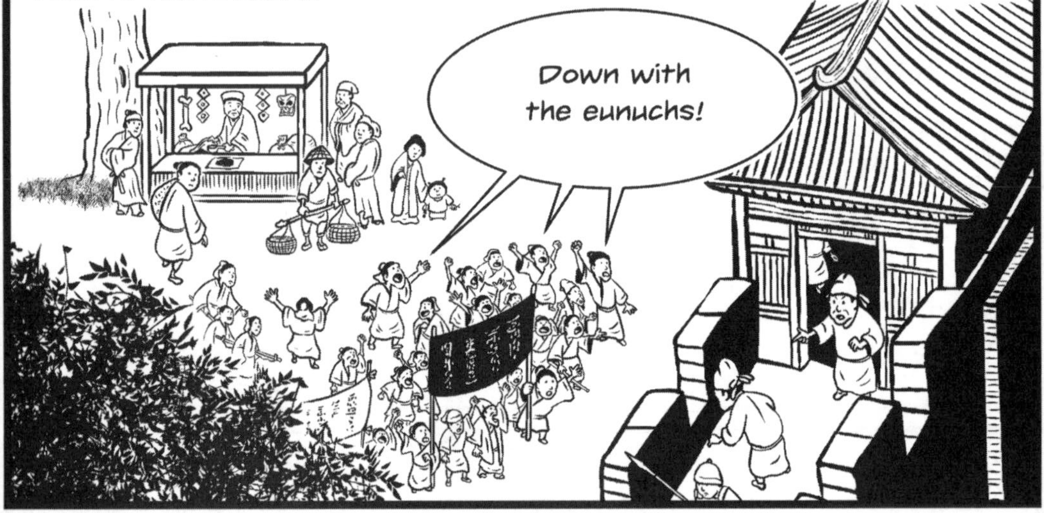
Down with the eunuchs!

Eunuchs mobilized the imperial guards to suppress the protest. Over 100 students were killed. Hundreds of officials were punished. Many were sentenced to death.

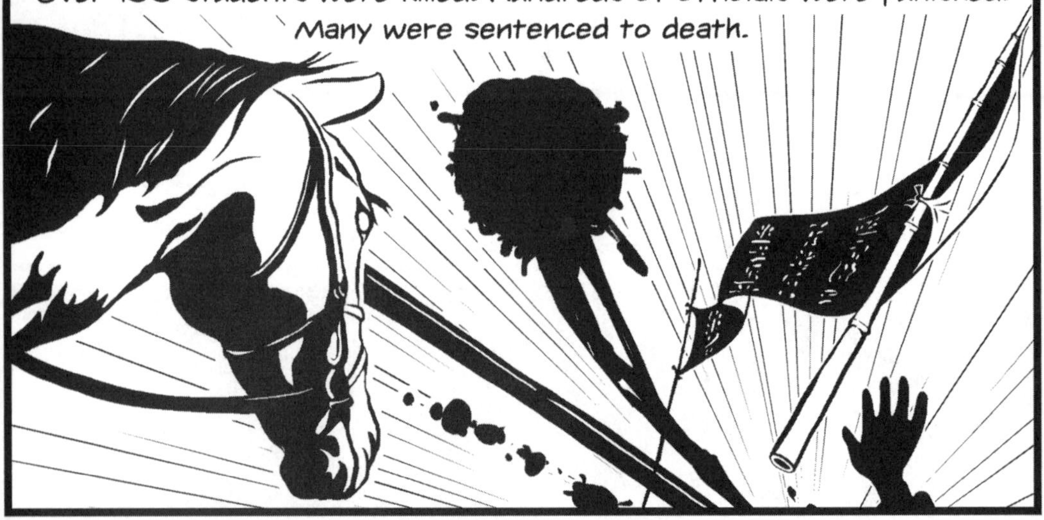

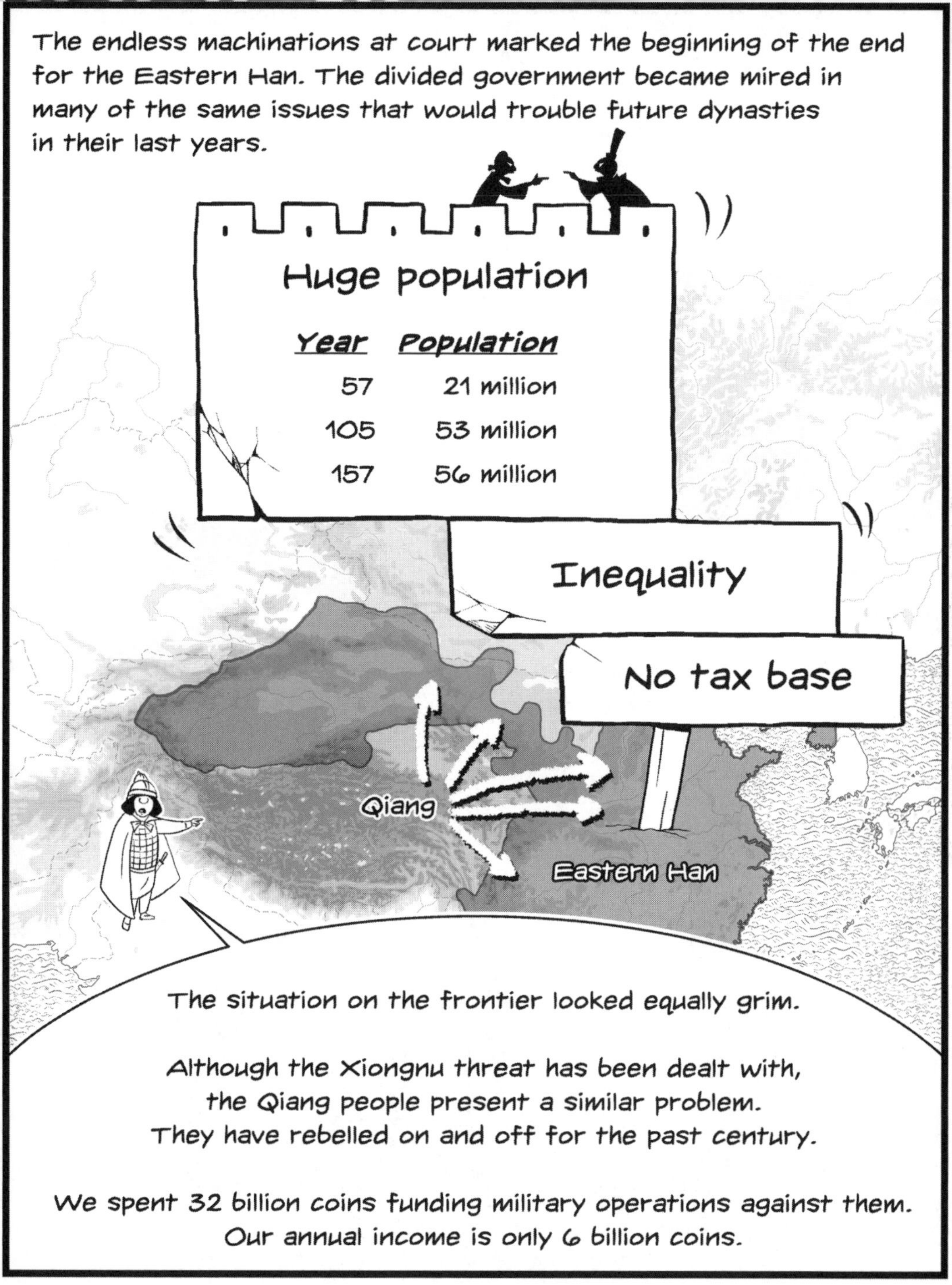

The endless machinations at court marked the beginning of the end for the Eastern Han. The divided government became mired in many of the same issues that would trouble future dynasties in their last years.

Huge population

Year	Population
57	21 million
105	53 million
157	56 million

Inequality

No tax base

Qiang

Eastern Han

The situation on the frontier looked equally grim.

Although the Xiongnu threat has been dealt with, the Qiang people present a similar problem. They have rebelled on and off for the past century.

We spent 32 billion coins funding military operations against them. Our annual income is only 6 billion coins.

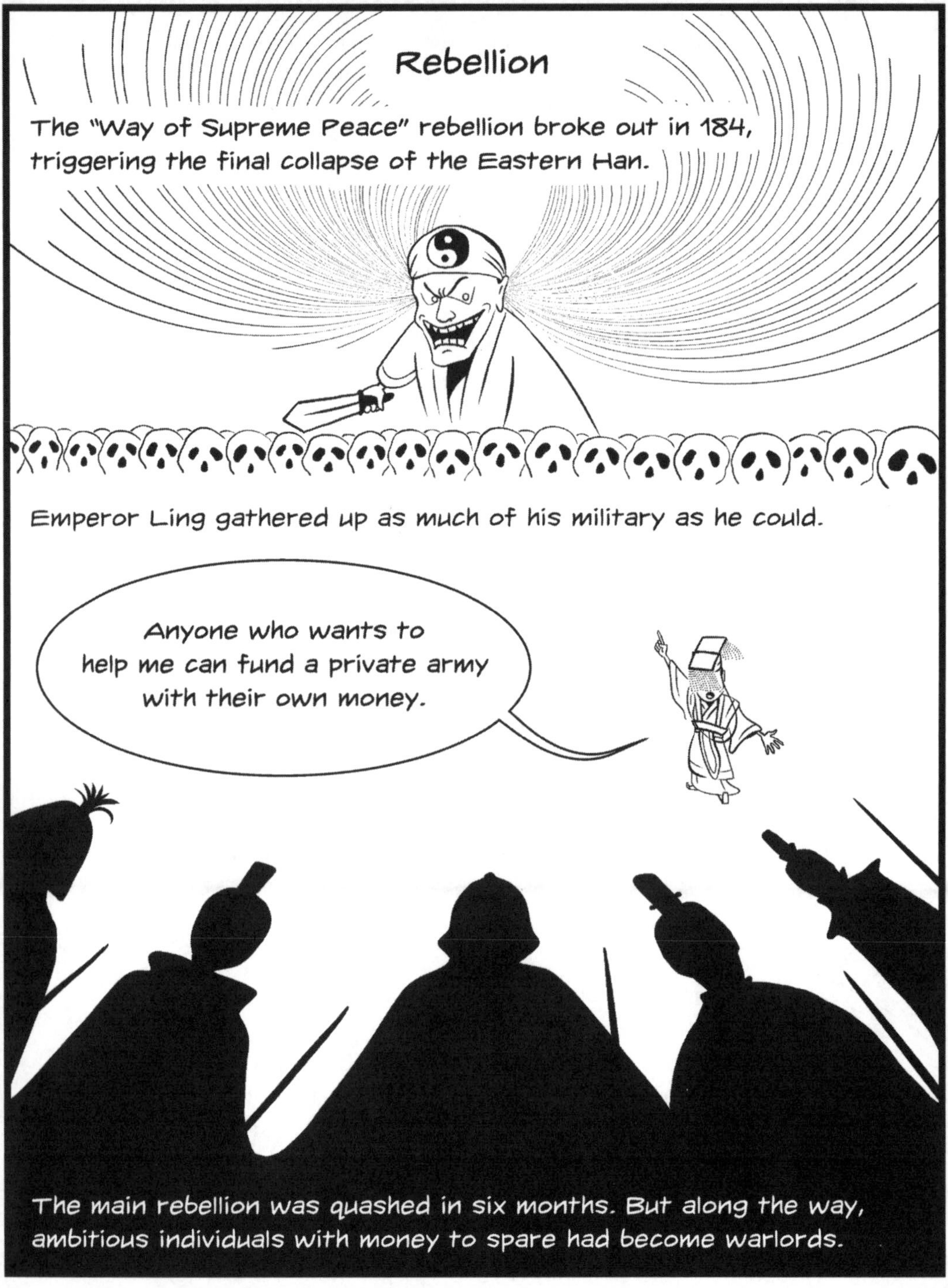
Rebellion
The "Way of Supreme Peace" rebellion broke out in 184, triggering the final collapse of the Eastern Han.
Emperor Ling gathered up as much of his military as he could.
Anyone who wants to help me can fund a private army with their own money.
The main rebellion was quashed in six months. But along the way, ambitious individuals with money to spare had become warlords.

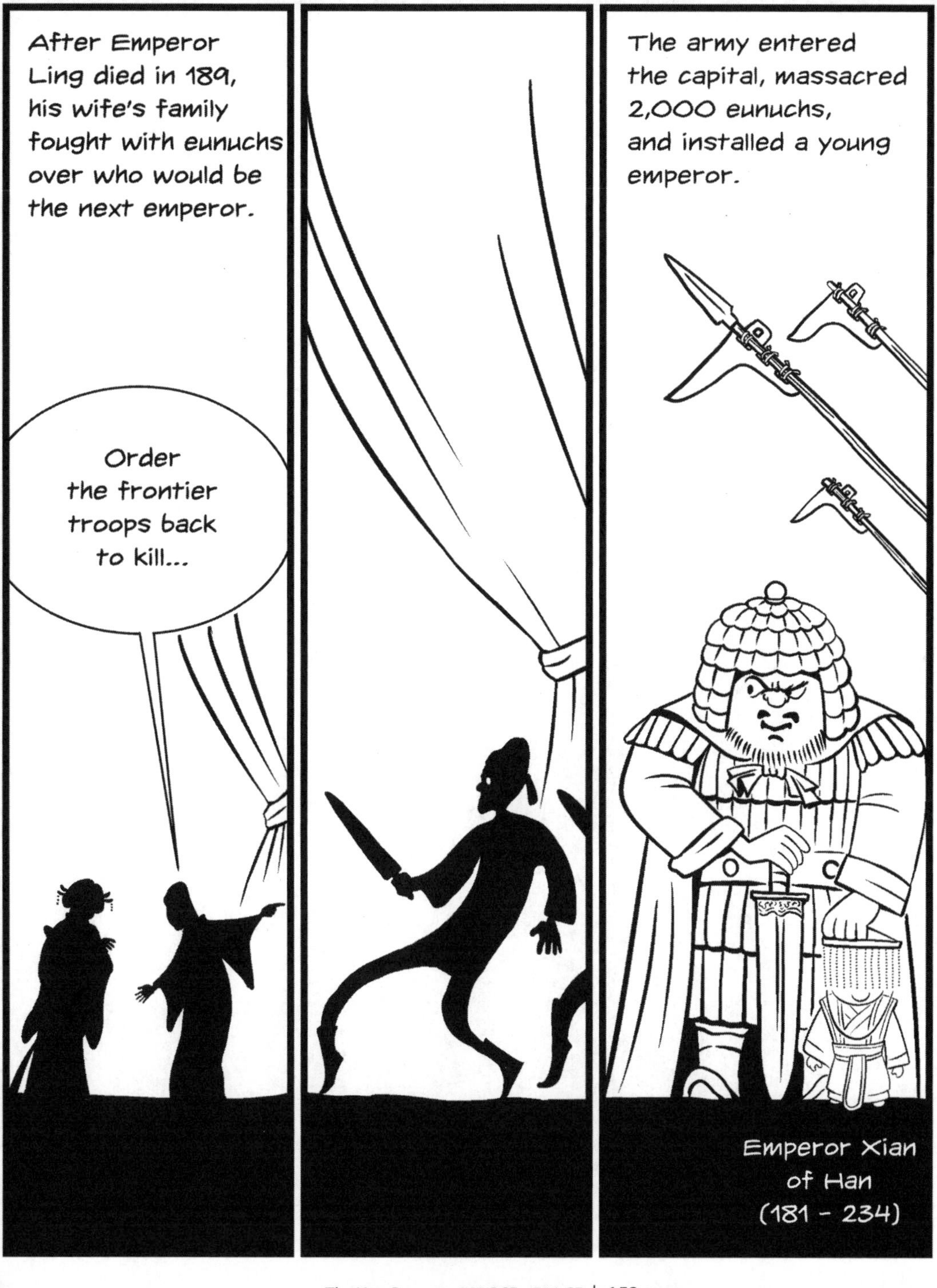

After Emperor Ling died in 189, his wife's family fought with eunuchs over who would be the next emperor.
Order the frontier troops back to kill...
The army entered the capital, massacred 2,000 eunuchs, and installed a young emperor.
Emperor Xian of Han (181 - 234)

As the last Eastern Han ruler, Emperor Xian was a puppet in the hands of warlords. The 400-year Han rule effectively came to an end.

The Han dynasty and its predecessor, the Qin dynasty, left a lasting and impressive legacy.

The short-lived Qin laid the foundation for a politically centralized model of government. The Han further consolidated power, projecting it over great distances for an extended period of time.

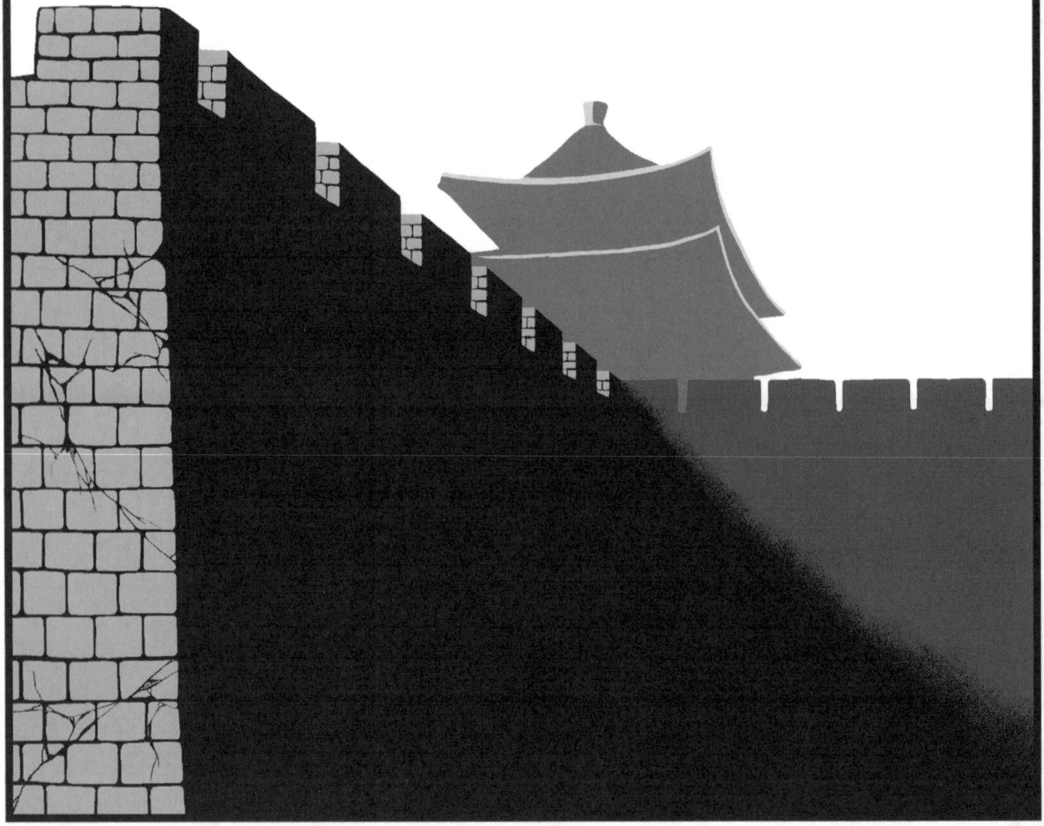

Together, the Qin and Han dynasties created a core region characterized by political and cultural unity. People began to call themselves Chinese and perceive China as a unified country.

This unification under the Qin and Han, however, was not to last. China soon found itself divided once more, this time for nearly 400 years as warring factions waged battle. That, however, is a different story.

To be continued...

NOTES AND SUGGESTED READING

Pronouncing Chinese names can be very difficult. To keep things as simple as possible I've kept all Chinese names in pinyin, the standard phonetic method for transcribing Chinese words.

The only exceptions are names previously romanized according to different standards that are now very common. An excellent example is the name of the philosopher Confucius. If I were to write it in pinyin it would be spelled *Kongfuzi*. Instead, I use Confucius, the name Jesuit missionaries gave him in the 16th century.

If you want to check your pinyin pronunciation there are a number of useful online resources available to you. An excellent web dictionary with audio capabilities can be found at www.mdbg.net. The Pleco app for iOS and Android phones allows you to check proper pronunciation.

In writing *Foundations of Chinese Civilization* I relied on a number of Chinese-language sources. These include *History of China* by Tongling Wang, *The General History of China* by Simian Lü, *China: A Macro History* by Ray Huang Renyu, and *A History of Chinese Philosophy* by Youlan Feng. Many of these books are classic histories and have more information than I could ever fit into a series, much less a single volume. If you read Chinese these books are worth investigating.

While there aren't a huge number of English-language resources that address ancient Chinese history in an accessible way, *The Early Chinese Empires: Qin and Han* by Mark Edward Lewis is very informative. I also suggest *Chinese Civilization: A Sourcebook,* 2nd Edition, by Patricia Buckley Ebrey, which collects original source material from Chinese history, including oracle bones, tax codes, and folk tales.

ACKNOWLEDGMENTS

To Sara, Elizabeth, Malcolm and Connor, Katelyn and Yifu, and many, many more children who have been born with a connection to China.

BOOKS IN THIS SERIES

Volume 1
Foundations of Chinese Civilization:
The Yellow Emperor to the Han Dynasty
(2697 BCE–220 CE)

Volume 2
Division to Unification in Imperial
China: The Three Kingdoms to the Tang
Dynasty (220–907)
TO BE PUBLISHED NOVEMBER 2016

Volume 3
Barbarians and the Birth of Chinese
Identity: The Five Dynasties and
Ten Kingdoms to the Yuan Dynasty
(907–1368)
TO BE PUBLISHED APRIL 2017

Volume 4
The Making of Modern China: The
Ming Dynasty to the Qing Dynasty
(1368–1912)
TO BE PUBLISHED NOVEMBER 2017